Award-Winning Plays From The Open Book
and The Stage & Screen Book Club

Incisions

Award-Winning Plays From *The Open Book*
and *The Stage & Screen Book Club*

INCISIONS

Edited by
MARVIN KAYE

With a foreword by
JOHN JAKES

And Six Award-Winning Scripts by
KITTY FELDE
JOSEPH P. RITZ
ALAN DAVID PERKINS
SKOT DAVIS
CE MCCLELLAND
AL SJOERDSMA, JR.

STAGE
&SCREEN
The Book Club for the Performing Arts

Garden City, New York

CONTENTS

FOREWORD

Whether you call it readers theatre, chamber theatre, or some other term, dramatized literature is a form that has always captivated me. It's a form I've been involved with as an adapter and director, with considerable pleasure.

What appeals to me is the simplicity of it. You don't need a lot of scenery or costuming, and only minimal lighting; not even that if your venue won't accommodate it. You have the world's greatest scene painters and costume designers and lighting directors at your disposal. I'm referring to your audience, whose imaginations will help dress and light any bare stage.

I was first involved in a performance of something other than a conventional play during the freshman year I spent at the School of Speech, Northwestern University. As a sort of final exam for a course called Oral Interpretation, we had to prepare an oral dramatization of a written work. Anything was suitable as long as it wasn't plucked from a play catalog.

In those days I was reading a lot of science fiction, and in my spare hours trying to write it. One sf writer, Robert Heinlein, had broken through into the *Saturday Evening Post*. In that magazine I read his story, "The Green Hills of Earth," all about Rhysling, the "blind poet of the spaceways" (I'm digging this up from fifty years ago, and hope I have the details right). I loved the story, and I chose it for adaptation.

I recall stumbling through the piece in front of a somewhat puzzled instructor and class. This was 1949, remember; science fiction was read and appreciated only by a very small (and, in the estimation of most others, peculiar) minority. I don't remember what grade I received, but I do know that for all my mistakes, I enjoyed trying to lift the different narrative and dramatic voices off the page in a way that perhaps Heinlein himself never imagined.

Jump to the 1980s. We were in our new home on Hilton Head Island, and I was a full-time novelist. The local little theatre where I'd acted a few times was restricted, by the paid director's choice and the vocal views of the majority of the audience to overly familiar comedies and musicals. This was—still is—the kind of conservative American audience I've described for years as wanting dinner theatre without dinner. That sort of theatrical diet struck me as too meager.

Just then I was a board member of our local Friends of the Library. Somehow that and my dissatisfaction with the little theatre's programming fused and brought up a memory of my Northwestern class; out of that came a trio of readers theatre performances I wrote and directed. Together, they opened my eyes to the form's enormous potential.

Our first show, *A Woody Allen Quartet*, consisted of adaptations of four of his short pieces. I wrote Allen's office for permission, which he generously granted, sans any fee. We presented the show on the plain fiber carpet of our small library, with no theatrical lights, only the glaring overhead fluorescents no doubt provided by the county's lowest bidder. Difficulties notwithstanding, the performances were packed, with a waiting list for cancellations. We didn't charge admission, but you had to join the Friends for a ticket.

Admittedly I had star power going for me. One of my actors was the gentlemanly and vastly talented Garry Moore, no longer with us. Garry had retired to Hilton Head after his stellar TV career. He performed Woody Allen's take on an address to a graduating class, and brought down the house.

For our next show we tackled F. Scott Fitzgerald's *Babylon Revisited*, again with my adaptation and the necessary permission of the agent for Fitzgerald's estate (cost us $25 as I recall; well worth it). We were back in the same minimalist "theatre," with the addition of a grand piano on our imaginary stage, and a pianist to provide an incidental score of tunes of the 1920s. Again, a success.

Finally, for the biggest hit of all, I adapted Erma Bombeck's *Motherhood, the Second Oldest Profession* for an all-female cast. We now had a light bar with four theatrical instruments and a small dimmer board, purchased for us by the Friends from the local little theatre. A simple light plot racheted up the emotion in Erma's heart-tugging material.

I knew Erma when we both lived in Dayton, Ohio, and she was just beginning her meteoric rise to fame. Her agent gave me permission to do the adaptation gratis. I was so pleased with the way the hour-and-fifteen-minute show worked, I wanted to expand it and try it elsewhere. The Westport Country Playhouse, of which I am, through a limited partnership, a fractional owner, expressed strong interest. Alas, Erma's agent wrote to say she wanted to try her own adaptation for Broadway. In her all too short life, she never had time to write the play, and my adaptation languishes in my files.

These shows gave me two other insights into readers theatre: it costs little or nothing to present, and amateur actors love the form. Armed with scripts, they can rehearse for two or three evenings and give creditable performances.

Later, using the second stage of our local playhouse, I directed a series of staged readings of dramas such as *Our Town* and *I Never Sang For My Father*. Audiences packed our four or five showings of each, but I never found these efforts as satisfying as creating something new.

That was the end of my association with readers theatre until my friend Marvin Kaye asked me to help judge one of these annual contests, which he and what was then known as The Fireside Theatre Book Club organized to develop new readers theatre material. You can see from this anthology that the idea has remained very much alive.

I regret that my career has kept me from writing more readers theatre pieces. At our new, multi-million-dollar Arts Center on Hilton Head, we have a lovely, flexible black box theatre that would be ideal for them. I am inspired by the work of a London-based company called Shared Experience. Shared Experience routinely adapts great long novels such as Dickens's *Hard Times* to what is essentially a presentational readers theatre format, with critical and popular success. Why not similar theatre all around the U.S.?

Of all the plays in this volume, I would direct your attention particularly to *Blood and Ivy*, about the Kent State tragedy. Its author truly understands how the form works: you take material from letters, or the press, or narrative fiction, or non-fiction, and turn it into something other than a four-wall play. A lot of the scripts submitted in Marv's annual contest are really four-wall plays. I look forward to the time when more playwrights grasp the nature and power of readers theatre and begin to create pieces that can't be mistaken for anything else.

Until then, you have some fine dramatic reading in store for you in this collection.

—John Jakes

Hilton Head Island
South Carolina
November, 1999

INTRODUCTION

In 1975, a group of professional actors, educators, singers and writers began The Open Book, New York's oldest continuing professional readers theatre ensemble. As this book goes to press, our company is observing its twenty-fifth anniversary of bringing our motto, "the best of all worlds of literature," to theatre lovers, amateur and professional, throughout America.

The Open Book often stages a conference and workshop at the Eugene O'Neill Memorial Theater Center in Waterford, Connecticut. Originally intended as a national forum for educating playwrights and other theatre professionals in readers theatre,* this event has evolved into a forum for workshopping new scripts, one of which last year went on to win the National Readers Theatre Playwrighting Competition that The Open Book cosponsors with the Stage & Screen Book Club.

The playwrighting competition has been running for the past six years. The winning scripts are produced in New York by The Open Book under the terms of the Actors Equity Association Showcase Code.†

In 1995, The Wildside Press published *Memorial* by Charles LaBorde, the winner of the first national competition, and three other finalist scripts, in *Readers Theatre, What It Is, How to Stage It*, a monthly selection of The Fireside Theatre (now the Stage & Screen Book Club). The following year, The Fireside Theatre itself published *From Page to Stage*, which featured the cowinners of the second competition, *The Most Dangerous Woman* by the late Ted Eiland, and *Kilroy Was Here* by Constance Alexander.

In this volume, I am pleased to bring to the Stage & Screen Book Club membership the winners of our third, fourth, fifth and sixth play contests: respectively, Kitty Felde's *Alice*, Alan David Perkins's *Nobody Knows I'm A*

---

*Readers theatre, a minimalist production technique that some directors and producers still confuse with staged readings, is not a way station in the development of a play, but an alternative performance style often more effective than traditional staging methods. Its parameters are discussed in The Open Book's two earlier anthologies. For further information, inquire via e-mail at theopenbook@Juno.com

†For further information, send a self-addressed stamped envelope to The Open Book, 525 West End Avenue, Suite 12 E, New York NY, 10024-3207.

Dog, CE McClelland's *Blood and Ivy: An American Anthem*, and Al Sjoerdsma, Jr.'s *The 82nd Shepherds' Play*, as well as two second place winners, Joseph P. Ritz's *Trappists* and Skot Davis's *Consider the Banana*.

Thanks to various judging panels, which have included, in addition to myself, Beth Goehring, former editor of The Fireside Theatre; Mark Glubke, editor of the Stage & Screen Book Club; the winning playwrights each year, and such distinguished theatre and literary professionals as Carol Higgins Clark, Professor Louis Fantasia, John Jakes, Greg Lehane, Morgan Llywelyn, Rex Robbins, Mary Stuart, Nancy Temple and Professor Judy E. Yordon.

In his appealing foreword, my friend and colleague John Jakes eloquently summarizes the virtues of readers theatre as an economical, comparatively simple production technique, with which I heartily concur on all but one particular, that of ease of rehearsal, at least in the New York market. It is not easy to find professional actors succinctly trained in vocal technique to achieve quality results without teaching them the rudiments of the form as it differs from traditional theatre.

The two distinguishing aspects of readers theatre as I have addressed them over the years as Artistic Director of The Open Book are vocal technique and presentationalism. I expect good readers theatre performers to have the skill to analyze their texts for sonority, rhythm, pace, onomatopoeia, essentially the inner music of each playwright's use of language. This takes a lot of drill, and though it is true that in some of our productions, the actors are permitted to carry the script (that being, after all, the name of the producing company) they are still expected to memorize their roles. Only a performer intimately familiar with his lines can begin to shape his speeches and play his interpretation with the subtle intimate adjustments required in live performance. In short, I expect readers theatre performers to have the skill of trained musicians. In addition to that, they must be familiar with presentational acting: the stuff of soliloquies and asides.

Readers theatre is always, to some extent, presentational because the underlying subtext of the performers must be that they have a work of literature that they enjoy so much they can't wait to share it with the audience. This "ür-message" implies direct eye contact at significant moments; as I often tell my actors during rehearsal, "That fourth wall can only be waist-high. You've got to look over it from time to time."

Most literature is easily adaptable to the form, but plays sometimes require special handling. During judging discussions for our national competition, John Jakes has more than once lamented the dearth of pure readers theatre scripts being submitted, and to some extent I agree with him. But reeducation takes time, and little by little over the years, The Open Book has seen an upturn in submissions of scripts especially suited to the form without further adaptation. It is especially gratifying when writers who sent earlier plays for judging reenter later competitions with increased awareness of the exigencies and characteristics of the form.

In the present collection, John Jakes especially recommends CE McClelland's *Blood and Ivy: An American Anthem*, as an excellent example of how the form works, and this is so. An earlier version of the play was brought to the O'Neill Theater Center, where it was read and discussed by conference attendees. The result was that the playwright went home, applied what he'd learned and entered it in the next competition, which it won.

Although the other plays in this volume are indeed, as John Jakes puts it, "four wall plays," each of them was easily adapted to The Open Book's production needs, with Kitty Felde's *Alice* and Alan David Perkins's *Nobody Knows I'm A Dog* especially simple to present presentationally.

During the six years The Open Book's competition has been running, our judges have read approximately one hundred new scripts a year, and of these the percentage of poor writing has been small. Only a handful of plays each year make it to the finals, but with more work, a lot of near-misses might become winners in subsequent seasons.

Indeed, when one reads the six excellent plays in this volume—all of them audience-tested, all of them superior evenings in the theatre—one wonders why some producers are still griping that there are no good new plays being written. If you know anyone like that, please give her or him a copy of this book with my compliments.

—MARVIN KAYE
New York, 2000

KITTY FELDE

Alice

Alice was the winner of The Open Book/Stage and Screen Book Club's third national playwrighting competition. Kitty Felde is an award-winning playwright, with six plays and a produced TV script to her credit. Her most recent play, *A Patch of Earth*, based on testimony from the Yugoslav war crimes tribunal, premiered October, 1999, at the Alleyway Theatre in Buffalo. The play has won numerous awards, including the 1999 Maxim Mazumdar New Play Competition. "My next project," she said, "is to find a home for *Bum's Rush*, my musical comedy about the Dodgers' move west."

A member of The Dramatists Guild and a California resident, Ms. Felde is an award-winning public radio journalist and Friday host of the talk show, *Talk of the City*, on National Public Radio affiliate KPCC (FM 89.3).

Alice premiered in February, 1997, at The National Theatre in Washington, D.C. and was produced by The Open Book in New York at The Miranda Theatre, opening March 8th, 1998, with Marvin Kaye directing the following cast:

ALICE ROOSEVELT LONGWORTH   . . .   NANCY TEMPLE
THEODORE ROOSEVELT   . . . .   MILLER LIDE

ACT I

TIME: June, 1971
PLACE: Washington, D.C.
AT RISE: The stage is dark. We hear a doorbell. There is a pause. We hear
           the doorbell again.

ALICE (*offstage*): I left the door open for you. Make yourself at home. I'll
be down in a minute.

(*We hear the sound of a heavy door opening and closing. Perhaps there
are street sounds heard briefly as the door opens and shuts. We hear footsteps climbing the half dozen stairs from the landing. The lights come up
to reveal a comfortably shabby drawing room. A fire burns in the fireplace.
A grand piano occupies one corner of the room, covered with bric-a-brac
and an odd collection of sheet music—everything from "Hot Time in the
Old Town Tonight" to "Let The Sunshine In." If we look closely enough, we
can see the tail of an ancient Siamese cat sleeping among the music
sheets, but only the tail. A pair of dusty old red journals are also resting on
the piano.*

*Nearly every inch of wall space is filled with something interesting—a
Flemish tapestry, a Sargent watercolor of the White House, ancient photographs of long-dead Asian emperors hung in elaborately carved wooden
frames. There is also a small cartoon with caricatures of Eleanor and
Franklin Roosevelt and a slightly moth-eaten tiger skin—head included,
minus just one paw.*

*There is a pair of well-worn armchairs and a wine velvet sofa. Old lace
antimacassars are on the armrests and an embroidered pillow in the center
of the sofa reads: "If you haven't got anything good to say about anyone
come and sit by me." A small table next to the sofa holds an old fashioned
black telephone and a well-worn personal telephone book. A curious looking pre-Inca figurine with scary-looking eyes perches near the phone. Books
of all kinds litter every available space, including a tattered copy of the* Ox-
ford Book of English Verse *held together with twine.*

After perhaps fifteen seconds, we hear ALICE again)

ALICE (*offstage*): Do sit down. Oh, not the chintz armchair. Joanna tells
me there's a wicked spring that's positively determined to attack unsus-
pecting guests. I think it's just her polite way of telling me to get new furniture. There, now what do you think?

(*We hear footsteps on the offstage staircase.* Alice Roosevelt Longworth *enters. She is 80-something, but moves with the grace and energy of a woman several decades younger. She has fiercely blue eyes, a chiseled face that once was quite beautiful, and a mass of white hair that won't quite stay in a bun. On top of her head she sports a very wide, flat-brimmed white hat covered with flowers. In her hands she holds a second flat-brimmed straw hat. This one is simple and black.* Alice *addresses her invisible guest*)

ALICE: I've been invited to Tricia Nixon's wedding and I can't decide
    whether my "chapeau de fleures" will upstage the bride. I suppose I could
    wear my all-purpose black straw. I just don't want her to think I'm mak-
    ing a statement of some sort—that I'm in mourning for her wedded life to
    come or some such nonsense.

(*Alice walks over to a mirror and models the hats for herself*)

No one wears hats any more—except the Queen Mother and the rest of us
ancient relics of the ice age. I think I'll go with the flowers. They're a bit
gaudy, but if anyone is allowed to upstage the bride at a White House
wedding, it ought to be me. After all, Father did his best to steal the spotlight at *my* White House wedding. It's true what they used to say: Teddy
Roosevelt wanted to be the bride at every wedding and the corpse at every
funeral.

(*Alice takes off her hat and tosses them both on top of the piano. Cat is surprised awake, meows and goes back to sleep*)

ALICE: Hush, Cat! No one asked for your opinion. Did you have any trou-
    ble finding the place? You might have asked one of the local tour guides.
    I understand they now stop out in front and tell visitors the place is
    haunted by the ghosts of Washington past. They're only half wrong, you
    know. (*Pause*) That nice red plant out in front? Yes, it is rather unusual. I
    hope you didn't touch it. The gardener tells me it's poison ivy. Wouldn't
    you like a cup of tea? (*Alice calls offstage*) Janie! Bring in the tea things,
    please!

(*To reporter*) What? Yes, I know this isn't a social call. But I've never
heard of a cup of tea and a bread and butter sandwich corrupting anyone.
Although I'll admit I do brew it a bit strong. Bob Hope and his wife came
to tea last spring. He accused me of steeping marijuana instead of Earl
Grey. Now, there's something to perk up my reputation with the younger

generation! On, come now. Do have a cup. All right. If you insist. You journalists today aren't as much fun as the old boys were. (*Calling offstage*) Janie! Never mind about the tea! (*To reporter*) My bread and butter sandwiches are quite famous, you know. Written up in all the best places. You're missing a good story there. Well, next time you come, then. (*Alice returns to the sofa and assumes a dignified pose*)

What sort of article did you say this was for? Oh, yes. That glossy magazine inside the Sunday *Post*. Tell me. Does anyone really buy those God awful collectible plates with pictures from *The Wizard of Oz*?

Well, you know my dear, I don't give interviews as a rule. I did more than enough talking back when I lived in the White House. But Joanna—that's my granddaughter, you know—Joanna says I should "share my slice of the historical pie" with the world before I pass on. She should know I have no intention of going anywhere. At least not at the moment. Now, then. What is it you want to know?

Oh, don't worry, dear. You can ask me anything you like. I don't bite, you know. I don't have the teeth for it any more.

Begin at the beginning, you say. Very well. I was born on the evening of February 12th, 1884. Abraham Lincoln's birthday. Father thought it was a good omen. It wasn't. Shortly after my arrival, people began dying.

I'm perfectly serious, my dear. My mother and grandmother died in the same house just hours apart, two days after I made my appearance in the world. It must have been a dreadful blow for my father, to lose his mother and his wife at the same time. My mother was Alice also. Alice Lee. Now *she* was beautiful. Truly beautiful. And I'm told both charming and frivolous. But I never heard that from my father. He never even mentioned her name to me. Not once. My Irish nurse was always reminding me to "say a prayer for your little mother in heaven." It was all quite awful, I suppose. Very bad psychologically and all that. But I survived.

Actually, from what I've heard, I'm not certain I would have liked my mother very much as a flesh and blood human being. Rather like Little Dora, the child bride, from Dickens. I once overheard Mother—my stepmother Edith Roosevelt—I always called her Mother—I overheard her say it was just as well Alice Lee had died before she bored my father to death.

No, I wasn't shocked to hear such a thing. Tact was never one of Edith's strong suits. She wasn't the wicked stepmother or anything of that sort. Although I do remember the night I got married, I was saying goodbye to the family, telling Mother it was quite the nicest wedding I'll ever have, and that I'd never had so much fun. And she, poor dear, obviously overexhausted by it all said, "I want you to know that I'm glad to see you leave. You've never been anything but trouble." It was quite fantastic. It just came out like that. I said, "That's all right, Mother. I'll be back in a few weeks and you won't feel the same way." And I was and she didn't. Well, at least I don't think she did.

I don't blame her for being tired. We were quite the group of little hellions. The six of us—four brothers, my sister Ethel and I—pretty much had the run of the White House while Father was President. Nothing was sacred. We used to slide down the main staircase on oversized tin serving trays. They were better than toboggans! Occasionally, we rode our bicycles upstairs in the family quarters. And we were quite famous for our First Family menagerie: the blue macaw named Eli Yale, a badger, my green snake Emily Spinach, named after my skinny Aunt Emily, oh, and the pony we smuggled into my brother Quentin's room one day when he was sick. All of it ended up in the papers, you know. It was a novelty having that many children in the White House and we were quite the center of attention. Especially me, I must confess. Father was quite annoyed that our escapades were always ending up in the newspapers. "And Alice," he'd say, "you're old enough to know better." It was Father's fault, really, that we turned out the way we did. He raised us to be "rough riders" just like him. And I suppose we were. We were certainly as headstrong as he was. Father hadn't a clue what to do with me. My smoking, for example. Oh, I know it's a rather unpleasant habit— butts, ashes, and such a nasty smell. But I find it quite pleasant once in a while. More important for me at the time, it truly annoyed my father. "Alice, you shall not smoke under my roof." "Very well, Father," I said, and sat myself up on the White House roof for my afternoon puff. It was that sort of behavior that prompted Father to tell his friend Owen Wister, "I can be President of the United States—or I can attend to Alice. I can't do both!"

(*We hear the deep, robust offstage voice of Theodore Roosevelt—a voice only Alice and the audience can hear*)

TR: Alice, you know that was a line Wister invented himself.

(*Alice rises to address the absent TR*)

ALICE: Yes, but it's such a good one. You used it yourself often enough while you were alive.

TR: Yes, but I was President of the United States.

ALICE: And I am the President's daughter.

TR: It's a bad habit to fall into, Alice—remembering exactly what you want to remember.

(*She returns to the sofa and addresses the reporter*)

ALICE: Father and I loved to argue. I would inevitably pick the opposite view of Father just to be provocative. Politically, however, we were two peas in a pod, Republicans through and through. It was truly the Grand Old Party in those days.

Though I must confess, I did vote Democratic once. Please don't tell President Nixon or he'll disinvite me to his daughter's wedding!

What's that? Vote for F.D.R.? God forbid! None of the family ever voted for Franklin in any election, at least so far as I know.

Run for office? Me? (*She laughs*) My dear, for a good portion of my life, women didn't even have the vote. Although I won't say I wasn't asked. After Nick died—Nicholas Longworth, my husband, you know. Yes, they did name that ugly congressional building after him. It's a typically American way to achieve immortality: serve faithfully as Speaker of the House for half a dozen years, and all anyone remembers you for is a God-awful federal office building. At any rate, after Nick died, it was suggested that I run for his congressional seat in Ohio. And even some talk that year that I be put on the ticket as the Vice-Presidential candidate! Can you imagine that? Back in 1931 no less! Of course, my running mate would have been Herbert Hoover. And I'm certain that as the first woman vice-president, I would have been blamed for the Depression. Why are we always trying to pin the tail of accountability on someone? Does fate necessarily get off scot-free? Blaming Hoover for the Depression is like blaming the people of San Francisco for the earthquake of 1906. But imagine sharing the ticket with that man! Could anything be more boring? The Hoover vacuum cleaner was more exciting. But, of course, it's electric.

It's rather nice to think back on the possibilities of public service, I suppose. But all that talk about running me for vice-president was just that. Talk. Americans weren't ready for a female in high office. They aren't ready today. Besides, running for office is enough to put one to sleep! Every two years, Nick would have to run for re-election in Ohio and as the dutiful wife, I would have to spend every other summer in that dreadful Ohio heat—

—Oh, no, my dear. It's far worse than August in Washington, Trust me.

We would ride from town to town, listening to the same speech over and over again. And I would smile and smile until my cheeks ached. Of course, I got even with Nick. I used to make faces at him from the Gallery when he was Speaker of the House just to make him laugh. And he did. Nick looked like the sort of fellow who took himself far too seriously, but he was always willing to laugh at himself.

A picture? (*She looks around the room and feigns surprise*) No, I don't suppose I do have a photograph of Nick anywhere about.

Well, he was about my height. Rather bald. He had the remarkable talent of making a woman feel she was the center of attention whenever he looked into her eyes. Of course, it only lasted until he found himself staring into the next lovely set of eyes across the reception hall. It was an amazing thing to watch Nick work a room. If I hadn't been married to him I would have fallen in love with him right then and there. But of course, I was married to him. The magic rather wore off on repeat performances.

TR: Alice, say something kind about Nick.

ALICE: Stay out of this, Father.

TR: He was an important man, Alice. He served his country and his party well.

ALICE: And every pretty lady in the District of Columbia. Father, his own colleagues described him as "the greatest womanizer on the Hill." Nick was a dreadful spouse. I can't think of one good thing to say about him.

TR: What about Paulina? (*Pronounced with a long "i"*) Even you must admit Nick was a damned good father.

(*Alice opens her mouth to answer, but her attention is again drawn back to the reporter*)

ALICE: Yes, we did have one child. A daughter, Paulina. We called her Kitz, after the German word for tickle—kitzeln. Cincinnati, where my husband is from, was quite the Bavarian town in those days. Kitz was a bit of a surprise. Nick and I had been married a full 18 years before she finally arrived. I was practically an old lady by then—41 years old! The family was a bit shocked, I think. My sister Ethel told me— No, I keep the picture of Paulina upstairs in my bedroom.

Yes, she did die quite young. Too young. Paulina was just thirty-one. Her daughter—my granddaughter lives with me now. Joanna. She should be back any time now—

Yes, I've heard the rumors. That's just what they were. Rumors. If you read the official coroner's report, you'll see it was ruled an accidental overdose.

I don't care what "some people" say! I know my own daughter, don't I?

I'm not upset. I agreed you could ask me whatever you wanted to ask. I'm a woman of my word—

(*The telephone rings*)

ALICE: Excuse me. (*Alice crosses to the telephone and answers it*) Hello. Yes, it is. Who? *Newsweek* magazine? (*To the reporter in the room*) Do you mind? (*Back to the telephone*) No, you're not interrupting. What's that? Miss Nixon's wedding? Yes, I am one of "the honored four hundred." Yes, I see. You're writing a story on the blessed event— no, I suppose it's not a blessed event until nine months after the wedding. What's that? What do I remember about my own wedding? Quite honestly? Not one damned thing! My pleasure. Goodbye. (*She hangs up the phone*)

ALICE: I suppose this is only the beginning. Every member of the press corps will have to have an Alice Roosevelt Longworth angle to their

Nixon wedding story. I'll just have to have Joanna answer the phone for the next week and a half. I'm sorry she isn't home yet. You would enjoy Joanna's company. She's a much nicer person than I am. But then, she's young yet.

(*Alice walks over to the piano to retrieve the dark, plain hat. She tries it on, looking into an imaginary mirror to judge the effect*)

ALICE: I think I will wear the plain one. I understand the bride-to-be is wearing a headpiece that rather resembles the classic Bouvier pillbox. I wonder if Mr. Nixon realizes his daughter is wearing Democratic headgear? I rather like the Kennedy clan. They're so very "all for one and one for all" among themselves, which is quite nice. (*Alice returns to the sofa, tossing her hat on the coffee table*) I suppose we were as well, to a certain extent. We were certainly all quite loyal to Father. Even today, he is my ideal of what a President ought to be. It was the greatest mistake of Father's life when he promised not to run for another term. And don't think I didn't tell him so.

TR: I'm a man of my word, Alice.

ALICE: Yes, and look what it got the country. Taft. (*To the reporter*) Father realized I was right when Taft gloated over the nomination and pretended my father had had nothing to do with it. Of course, I got even for Father. I buried a voodoo in the garden the night before we left the White House.

Don't laugh. I'm serious. And it seemed to work. The weather on Taft's Inauguration Day was truly foul. The snow turned to slush and President Taft had to make his speech from inside the Senate Building. And then Nellie Taft suffered a stroke two-and-a-half months later. It wasn't the first time I'd worked my "magicks" for Father.

Magicks. You know, little bits of sorcery. Jinxes. Murrains.

(*Alice picks up the figurine on the telephone table and strokes its ears*)

ALICE: Sometimes I'd cross my fingers, other times simply utter small spells. It was most effective.

TR: Alice, I wish you'd stop with this superstitious nonsense!

ALICE: You can't argue with success, Father. That nasty little man Leon Czolgosz may have pulled the trigger and put two bullets into William McKinley. But it was I who put you into the Oval Office.

(*To the reporter*) My entire sixteenth year, I was weaving spells to rescue Father from the obscurity of the vice presidency. And it worked. President McKinley survived the assassination attempt, but died a few days later of septicemia. The doctor who performed the emergency surgery decided not to remove one of the bullets still lodged in his back.

When I heard the news, I put on a long face. And then my brother Ted and I went outside and danced a little jig.

Well, yes, someone did take a shot at Father once upon a time. It was after we left the White House and Father had decided to make another run for Presidency. A small, crazy man shot him in the chest—in Milwaukee of all places! The bullet fractured a rib and lodged near his lung. But Father insisted he be driven to the auditorium. "I will make this speech or die," he said.

TR: A bit over-dramatic in retrospect.

ALICE: I thought it was marvelous! The bullet didn't stop Father. He called it "an amazingly interesting experience."

(*To the reporter*) You know, sometimes I think there was a jinx on that entire 1916 campaign. It was the year Nick lost his Congressional seat. And the year Republican party leaders changed the rules and cheated Father's followers out of their credentials at the convention. That was why Father formed his own party. The Bull Moose Party. Father survived the assassination, but lost the election. But then, so did Taft.

The Bull Moose Party? That's what everyone called it. It's official name was the Progressive Party. But of course Father was the Bull Moose. A newspaperman asked him how he was feeling after the shooting.

TR: Fit as a bull moose!

ALICE: And the rest, as they say, is history. Do you know his campaign song? My brothers and I used to sing it at the top of our lungs as we'd tramp around the woods of Sagamore Hill.

(She rises and moves to the piano bench. She puts the sheet music for "Hot Time in the Old Town Tonight" in front of her and plays, singing)

> Roo-See-Velt
> And his riders bold and rough
> Showed that they
> Were made of good old stuff
> Now the country
> Needs you, sure enough
> So Teddy's marching
> To the White House
> Tonight!

(She finishes with a flourish and takes a bow)

ALICE: Thank you, my dear. We were well-trained young women in my day. We could play the piano—a little. Play at cards—a little. Recite a bit of amusing poetry—ahem:

> "B stands for Bear. When Bears are seen
>   Approaching in the distance,
> Make up your mind at once between
>   Retreat and Armed Resistance.
>
> A Gentleman remained to fight—
>   With what result for him?
> The Bear, with ill-concealed delight,
>   Devoured him, Limb by Limb.
>
> Another Person turned and ran;
>   He ran extremely hard:
> The Bear was faster than the Man,
>   And beat him by a yard.
> Moral?
> Decisive action in the hour of need
> Denotes the Hero, but does not succeed."

Of course, proper young ladies were also required to stay enough abreast of world affairs to keep the conversation going at dinner. That's about all that was expected of the fair sex in my generation.

Oh, yes, there were exceptions to the rule.

My cousin Eleanor? (*She pauses*)

TR: Alice!

ALICE: Yes, I suppose Eleanor did accomplish a great deal in her life, though I wouldn't say it was all for the good. Especially her influence on Franklin's policies. I'm convinced the New Deal was ten percent Eleanor and ninety percent mush.

Eleanor and I were thrown together quite often as children. Our fathers were brothers. Uncle Ellie was a tragic story: an attractive and intelligent young man who ruined himself with drink. Eleanor was kept away from him, so naturally she doted on him. In a way, we both suffered the deprivation of a parent. But while she responded to her insecurity by being goody two shoes and virtuous, I responded by being boisterous and showing off.

TR: I hardly think you can attribute your bursts of outrageous behavior to such psychological mishmash.

ALICE: Perhaps you're right, Father. Perhaps I just took after you in that way.

Some writer once stated that I was frightfully put out because Eleanor was supposedly so much more like my father than any of his own children. Oh, in some respects she probably was. He certainly had a do-gooding side to him, too, which I'm all for, as long as you don't have to do it yourself. And yes, I suppose he was very fond of her—although he terrorized her as a child.

TR: I did no such thing!

ALICE: Father's way of teaching us to swim was to toss us off the pier and see if we came up.

TR: Never lost a pupil.

ALICE: Eleanor hated it, but she never said a word. I, on the other hand, snarled and cried my eyes out.

TR: The tide rose several inches every time you had a swimming lesson.

ALICE: Father gave the bride away when Eleanor married Franklin. Foolish girl, allowing herself to be upstaged like that. She even asked me to be a bridesmaid. I think Franklin was very much in love with Eleanor when he married her. But she could never cope with Franklin's romantic affairs. My sister Ethel told me she remembers Eleanor weeping on her shoulder when she became engaged, saying: (*She imitates Eleanor's "high, emphatic" voice*) "I shall never be able to hold him. He is so attractive." Poor Eleanor! It was all rather pathetic. A smart wife should be able to manage her life around her husband's infidelities. (*Pause*) Not that I would have any firsthand experience with such things, you understand.

You know, there are stories floating about that I was interested in marrying Franklin myself and was quite put out when he chose Eleanor instead. Nothing could be further from the truth! I don't think it crossed either of our minds for a moment—though he did dance with me twice at my coming out party. Rather badly, I might add. But we did enjoy each other's company. Franklin and I could have had a lot of fun together if the Presidency hadn't come between us. I remember in 1904, we all wondered whether Franklin would vote for his party or for his cousin. And he chose his cousin. We, of course, never returned the favor.

I think the bad feelings between us grew out of the fact that my brother Ted had been brought up to become the second Roosevelt to occupy the White House. Poor Ted! Watching Franklin follow in those same Roosevelt footsteps with those large Democratic overshoes was just too terrible to contemplate! I think the final straw came when Ted ran for Governor. Father's path to the White House included a term as New York Governor, so naturally Ted would have to run as well. But Ted lost to Al Smith—in large part because Eleanor decided to drive all over the state with a teapot strapped to the chassis of her car.

A teapot. You know, to imply that Ted had connections with the Teapot Dome scandal. Her little stunt effectively ended my brother's political career.

I suppose what galled me the most about Franklin—I never, ever called him "Mr. President," you know, just to be spiteful. And it did get under his skin. His teeth would clench that cigarette holder just that much tighter every time I'd say it. But what upset me most about a Hyde Park Roosevelt occupying the White House was the thought that my Father was going to be forgotten.

TR: Nonsense!

ALICE: It was humiliating to read Alexander Woolcott's column in the *New York Times* proclaiming the Oyster Bay Roosevelts had become "the out of season Roosevelts." Ted said it best. This was back when Ted was Governor General of the Philippines. Reporters kept asking him what his relationship was to the new president. "Fifth cousin," he said, "about to be removed."

TR: That's quite good! I never heard that—"fifth cousin, about to be removed." Hah hah!

(Alice turns back to the keyboard and pounds out a slightly off-key rendition of "Happy Days Are Here Again." The telephone rings again. Several times. Alice finally stops mid-phrase and crosses to the sofa to answer it)

ALICE *(to the reporter)*: So sorry. *(She picks up the phone)* Hello. It is. I am. *People* magazine? I don't suppose you're calling to send me a free subscription. No, I didn't think so. The Nixon wedding. Yes, I'll be there with bells on. No, dear. Not real bells. It's just an expression. What's that? No, I'm sorry to say I was not invited to the shower Mrs. Agnew threw for the bride. *(Pause)* No, dear, I did not wear what was popularly called an "Alice Blue" gown at my own wedding. That was just nonsense some dressmaker came up with, this odd color of blue that supposedly matched my eyes. No, dear. I wore white to my own wedding. And orange blossoms. What's that you say? No, it is decidedly *not* true that I swung the sword we cut our cake with over my head like a Cossack. Goodbye!

(She hangs up the phone and returns to her guest)

ALICE: Are you covering the Nixon wedding? Pity. You're missing out on the media event of the summer. I understand reporters outnumber the guests nearly two to one.

Yes, as a matter of fact, I do like President Nixon. He's what I call level-headed. I suspect he knows quite a bit about what goes on in the world. And when he needs advice, he's not afraid to consult an expert.

Oh, yes. Secretary Kissinger is quite bright, too. And a terrible flirt at dinner parties. And since he makes it a point to flirt with me, he must be a brilliant diplomat. But I was actually talking about the other experts

Mr. Nixon relies upon. He once told me—now, this is off the record, of course—that he chats regularly with some of our former Presidents.

No, no. Not President Johnson. I mean the *very* former Presidents. Mr. Nixon tells me he periodically convenes a summit in front of the White House presidential portraits. I understand he especially appreciates President Madison's perspectives on the economy. Well, I suppose if you're going to get advice, it may as well be from someone who isn't seeking for political favors. Unless, of course, Mr. Madison is hinting around for a few dollars for a presidential library.

Oh, no. I don't think that sounds particularly crazy at all. I think it makes perfect sense to listen to our ancestors. Especially the former Presidents. Who better to give advice than someone who once held the job? I rather like the notion that the White House is saturated with the wisdom of past presidents, don't you? It's comforting, in a way. It's the same sort of feeling you get about many old houses, houses with history. Like this one. (*She notices that her guest is a bit uncomfortable with the subject*) Of course, who would I talk to?

(*She points to the cartoon of Franklin and Eleanor*)

ALICE: Franklin hasn't spoken to me since I called his ideas rubbish. And you couldn't pay me enough to listen to that dreadful voice of Eleanor's. I do a marvelous Eleanor impression, by the way. It was so famous at Washington dinner parties, even Eleanor herself asked to see a performance. Would you care to see it? (*She flashes a large-toothed smile*) It's all in the Roosevelt teeth, you know. That's why I seldom smile in family portraits.

(*Alice looks at her watch*)

ALICE: Oh, dear. It is getting late, isn't it? (*She rises*) Yes, well, maybe you're right. We'll just call it a day. Next week? Yes, Tuesday is just fine.

Oh no, my dear. The pleasure's been mine. Next time you come, bring your appetite. I'll have bread and butter sandwiches waiting for you. All right, dear, if you want to show yourself out. Just flip the latch when you go. I don't want another lost Turkish Ambassador wandering in here by mistake. The last time one got in, it nearly caused an international incident. Goodbye, dear!

(*We hear the sound of the door opening and closing, locking shut. The telephone rings. Alice answers*)

ALICE: Encyclopedia of White House weddings. Oh, Joanna! (*She laughs*) Yes, well the phone has been ringing off the hook with nuptial inquiries. Everyone and his sister wants me to compare the Tricia Nixon affair to the party Teddy Roosevelt threw for his daughter. I think I'll start making up lies. Oh, don't sound so scandalized, Joanna. After all, who would know? I'm the only one who was there who's still breathing. What's that, dear? You go right ahead. Don't worry about me. Janie will feed me and I'm dying to finish the new Lash biography of Eleanor and Franklin. I'm hoping he's nastier on the subject than I am. Yes, dear. Goodnight.

(*She hangs up the phone. She sits quietly for a few moments on the sofa. She then sifts through the mountain of books on the coffee table, looking for her biography. She then looks under the sofa, leaning over in a very unladylike fashion. She finds several books, and examines one in detail*)

ALICE: I wondered what happened to my Belloc collection. (*She blows the dust off the book, looks through it, then tosses it on top of a large stack of books. It makes a bit of noise. Cat meows loudly*)

So sorry, Madame Cat. Now, where did I put that book?

(*She putters around the room, looking for her book*)

TR: Try behind the piano.

(*She looks behind the piano*)

ALICE: Ah, here it is.

(*She finds a seat and begins to read*)

TR: I appreciate the kind words to that reporter about your dear Papa.

ALICE: Not at all.

TR: You might have been kinder to your cousin Eleanor, though. I don't see why you have to sound so bitter whenever you mention her name.

ALICE: Father, please!

TR: The two of you seemed to get along quite well together when you were young.

ALICE: I don't remember it that way.

TR: Eleanor was a marvelous girl! Bright, courageous. She wasn't afraid to get her hands dirty and tackle the difficult tasks.

ALICE: And I was.

TR: I didn't say that.

ALICE: You didn't have to. Your meaning is clear. Out with it, Father. You're disappointed in me, aren't you?

TR: Disappointed? Not exactly.

ALICE: I never lived up to your expectations, did I?

TR: You're a bright girl, Alice. Far brighter than any of your brothers.

ALICE: And you expected me to "make something of myself." Well, I'm sorry, Father. I did the best I could. I was the dutiful wife, the perfect mother, I even entertained politicians in my home on a regular basis. If that's not a qualification for sainthood, I don't know what is. I know I'm not what you had in mind, Father. I know I'm not out saving the world the way Eleanor did. I'm just not interested. To be perfectly frank, I'm far more interested in me.

TR: Alice!

ALICE: I'm me, Father. I may be my father's daughter, but I'm still me. Can't you accept that?

(*Alice crosses to the piano and picks up one of the journals*)

I don't know why I'm defending myself to you of all people. It was your motto I took to heart and patterned my life after. You always told us: (*she reads from the journal*) "Have a good time as long as you live." And by God, I have!

TR: You've forgotten the second half of that maxim: "Do something worthwhile with your life." Alice, have you ever thought about what they are going to write on your tombstone after you're gone? Gadfly.

ALICE: I beg your pardon?

TR: That's what they'll write. Gadfly. An "intentionally annoying person who stimulates or provokes others, especially by persistent irritating criticism."

ALICE: Thank you, Mr. Webster. I see nothing wrong with that for an epitaph. Socrates declared gadflies were necessary to sting the mule of society.

TR: Yes, but you could have been one of those leading the mules, Alice, not simply throwing barbs from the sidelines.

ALICE: What do you want from me, Father? Do you want me to rush out and volunteer for the Peace Corps? Don a Santa suit and ring that little Salvation Army bell? Perhaps rescue puppies from the animal shelter?

(*Cat meows*)

Just fooling, Cat. Listen, Father. I don't need to defend myself to you any more. I've accomplished quite a few things in my lifetime. I used to punch up your speeches, you know.

TR: You're a good writer, Alice. When you actually sit down and put pen to paper. It's a shame you don't at least answer your mail.

ALICE: What about my work to defeat the League of Nations? You can't say I did nothing there. I was a lobbyist before anyone had even invented the word. Does my political work count for nothing?

TR: And Kitz?

ALICE: Father, don't.

TR: What about Paulina?

ALICE: It wasn't my fault. She was unhappy. I know that. But she should have been stronger.

TR: Like you?

ALICE: Like you, Father.

TR: And if she wasn't? (*Pause*) Alice?

ALICE: What should I have done differently, Father? I know what it was like to grow up under a spotlight, so I kept Kitz out of the public eye. No one was snapping pictures of her every time she turned around. Of course, it was easier for Paulina. Her father was just Speaker of the House, not President of the United States.

TR: Alice.

ALICE: I did my best to keep her away from Washington entirely. I sent her to the best boarding schools. And to Vassar. She's the one who chose to drop out after two years and go to secretarial school. I did everything I could to protect Kitz from being hurt. Didn't I tell her that her marriage was a mistake? What more could I have done?

TR: You could have loved her imperfections a little more.

ALICE: And when was a Roosevelt ever allowed to be imperfect? (*Pause*) Why can't I speak to her, Father, why?

(*There is no answer*)

Why is it you that haunts me, Father? Just give me a moment with her. Please.

(*TR remains silent*)

Father. Father, please! (*She rises and crosses downstage*)

ALICE: Kitz? Kitz, can you hear me? It's Mummy, darling. Kitz? (*Pause*) Kitz? I miss you, sweetheart. Kitz, I love you.

(*The lights fade to black*)

ACT II

*The lights come up as before. Once again, the stage is empty. Books and
mail are stacked everywhere. Cat is nowhere to be seen. A tea tray has been
wheeled on stage. There are Chinese rose medallion tea cups and saucers,
silver spoons and forks, heavy white linen napkins, a teapot, a creamer, and
a sugar bowl. There are a variety of cakes and cookies—homemade, of
course—as well as a loaf of unsliced bread, a butter dish, and a very large
knife. A silver tea kettle sits atop a small flame, quietly whistling and bub-
bling unattended.*
The telephone rings several times.

ALICE (*offstage*): Janie, those boxes go back on the top shelf. All right, I
can hear you ringing. Here, Janie. Take these, please. I'll answer the telephone. Now, mind the dust. No, I'll take those two with me.

(*Alice enters, carrying two dusty diaries. She handles them with care, looks
at them a moment, then sets them down on the piano and crosses to the
phone*)

Yes? That's right. *Life* magazine, you say? Oh, yes. It was a lovely wedding, wasn't it? A bit soggy I suppose. What was it the President said?
"A soft rain caresses the marriage." Spoken like a true politician! Of
course, that's all well and good if you don't have to spend an eternity sitting under a hair dryer once a week. Perhaps Martha Mitchell had the
right idea with that silly parasol she carried. Although with the ruffles
and hoop skirt, it looked as though she was auditioning for "Gone With
the Wind."

What's that? Well, I hope you're not going to use the picture they printed
in the *Times*. That young Marine with all the braid under his arm looks as
though he was planning to snatch my purse!

(*The doorbell rings*)

ALICE (*to her caller*): Just a moment, if you please. (*She shouts upstairs*)
Janie! The door! Never mind. (*To the door*) I'm on the telephone, dear.
Come right in!

(*Alice returns to her phone call. We hear the door open and shut*)

ALICE: What's that? (*She sighs*) Well, to be quite frank, my supply of original thoughts about the White House wedding of nineteen-ought-six has
been completely exhausted.

(*Alice smiles at the invisible reporter from* Parade *magazine. She motions to
her to take a seat while she finishes her telephone conversation. She indi-
cates that she is bored to tears with the topic*)

ALICE: Suffice it to say that I was there and I wore white. Oh, and F.D.R.
adjusted my veil for the photograph. What's that? Yes, I believe we did receive quite a number of wedding presents. I think at the time I said I'd
take anything but a red hot stove.

TR: And she'd have taken that, too, if it didn't take too long to cool off!

ALICE (*laughing politely*): Yes, my father had quite a sense of humor,
didn't he? You're quite welcome. Goodbye.

(*She hangs up the phone*)

I serve notice right now, I'll talk about anything but weddings! You'd
think there was no other news at all. And by the way, what did you think
of those Vietnam papers that showed up in the *New York Times* this
week? I can just imagine that Daniel Ellsberg person spending every
night at the copy machine, risking national security for the benefit of
the American reading public. It's rather like a Saturday afternoon movie
serial, isn't it? I can hardly wait until tomorrow to read the next install-
ment. (*Pause*) All right, you needn't ask. The wedding was rather nice.
The Nixon/Cox affair, I mean, not mine. Oh, mine was quite nice, too.
If I do say so myself. But such an interesting assortment of wedding
guests at the Nixon/Cox affair. A truly inspired mix of saints and hooli-
gans. Of course, it was hard to tell which was which. Ralph Nader shaking hands with Billy Graham. Doesn't that man ever shave? Mr. Nader,
I mean. Not the Reverend Graham. (*She whispers*) I was told "fast"
Eddie Cox used to be a Nader's Raider. Imagine that! Marrying him was
probably Tricia's ultimate act of rebellion. Undoubtedly, "Fast Eddie"
will turn into a dull senior partner at some corporate law firm and end
up fighting against Mr. Nader's organization in court. Oh, and speaking
of presidents' daughters, did you hear about Luci Nugent and J. Edgar
Hoover? All she did was give him a small peck on the cheek after the
ceremony. J. Edgar nearly had a heart attack, acting as if a Cuban assas-

sin had finally found him. A most interesting day. But I'm exhausted. If I'm still around for Joanna's wedding, I'm going to encourage her to elope to Las Vegas.

No, Paulina was married in Massachusetts. A small wedding, really. Her husband was a playwright. Such an unstable profession, don't you think? I suppose that's why he went into the manufacture of firearms.

(*She notices the teapot and removes it from the flame*)

A cup of tea? You can't refuse me this time, I have my witch's brew ready and waiting.

(*She splashes some of the boiling water into the teapot to warm it up. She adds several teaspoonsful of black tea and fills the pot with water, covering it with a tea cozy*)

Bread and butter?

(*Alice takes the entire loaf of bread into her hands, spreads butter liberally on the cut end, then takes the enormous knife and carves one very thin slice of buttered bread, which she places on a plate with a piece of cake and a few cookies. She repeats the same procedure for herself*)

The English have perfected the art of sliced bread and butter sandwiches. I am eternally grateful to my Auntie Bye for marrying a Brit and sharing the technique with the "colonists." The secret is to butter the bread before you slice it. Then, with the sharpest knife in the house, slice the bread thin enough so you can practically see through it. Paulina always had such difficulty making the slices thin enough. (*She demonstrates*) There! Now, how do you take your tea?

(*Alice pours a cup of tea, adding milk and a teaspoon. She pours herself a cup, adding a slice of lemon and sips contentedly*)

Ah. You wouldn't think it to look at me, but I can be a very crabby old lady if I don't get my cup of Earl Grey every afternoon. Sometimes I think if I can become this enamored of simple black tea, imagine what I'd be like with opium! Do you know when I was a teenager and they were digging around in my mouth trying to fix my teeth, it was cocaine they gave you for the pain. A rather heady experience, I can tell you. I quite enjoyed it. Alcohol never did much for me, though. Perhaps it was seeing poor Eleanor's father in his cups once too often.

TR: Tragic case. I should have spoken more to him about his imprudence.

ALICE: Some say my Uncle Elliott simply suffered from the constant disappointment of not living up to his father's expectations. My grandfather Roosevelt was apparently quite a taskmaster.

TR: Not at all! Father was honestly the best man I ever knew! I owe everything to him. I never would have outlived my asthma if my father hadn't taken me on those 20 miles hikes to strengthen my lungs. It's not unlike my insistence that you children march through Rock Creek Park or read a book a day.

ALICE: Yes, quite a taskmaster, "old man" Roosevelt. Drink your tea, dear. It's getting cold.

This cushion? (*She picks up the embroidered cushion on the couch and reads aloud*) "If you haven't got anything good to say about anyone come and sit by me." Yes, I'm afraid I did coin that phrase. I've always said it takes a bit of malice to be a good hostess. But do be careful, my dear. Dozens of "bon mots" have been uttered in and around Washington, all attributed to me. It's positively scandalous! People think they can say any horrid little thing and get away with it as long as they say it originated with Alice Roosevelt Longworth. For example, now while I will take credit for the observation that Wendell Wilkie sprang from the grass roots of America's country clubs—the quip about Thomas Dewey wasn't mine at all. I overheard that one at my shoe repair shop. Oh, you know the line. "How do you expect people to vote for a man who looks like a bridegroom on a wedding cake?" (*She laughs. There is a pause*)

TR: Gadfly, Alice.

ALICE: Stop it, Father.

TR: Nothing but a gadfly.

ALICE (*to the reporter*): You know, I have done more with my life than just comment on Washington's political scene throughout the ages.

No, it's not true—as you say—that I've never been *for* something. Not true at all. I've contributed quite a bit to the American political landscape, if I do say so myself. And I am not, as one of my lesser beloved cousins once remarked, "so much of my Father without the purpose." I've had purpose aplenty! For most of my adult life, I've been a regular fixture in the Senate Gallery. I do love a good debate. At Republican National Conventions throughout the years, I was frequently consulted on platform matters and even candidate choices. And you might say I was one of the most instrumental forces in seeing that Mr. Wilson's League of Nations proposal died a well-deserved death. Oh, it's ancient history now, but it was a matter of the future of the post-war world as we knew it back then. You know the League idea—a sort of primitive United Nations you might say—although certainly more dangerous at the time! My father compared it to the unconditional surrender of Germany in 1919.

TR: It practically called for the surrender of the United States to the sovereignty of the League! Not that I think mankind shouldn't try to solve its problems in a worldwide arena. Why—

ALICE: Wilson was the worst kind of fool. We used this house as the unofficial headquarters for anti-League activities. We would sit around and plot our strategy—feasting on scrambled eggs and port. And when we weren't working, I would compose bawdy ballads and limericks about dear President Wilson.

(*Again she returns to the piano, singing to the tune of "Yankee Doodle"*)

ALICE:

> Mr. Wilson came to Paris
> Just to sign a treaty
> Perhaps his trip to see 'Le Follies'
> Sent him home with V.D.
> "Monsieur Woody, keep it up!"
> So 'Les Danseurs' told him
> While distracted by such matters
> A bill of goods they sold him!

(*She pounds out the tune to "Shave and a Haircut, Two Bits" for the big finish*)

Just "un peut risque, n'est-c-pas?"

The papers got wind of our little group, and labeled me "the Colonel of Death"—of all things! Well, they could call me what they liked. It was a cause worth fighting for. And we won. We got more than a third of the Senate to sign a promise not to vote for the League. And it died the legislative death it so soundly deserved. Of course, I worked a bit of my own private influence, as well. When the President returned from Europe, I was part of the unofficial welcoming party. I followed Mr. Wilson to the White House. Standing on the curbstone, I crossed my fingers, made the sign of the evil eye, and said: "A murrain on him! A murrain on him!" My travelling companion kept saying: "Don't let anyone hear you!" He was afraid the Secret Service would pick me up and I'd never be heard from again. The spell worked better than I'd expected. Mr. Wilson collapsed from fatigue and nervous exhaustion on a train in Wichita, Kansas. One month later, he suffered a stroke. An appropriate end, don't you think? Blood vessels exploding in the brain of the man known as "the thinking man's president"?

TR: Alice! I think you've really gone too far this time.

ALICE: I did it for you, Father! (*To the reporter*) I don't say this with particular pride. But Wilson had crossed my father. He refused to grant Father's request to raise a division of fighting men—a sort of revival of the Rough Riders—to assist in the War. Even Clemenceau wrote to Wilson, asking him to change his mind. He refused. I'm certain the decision was made solely for political reasons. My father was a very popular man. Wilson knew that if Father returned from Europe triumphant—as he had from San Juan Hill—Roosevelt would be impossible to beat at the polls. Oh, yes, Father was seriously considering another run for the presidency in 1920. Only his death prevented him from winning back the White House. As for Mr. Wilson, he should have known I never forgive those who injure the people I love.

TR: Alice! Is this how I raised you? My God, girl. What happened to compassion? To reconciliation? What did I teach you about good sportsmanship, if nothing else?

ALICE: I thought you would be pleased, Father. I was just doing my part to see that your legacy lived on.

TR: Quite a legacy: dirty tricks and black magic. You did it for yourself, Alice, not for me. You couldn't bear the thought of never returning to the White House, relinquishing forever the title of "Princess Alice."

ALICE: And what about you, Father? You were never content to simply fade away from public view. You missed the conspicuousness of the presidency as much as I did. But you always found a way to get your name into the papers anyway, thereby ensuring that the legend and legacy of Theodore Roosevelt would live on.

(*Alice turns to the reporter in a slightly disingenuous fashion*)

It was really up to my brother Ted to carry on my father's legacy. Such things *always* fell on Ted's shoulders. Did you know that my father was named after his father? So, actually, Ted, Junior, should have been called T.R. the Third. (*She shakes her head*) I thank God sometimes that I hadn't been born the eldest son. You can imagine how difficult it must have been to live up to the name of Theodore Roosevelt. Poor Ted. At one point, the doctors believed he was on the point of "nervous prostration." They scolded my father for pushing Ted too hard.

TR: But I vowed thereafter never to press Ted either in mind or body.

ALICE: Ted always worried for fear he wouldn't be worthy of his father.

TR: Worthy of me? I was so very proud of him. He won honor not only for his children but, like the Chinese, he has ennobled his ancestors. I walk with my head higher because of him.

ALICE: And what about me, Father. What about me? Did I ennoble our ancestors?

TR: And what of Paulina? Did you ever tell her you were proud of her, Alice? She was such a fragile little thing.

ALICE (*to the reporter*): Of course, I know how difficult it is for a parent to balance high expectations with a gentle touch. It may come easy for some people. But not for a Roosevelt. Besides, you can't say it scarred anyone's childhood, exactly. Look at my brother Quentin. He should have been the eldest son. Quentin was so much more like my father than any of us. And he had no illusions of grandeur about being the President's son. Quentin's idea of a good time was to tromp around on the furniture in the Lincoln Bedroom wearing stilts. Once he stopped traffic in Dupont Circle, making awful faces at people passing by.

TR: One of them was me, I seem to recall.

ALICE: Father's open carriage happened by—I think Father was sitting with a bearded dignitary of some sort. Quentin made his worst face. (*She demonstrates*) Father could have ignored him. But being Father, he didn't. He responded with the most horrible grimace he could muster. (*She again demonstrates*)

(*Alice and TR laugh*)

TR: "Quentin Roosevelt," I said to him, "you have nearly succeeded in making a fool of me in public. I had the idea of asking you to hop in and ride the rest of the way with me. But on second thought, I have concluded that it is entirely too dangerous for me to be seen with you."

(*TR continues to laugh as Alice continues*)

ALICE: My brothers would do anything for my father. Anything. Every one of them rushed off to fight in the war. "Filling in for Father," they used to say. Ted was gassed and shot in the leg.

(*TR's laughter fades out*)

Archie was badly wounded by a shell. Kermit survived malaria and brought back great honors. Quentin never came home. He was a pilot, but he should never have been allowed to fly. He was as blind as Father. He passed his physical by memorizing the optician's chart.

TR: Enough, Alice. I'm not so foolish that I don't recognize my role in Quentin's death. I know he enlisted simply as a sign of respect for me. I could have told him it wasn't necessary. I can't think of anyone I respected more than Quentin.

ALICE: Certainly not Alice. But surely, Quentin's death wasn't entirely your fault, Father. After all, it wasn't you who assassinated that Austro-Hungarian archduke. (*To the reporter*) It was a war the United States just couldn't sit out. It was the aftermath that was truly criminal. President Wilson was lauded for his "great moral leadership" for trying to ram his Fourteen Points down everyone's throats. Father knew it was a settlement the Germans couldn't live with. And they didn't. The Second World War was a festering boil that finally burst. Again, the Roosevelt boys answered the call, just as their father would have wanted them to do. My brother Kermit died just after Pearl Harbor was bombed. Archie was wounded a second time. And Brigadier General Theodore Roosevelt, Jr., died of a heart attack on the battlefields of France, a week after D-Day, when he landed with his troops at Normandy.

(*There is a pause. Alice quotes*)

> "The tumult and the shouting dies;
> The Captains and the Kings depart:
> Still stands Thine ancient sacrifice,
> An humble and contrite heart.
> Lord God of Hosts, be with us yet,
> Lest we forget—lest we forget!"

Yes, Kipling. No need to end on such a sad note, my dear. Life is really not so glum for this old lady. Even if I have outlived nearly everybody I know. There will always be new tragedies to read about.

(*She gestures to the* New York Times *and its article about the Pentagon papers*)

Our own little war in Indochina, for example. The Vietnamese Embassy is right down the street, you know. Last year, those Weatherman people stormed the place. And then the police responded with tear gas, of course. It's not half bad, you know. Tear gas, I mean. I stuck my head out my front door just to clear my sinuses.

How about a fresh cup of tea? No? You don't mind if I fortify myself with another cup?

(*She warms up the teapot with more hot water and pours herself another cup*)

Hmm? Oh, Eleanor again. I had a lot of admiration for Eleanor. But I became bored with her type of piety. I can still see those large, blue eyes fixed on "one," worrying about "one," wanting "one" to know that—in her, "one" had a friend. The woman never used the second person singular. Eleanor always wanted to discuss things like whether contentment was better than happiness. And did they conflict? Things I didn't give a damn about. And I'm certain Franklin didn't either. When he started seeing Lucy Mercer, I encouraged the relationship. I was delighted Franklin was having a good time. He deserved a good time. I tried to tell Eleanor about it once upon a time, but she refused. (*Again, Alice imitates Eleanor's voice*) "I do not believe in knowing things which your husband does not wish you to know. So I think I will be spared any further mysterious secrets." Poor Eleanor.

TR: Poor Alice. Nick was a bit of a devil as well, wasn't he?

ALICE: I could understand young Lucy being entranced by Franklin. Myself, I always liked older men. Attraction for me had very little to do with sex. It was more closely connected with a certain vitality, a sense of humor, and a mental affinity. That was when the mayhem started.

No. I was not referring to anyone in particular.

(*Alice is a bit taken aback by the reporter's next question*)

Senator Borah? Well, of course I knew him. I wouldn't be much of a Washington hostess if I didn't know the head of the Senate Foreign Relations Committee. Bill Borah and I were dear friends for many years.

Know him in the Biblical sense? I haven't heard that expression since before the flood.

TR: Alice!

ALICE: No, it was not true we ever considered calling her "De-borah."

Poor little creature. For several days, she had no name at all. Eventually, we called her Paulina after my favorite figure in the Bible. Paul always wrote so eloquently on the virtues of self-denial.

TR: Alice, what's this about Bill Borah?

ALICE: I don't care to talk about it, Father.

ALICE (*to the reporter, laughing*): Oh, I'm certain the busybodies of this town have speculated for decades that Paulina was not Nick's child. Absolutely absurd! I imagine people say such things about any child born nearly 20 years into a marriage.

TR: If one of my daughters—or one of my sons, for that matter—even considered a relationship of this sort outside the confines of marriage—

ALICE: Enough, Father. I'm well aware of your moral sensibilities. You always act as though you were the original recipient of the Ten Commandments. I don't need your sermonizing at this late date.

(*Alice to both her audiences*)

Now listen to me. Whatever else he was, Nick was indeed Paulina's father—in every sense of the word. Paulina adored him. And he was devoted to her. He would bring her to the Hill to meet his colleagues every chance he could. Half of Congress used to fight for an invitation to her little birthday parties. (*Pause*) I often wonder if things might have been different for her if Nick had lived just a little bit longer. She was just six years old when he died. So young to lose a parent.

(*Alice retrieves her public face*)

But it does no good to live in the past. If you plan to live as long as I have, you must keep your eye on the future. That's where life begins.

(*She rises*)

(*Insincerely*) My dear, it's been lovely chatting with you. I'm so pleased you could come to tea. But now, I'm afraid I must send you home. My granddaughter Joanna is bringing over a few friends this evening and I must make the place presentable. Or at least put a few books away so that people will have a place to sit down. May I show you out?

(*We hear the sound of Cat hissing and shrieking*)

Oh, dear. I wondered where he'd disappeared to. Don't apologize, dear. Cat has been stepped on more than once, I can assure you. I hope you're not bleeding too badly. That is a bit of a nasty scratch. Here, let me get you some mercurochrome—(*she turns to walk upstairs*)—all right, if you wish. At least let me walk you to the—(*we hear the door slam*)—door. Oh, dear.

(*Alice addresses the unseen cat, which is directly down center*)

Good for you, Cat. I'd have scratched her eyes out myself, but my nails are a bit too short.

TR: Alice—

ALICE: No, Father. There'll be no more discussion about Paulina's paternity.

TR: Then what about your own? You made it very clear to that reporter that you find fault with quite a bit of my parenting. Quentin's death. Ted's nervous exhaustion. Are you that angry with me, Alice?

ALICE: Are you that angry with *me*, Father? Why are you tormenting me with questions about the way I raised Kitz? Implying I didn't love her enough. And this from you of all people!

TR: Alice, you know how much I love you.

ALICE: Do I?

TR: Alice, of course you do.

ALICE: I took your advice, Father. I've done a bit of organizing, cleaning out old papers and such. I found your letter to Auntie Bye. (*Pause*) Why did you try to give me away as a child?

(*There is no answer*)

You heard me, Father. It's too late to deny it.

(*She crosses to the piano and picks up a dusty journal. She pulls out a dusty, yellowed letter*)

(*Reading*) "If you wish, you shall keep Baby Lee. I, of course, shall pay the expense." Baby Lee. You couldn't even use my name.

TR: Alice.

ALICE: Yes, Alice. Alice Lee. Just like my mother.

TR: Alice, please. It was a mistake. A terrible mistake.

ALICE: What was a mistake? My finding the evidence in your own handwriting?

TR: I believed—and I know the conclusion was erroneous—but I believed at the time that if I put the child—

ALICE: Me, Father.

TR: Yes, you, Alice. If I could put you out of my sight—out of my conscious memory—then perhaps I could also forget the overwhelming loss of my sweet Alice Lee.

ALICE: You never forget that kind of loss, Father.

TR: Yes, I know.

ALICE: I did love Kitz, Father. More than you know.

TR: More than she knew.

ALICE: And that was my "great mistake," Father. Something I'll never be able to forget.

TR: Perhaps not forget. But at least forgive. Alice, please believe me now when I tell you that you are the dearest thing to my heart.

ALICE: Truly, Father?

TR: Truly, Alice.

ALICE (*pause*): Then what changed your mind, Father? About me, I mean.

TR: I'd like to say I had the change of heart. But it was Edith. She insisted that you come live with us—she insisted you were as much an important part of this family as she was.

ALICE: Funny. I never thought of Edith in that way—a champion of little Alice.

TR: You know I'm your greatest champion now, don't you, Alice?

ALICE: You have an extraordinary manner of showing it, Father.

TR: I don't apologize for the high standards I set for you, Alice.

ALICE: No, I don't suppose you would. Tell me one thing, Father. Did you ever regret not leaving me with Auntie Bye?

TR: Every day I'd read about your latest escapade in the newspaper. No, truly, Alice, there's never been a day in my life that I haven't been proud to say you are my daughter. And what about you, Alice? Would you rather have grown up with Bye?

ALICE: I don't know. I'm sure it would have been much better for me "psychologically" and all that. But truth be told, it was rather fun having Theodore Roosevelt for a father.

TR: It's not just the Presidential trappings, I hope.

ALICE: Well—

TR: Alice!

(*She laughs*)

ALICE: No, truly, Father. I'm very glad I ended up with you. You're the best man I ever knew. (*Pause*) Although I rather like the idea that you, too, possessed a few flaws. It makes life a bit easier for the rest of us wee humans.

TR: I love you, Alice.

ALICE: I know, Father. Thank you.

TR: Good night, girl. Oh and Alice, do one small favor for a former President, will you?

ALICE: What's that, Father?

TR: Do something about your mail. It's disgraceful, seeing it stacked up like that.

ALICE (*smiling*): Goodnight, Father.

(*She walks over to the piano where a mountain of mail is stacked high. She sits at the piano bench and takes a stack in hand. She looks at it idly and picks out a melody on the piano with her free hand*)

TR: And Alice—

ALICE: Hmm?

TR: Kitz sends her love, as well.

ALICE: What!?

(*The rubber band on the stack of letters is so old, it snaps off and the letters scatter to the floor. Alice bends over to pick up the letters and one catches her eye. She opens it up and reads aloud*)

"My dear Alice. I am shocked that this great grief has come to you. And I am glad that you have the small grandchild. If there is anything I can ever do for you, please let me know. With my deepest sympathy. Affectionately, Eleanor."

(*Alice slowly reacts to the letter, to the reality of the loss of her daughter*)

Kitz. Oh, Kitz!

(*The phone rings again. Alice recovers her public face and answers her phone*)

ALICE: Hello. Joanna! I was just thinking about you. No, dear. I'm fine. I haven't forgotten. I'd be delighted to entertain your friends. I'll see you then. Goodbye, dear.

(*Alice slowly returns to the piano and plays "Alice, Where Art Thou Going"*)

> Alice, where art thou going
> Where can we spend the day
> Alice, we'll make a dead swell showing
> If it costs my whole week's pay

My coin was made for blowing
Girlie, it's up to you
Sail or ride or roam the sands
Or sit and listen to the bands
Alice, where art thou going.

(*The lights fade to black*)

JOSEPH P. RITZ

Trappists

Joseph P. Ritz's long career as an award-winning journalist and playwright is distinguished by several national and state awards that he has won in both professions. He wrote part of a series of articles, *The Road to Integration*, which won a Pulitzer Prize, and is also the author of a book, *The Despised Poor*. His other plays include *Copy Desk, Family Honor, Inside Passage, I. R. S.*, and *The Harvest Years*, a finalist in one of The Open Book/Stage & Screen Book Club competitions. He is a resident of upstate New York.

An earlier version of *Trappists* called *Abbey of the Monaghalia*, was one of four winning plays in the Drama League of New York's Plays in Progress Competition. A later version, *Acts of Contrition*, was staged by the American Ensemble Theater. It became *Trappists* when it was polished at the University of Massachusetts' Theater in the Works festival. In 1994, it won the Christians in Theatre Arts competition for best play, and in 1997 was first runner-up in The Open Book/Stage & Screen Book Club's fourth national competition.

The Open Book's production of *Trappists* is scheduled to open April 6th, 2001, at the 78th Street Theatre Lab, Manhattan, with Marvin Kaye directing the following cast:

MEREDITH MALLORY	ALICE KING
DOM GREGORY	RJ LEWIS
SUSAN SHAWNESSY	JONA TUCK
THOMAS HOGAN	WAYNE MARKOVER

CHARACTERS

Meredith Mallory   A reporter for the magazine, *Quote*. She is in her early thirties. She dresses casually as evident by the fact that when we first see her she is wearing slacks, a blouse and sweater with a little jewelry, a gold chain, earrings.

She is neither cute nor beautiful, a strong-minded, intelligent woman who doesn't take great pains with her face or attempt to be sexy.

She can be naive and charming when it suits her purpose. She has a wit with an edge to it which she cannot entirely suppress. She is a talented journeyman in a cynical profession and her suspicious outlook partly reflects her training and experience.

Dom Gregory   Abbot of Our Lady of Champlain monastery. He is a tall man in his mid-fifties or maybe sixties. He gives the appearance of being stretched out, as though he were a figure in an El Greco painting. He wears the white robe and black scapular of a Trappist. Around his waist is a brown belt, also part of the habit. He wears sandals.

He is a gentle man with a sense of humor, quick to smile and to ease a difficult situation with a joke, yet there is steel there and his authority shows through his quiet demeanor.

Susan Shawnessy   A nurse in St. Jude's Hospital. She is a raven-haired young woman around 30, fair-skin, blue eyes, Irish-looking, a pretty, alert, and intelligent female, yet a romantic whose passions are close to the surface. She is a devout Catholic.

Thomas Hogan   A monk, as Dom Gregory.

He is in his early forties. He is less self-assured and dogmatic than one would expect from someone who wrote a best seller at the age of 25 and whose books are still popular among readers with an intellectual or religious bent. There are two elements in his nature which are unexpected and paradoxical for someone who has chosen a lifetime of obedience and solitude:

At the core of his character remains a stubborn and re-
bellious spirit and a need for companionship more material than the love of God.

SETTING

The stage is divided into two sections. One is the abbot's office in the
monastery, a room with grey stone walls, a statue of St. Benedict and the Virgin Mary holding the Christ child are on either side of the abbot's desk. The top
of the desk is clean, except for one or two sheets of paper, two ballpoint pens
sticking out of a holder, a Bible, and a large, ornate candlestick. A filled bookcase is behind the desk. A crucifix hangs on the wall. If possible, there is a
window on one side of the desk. There is a feeling of simplicity and greyness.

On the left downstage is a wooden, high-backed swivel chair that hides
anyone sitting in it from the audience's view when the back faces the audience. On the wall is an inscription, "Pax Intrantibus."

The other half of the stage is an outdoor scene. There is a small garden
in the foreground and a stone path that encircles a statue of Our Lady of
Lourdes. There may be flowers planted around the statue. A bench is in front
of it. The path leads upward to a woods and a grassy area where an old fallen
tree is little more than a log that can be sat on. The woods become denser
and wilder as the path climbs toward the rear of the stage. A scrim of grey
cloth, resembling as much as possible the grey stone wall of the monastery
wall, blocks the abbot's office from the audience's view when that portion of
the stage is not lit.

ALTERNATIVE SETTING

Four tall stools are set in a semicircle on the stage. Each is lit by an overhead
light. Downstage are two wooden benches on which the scenes between
Hogan and Susan and Susan and Meredith are played.

Dom Gregory is alone downstage at curtain. Meredith walks in on him
from the darkened stage. The other actors appear from the dark when they
enter a scene and remain on stage throughout the play.

The actors are lit only during the scene in which they appear. There are no
props. Gregorian chants play under the actors in parts of the scenes in the
abbey.

The recorded sounds of birds can also be used effectively in the woodland
and garden scenes.

ACT I

TIME: The present. Late spring.

AT RISE: It is evening. Dom Gregory, dressed in the white robe and black scapular of a Trappist monk, lies prone on the floor in front of his desk with his arms stretched out in the form of a cross. He is reciting the eighth psalm of David in a low voice, but which is strong enough to carry to the audience. In the background the muffled sound of monks' voices singing the Salve Regina can be heard.

    Meredith enters and knocks on the desk to get Dom Gregory's attention.

DOM GREGORY: Oh Lord, Our Lord, how admirable is Thy name in the whole earth! For Thy magnificence is elevated above the heavens. Out of the mouths of infants and of sucklings Thou hast perfected praise, because of my enemies, that Thou mayest destroy the enemy and the avenger. For I will behold Thy heavens, the works of Thy fingers . . .

MEREDITH: Is this where they make the Benedictine?

(*Dom Gregory lifts his head and looks at her surprised and puzzled. He slowly rises*)

DOM GREGORY: Whiskey. It goes into our fruit cakes. Is something wrong?

MEREDITH (*extending her hand*): I'm Meredith Mallory.

DOM GREGORY: You?

MEREDITH: You must have gotten a letter from Dom Ignatius.

DOM GREGORY (*hesitates before taking her hand with some reluctance*): I didn't expect a **female** reporter. The name . . . well, you've come many miles.

MEREDITH: About five hours from New York.

DOM GREGORY: You must be tired.

MEREDITH: I got a late start.

DOM GREGORY: You've created an awkward situation. (*Meredith looks surprised and annoyed*) This is not the place for us to talk. (*Meredith gives a slight shake of her head. Dom Gregory walks to the door and opens it*) I'm afraid I must ask you to leave. (*Meredith sits defiantly on one of the chairs*)

MEREDITH: Why?

DOM GREGORY: Women are not permitted here. Many of the ancient rules have been relaxed, but . . .

MEREDITH: Women reporters these days invade many male bastions.

DOM GREGORY: This is not a men's locker room in a sports stadium.

MEREDITH: If you send me away I'll raise holy hell. It will be all over the media. You agreed to an interview. You refused when you found I'm a woman.

DOM GREGORY: That's not quite . . .

MEREDITH: How do you think it will sit with the younger women in the church? They're speaking out against your male rules. Think about it. You'll have to use force. I'll put up a wicked struggle. You could be charged with sexual assault.

DOM GREGORY (*picks up the phone*): I don't like calling the sheriff. (*He begins punching numbers*)

MEREDITH: Come on, father. Women come here frequently.

DOM GREGORY: They are not allowed inside the cloister except . . . (*He pauses and slowly puts down the phone*) On some occasions we have to comply with federal regulations—deliveries, medical emergencies, those kinds of things. Women are in so many occupations today. We obey all the laws.

MEREDITH: I've come a long way.

DOM GREGORY (*sits behind his desk, recognizing defeat*): I would have arranged for an interview outside the cloister. Women quite often ask questions when they come to the abbey. They have a curiosity about men living most of the day in silence—without feminine companionship. You're the first woman to be in this office. I would have liked to have seen the expression on Brother Gatekeeper's face when you said I had agreed to see you.

MEREDITH: He was the monk by the gatehouse? Big bushy eyebrows? They covered half his forehead. He didn't want to let me in. You aren't bothered by call girls are you?

DOM GREGORY: I don't think we're very good prospects.

MEREDITH (*laughs*): If you could have seen the look on your face just then. I'm just kidding, father.

DOM GREGORY: Brother Gatekeeper probably didn't expect a visitor at this hour.

MEREDITH: I got such an angry look.

DOM GREGORY: What we are not allowed to say in words here we often express in looks or gestures. There is a sign language in the monastery which has 600 characters. I suspect it will die out eventually. Since the rules have been relaxed I've noticed a tendency to expand the definition of necessary language.

MEREDITH: You'd think I'd come in the middle of the night.

DOM GREGORY: The song that's just ending is Salve Regina, hail to our queen, the mother Mary. It's sung at bedtime.

MEREDITH: It's only a little before seven.

DOM GREGORY: The day begins here at two in the morning with the signing of the Little Office of the Blessed Virgin Mary.

MEREDITH: I should have waited until morning. I got off on the wrong exit. Those narrow roads. I got caught behind one of those logging trucks. It crawled up the hills. The bastard . . . the driver wouldn't let me by.

DOM GREGORY: Our supper is over, but I'm sure we can boil a potato or two. You'll find our cheese excellent.

MEREDITH: No, thanks. I ate on the road, steak. I've heard about your meals. Never go to a Trappist monastery for the food, or the dinner conversation.

DOM GREGORY: Do they say that? Our fruitcakes are prized.

MEREDITH: Hogan called this place a fruitcake factory.

DOM GREGORY: So I've heard.

(*Meredith takes a small tape recorder from her pocket and puts it on the desk*)

MEREDITH: You don't mind if I put this interview on tape? It saves a lot of writing.

DOM GREGORY: It must be useful in your occupation. We have little use for one here. (*Dom Gregory opens a deep drawer in his desk and takes out an unopened bottle of sherry and two glasses*) Would you care for some sherry? I was given this bottle last Christmas by someone who knows how much I enjoy it.

(*Meredith nods*)

MEREDITH: I wish I had your will power.

(*Dom Gregory pours the wine into two small glasses and hands one to Meredith*)

MEREDITH (*taking a sip of the wine*): It's good. Not too sweet. Made by monks?

DOM GREGORY (*nods*): In France. (*He reaches across the desk and turns off the tape recorder*) Your letter to the abbot general indicated you are an admirer of Father Francis. I tell you in all honesty, I would not have invited you here had I been consulted beforehand, not even if you were a male. We have had some bad experiences with some members of the press, especially since some of Father Francis' journals were made public. Some writers come here with preconceived ideas. They invent things to conform with their notion of truth. Did you come here looking for a means to discredit our way of life? That's the kind of thing that sells today.

MEREDITH: There's always been a fascination for martyrs. I'm looking for the man some people in the Catholic Church are calling a saint for our times. Ever since the miracle . . .

DOM GREGORY: I wish he had healed a less public figure.

MEREDITH: It's an interesting coincidence that the miracle occurred just before the start of her new series.

DOM GREGORY: I've never seen her on television. We are cut off from much of the distractions of the world. (*He reaches over and turns on the tape recorder*) What do you wish to know?

MEREDITH: Why don't we start by sorting out the facts about his death. You were in El Salvador?

DOM GREGORY: We were attending a conference on contemporary monastic life and its meaning in society today. Cardenal was to have been there. He had been a novice under Father Francis's guidance, you know. It was a climactic time for Father Francis, the whole Central American trip. He had his great mystical experience there. He at last came to the place where time stopped.

MEREDITH: You were there to watch him?

DOM GREGORY: I was there as the abbot of a major U.S. monastery. It was I who arranged for the invitation of Father Francis.

MEREDITH: Why? You refused permission for him to leave the abbey for 24 years. Even when you were pressured by the Vatican. The pope . . .

DOM GREGORY: The pope expressed much interest in Father Francis's writings. He sent him a stole he had worn himself. Rome would not have been a good place for Father Francis.

MEREDITH: Why? There are rumors he didn't intend to return here.

DOM GREGORY: The Abbey of Our Lady of Champlain is not a prison. Father Francis could have left freely any time he wished. Many do. Are you looking for a sensation?

MEREDITH: I'm looking for the truth. We got off to a bad start, but it was God who made me a woman.

DOM GREGORY: The last person who was here asking questions was a young Franciscan nun trying to obtain evidence for his beatification.

MEREDITH: You don't think he was a saint?

DOM GREGORY: Thomas? A saint is anyone who gets to heaven. It's quite possible that Father Francis is among them. (*With a hint of wry sarcasm*) He was a saintly man.

MEREDITH: Many people say so. There are some questions. You had a quarrel with Hogan the day he was killed.

DOM GREGORY: We had a discussion. Father Francis was by no means a team man. Sometimes living with a prophet can be difficult.

MEREDITH: Even here where half the day is spent in prayer?

DOM GREGORY: Even here we remain men, with all the weaknesses of men: anger, pride, deceit, spitefulness, ambition, jealousy. We try to root them out, but it's a struggle that has to be renewed each day.

MEREDITH: And what about the sins of the flesh? What about lust? Lust for women—and for men?

DOM GREGORY: Those are human weaknesses. We do what we can to guard against them. No particular friendships are allowed here.

(*The lights go up on Hogan in the garden*)

HOGAN: I asked for solitude. I know now, it's not what I wanted.

(*Susan Shawnessy enters. She wears a frilly white dress. Her hair is undone, so that it hangs below her neck. She is breathless and nervous*)

SUSAN: The grass smells almost like wildflowers. A monk was cutting it.

(*Hogan, surprised, walks rapidly toward her with his arms outstretched as if to embrace her. She runs toward him. A few feet before they come together he drops his arms and she slows to a walk*)

HOGAN: I was afraid you wouldn't come.

SUSAN: I was afraid you asked me only out of politeness. The poems brought me here.

(*They walk together without touching. Susan looks at the flowers, smells some of them. Hogan toys with a small crucifix which hangs from a string around his neck*)

HOGAN: Did anyone question you?

SUSAN: No. Brother Gatekeeper looked grim. I think he sees me as a temptation of the flesh. I feel like it. Some of the monks looked at me like—like a man looks at a woman.

HOGAN: We are all men here. We think about women, sometimes, even in prayer.

SUSAN (*teasing*): Is that when you thought up the poems you sent?

HOGAN: They were written on impulse. The next day I would have destroyed them.

SUSAN: I was touched. Usually people send me funny verses from Hallmark.

HOGAN: Now you know what an inadequate poet I am. My poems are published only because Trappists are such curiosities.

SUSAN: I don't believe that. Will you publish any of the poems?

HOGAN: The censors wouldn't allow it. The order protects my image. They were a foolish impulse.

SUSAN: I'm glad you sent them. I've enjoyed your letters for, gosh, so many years. But the poems, they were something special.

HOGAN: I had wondered all these years what you were like in person.

SUSAN: How did you imagine me?

HOGAN: It changed from time to time. Sometimes your hair was the color of redwood. Sometimes black as walnut bark. You wore glasses—big lenses with a plastic frame. You were always smiling. . . . I think I thought so because of your funny letters.

SUSAN: I moved heaven and earth to be your nurse. You can't imagine how many favors I owe.

HOGAN: I wondered at the coincidence. Then I accepted it as something ordained by God.

SUSAN: The time I was here before, when I was studying your poems and wanted to see the place you stayed . . .

HOGAN: Before you first wrote me . . .

SUSAN: I must have seen you in the chapel then, but I didn't know what you looked like. There was a sign by the cloister: "Women forbidden to enter under pain of excommunication." It was as though we were something evil that had to be avoided.

HOGAN: That sign is gone. Now women drive some of the trucks that deliver flour and pick up fruitcakes. A monk has many more temptations.

SUSAN: More than the Latin mass has changed since Vatican II.

HOGAN: Yes. I was surprised when I saw my face in a mirror. I had grown older.

SUSAN: I couldn't stand not knowing if my face was dirty or whether my hair was out of place. I wish I had known you then, I would have been your mirror. (*She sits on a bench placed near the path and quickly changes the topic*) Do you still use sign language?

HOGAN: Yes. But not as much. (*He puts his thumbs on his temples and spreads his fingers widely so that they suggest antlers*) This is a deer.

(*Susan laughs. Hogan twists an imaginary mustache with his thumbs and forefingers*).

SUSAN: Let me guess. A cat!

HOGAN: YES!

SUSAN (*imitates a cat*) Meow. Let's see if I can guess another one. (*Hogan makes a fist, brings it to his mouth and misses the knuckles of his forefinger and middle finger and then opens his hand*)

SUSAN: A punch in the mouth? That's wrong, isn't it? (*She laughs uncertainly. Hogan nods*) Um. Kiss. I want to kiss you. (*Hogan shakes his head*) I didn't think so. (*She giggles*) Do I have twenty questions?

HOGAN: If you wish.

SUSAN: No. I give up.

HOGAN: Peace.

SUSAN: Peace? That was harder than the others. What's the sign for doctor? (*Hogan makes an imaginary injection on his left forearm with his right hand*) Oh, an injection. You could use that one for nurse. Let me think of something else. An iron. Like ironing clothes. (*He makes the motions of a man ironing something*) Sew. To sew something. (*He holds out his left hand with his palm down, then, with his right hand, pantomimes putting a needle and thread through his fingers*) Those were easy. I expected something more obscure. Is this a woman? (*She outlines the curves of a female figure with her hands. Hogan shakes his head. He makes the Cistercian Order's sign for a woman by placing his right index and middle fingers on his forehead and drawing the fingers across the forehead from left to right*) That one *is* obscure. I wonder where it came from? What's the sign for love? (*Hogan traces a heart on his chest and holds both hands over the area*)

HOGAN: It's also the sign for want. It's not used very often.

SUSAN: Love?

HOGAN: You wouldn't tell a brother monk you love him.

SUSAN: It's terrible to go through life without anyone saying they love you.

HOGAN: We know we have the love of God.

SUSAN: That's such a quiet love. We have to tell it to ourselves.

(*The lights go up on the abbot's office*)

DOM GREGORY: In the early days of the church Father Francis might have been canonized by popular acclaim.

MEREDITH: The order mailed copies of his journal to the major newspapers. Did you think it would stimulate popular acclaim?

DOM GREGORY: His writings brought people closer to God.

MEREDITH: The journal was censored. There are large gaps in the final two years.

DOM GREGORY: There were references to persons still living. It was felt they might cause some needless embarrassment.

MEREDITH: He was away from the abbey quite a bit during that period.

DOM GREGORY: He had several illnesses in those years. He was hospitalized for several weeks, an operation for chronic osteomyelitis.

MEREDITH: He was a man who would fill three sheets of paper on the death of a robin. It's funny the journal never mentions his hospital stay. What hospital was it?

DOM GREGORY (*uncomfortable and, for a moment, at a loss for words*): Are you writing in a medical journal? Usually the public is more interested in the way we live in the abbey.

(*During Meredith's following lines, Dom Gregory walks into the garden*)

MEREDITH: Something must have happened in the hospital. Did you know any of the nurses?

(*The light goes out in the abbot's office. Dom Gregory is alone in the garden. Susan enters the garden dressed in her nurse's uniform, carrying a book*)

DOM GREGORY: Can I help you? (*Susan registers surprise before she can answer. He adds jokingly*) I hope you're not looking for a hospital.

SUSAN: Actually, I'm looking for a former patient. I'm from St. Luke's . . . in Albany.

DOM GREGORY: You've traveled a long way.

SUSAN: Only seventy miles. A hour and a half when the traffic is light.

DOM GREGORY: I'm Father Gregory. You've been here before.

(*Susan nods and shakes his hand. He holds it for a moment*)

SUSAN: Once or twice . . . briefly. Susan Shawnessy. I think you know that. It's a beautiful setting. All the trees and the green hills. I came to return this book. Father Tom's a wonderful writer. I'm not sure I understand all his poems, but I love the words. The order must be awfully proud of him.

DOM GREGORY: All that way just to return a book.

SUSAN: A nice day for a drive in the country. I play all my tapes in the car, the Beatles. I had nothing important to do for the afternoon.

DOM GREGORY: You must have come straight from the hospital.

SUSAN (*looks at her uniform as though she were surprised to see it on herself. She nervously gives it a tug here and there*): I was in a hurry. I must smell of iodine and peroxide. I have to get back.

DOM GREGORY (*holds out his hand for the book*): I'll be glad to take the book.

SUSAN (*clutching the book tightly*): No. I'd like to say hello—as long as I've come all this way.

DOM GREGORY: I thought as much. (*A beat*) Too close a friendship would be dangerous for Father Francis. (*Susan shakes her head in denial*) You're Catholic?

SUSAN: Yes.

DOM GREGORY: Then you know the danger. God has blessed you with physical beauty. Even by a casual glance, you arouse temptations in a man. They can put his soul in peril. If the friendship you are developing with Father Francis should ripen into something more serious, in a few months, a year, when one of you breaks if off—and one of you will surely break it off—it can only bring anguish. I tell you this in all charity. Father Francis will never leave the abbey. Break it off now, while you still have happy memories. (*Hogan appears in the path behind Susan. Dom Gregory sees him*) Here's your friend now. Father Francis, there's a beautiful girl here to see you. No wonder you stayed in that hospital so long.

HOGAN (*taken aback to see Dom Gregory there*): Reverend Father. I see you've met my favorite nurse. Her care made me forget my pains.

DOM GREGORY: I'm not surprised.

SUSAN: You both see too few women.

DOM GREGORY: If you will excuse me. I have a postulant waiting in the office. (*To Susan*) Remember what I told you.

HOGAN (*looking after the departing Dom Gregory*): I imagine he was referring to me.

SUSAN: I won't be able to come again. He didn't say so in so many words, but . . . that sign is still up. I shouldn't have come.

HOGAN: I have been looking forward to your visits. I will miss our talks. When I lay in that hospital bed, I started to count the minutes before your shift—after that first day.

SUSAN: I couldn't stop talking. I must have been a pain. I thought I could perk up. You looked like you needed it.

HOGAN: All those questions about the liturgy and women priests.

SUSAN: I was nervous. I couldn't think of anything else to say. I don't get many priests as patients. Your elegy for Martin Luther King was required reading in my American Lit class. You were an important literary figure. I was afraid to touch you. When I gave you a bath I trembled.

HOGAN: I noticed.

SUSAN: I felt almost as though I was committing a sacrilege, especially when I brought the bed pan.

HOGAN: That makes mortals of us all. A monk doesn't get such tender care in the monastery infirmary. Some nights I lie in bed wishing for the old, familiar pain to return so you can nurse me to health again.

SUSAN: Oh, you're like most men. You just want a substitute mother. (*She sits on the bench and picks up the book*) I don't understand many things in your books. There's a couple of poems that are over my head. (*She opens the book and begins to read*) "The bottom of the earth has come and builded in my quiet room, The earthworms and the serpent's home, Whose it is most, most hell to be . . ."

(*Hogan takes the book from her and gently closes it*)

HOGAN: That was written a long time ago. It was a work of youth, too gloomy and undisciplined. I am trying to live it down.

SUSAN (*extends her hand to Hogan*): I'm sorry I can't stay very long. I didn't realize it would be our last meeting. (*They walk together along the garden path, close together, but not touching*) You can still write. (*She touches his arm lightly with her fingers. She jerks her hand back as though stung by an electric charge and puts her hands behind her back*) We must be a source of temptation for priests. I think some of them hate us for it.

HOGAN: We don't often see young and pretty women here.

SUSAN: You live in a fortress intended to keep us out.

HOGAN: I think Dom Gregory regards your presence as an occasion of sin. (*Susan nods in agreement*) I'm going to see a specialist Wednesday. His office is near the hospital. Will you meet me? It will be more than an hour before I can get a ride back.

(Susan gives a tentative shake of her head, but her face shows that the idea interests her)

SUSAN: A Trappist monk with a girl? Vatican II can't have changed things that much.

HOGAN: I was planning on wearing civvies. A cowl would be ostentatious. Our order does not require a monk to be a public oddity.

SUSAN: I'm on duty Wednesday.

HOGAN: Your shift doesn't start till three. I remember your schedule. The yellow pill at 3:30 delivered by the nurse with the crooked cap and the bright smile. Meet me. We could have lunch by the river.

SUSAN: Oh, Thomas, I would like to. I really would. We could forget that you're a priest for just a little while.

HOGAN: I will not be leaving the monastery again. After 19 years of pleading, I'm being allowed to become a hermit. I'm building a shelter out of river stones and some wood left over when they built new choir stalls in the chapel. I will be very much alone. I want to see you for one hour. We'll talk about all the foolish little things that come to mind. Just two people without any sense.

SUSAN: For someone who has taken a vow of silence, you talk a great deal.

HOGAN: It's a *rule* of silence. It applies inside the cloister, not here. We could sit and talk of weather like old friends. *(They gradually come closer together as they talk)*

SUSAN: It's rained so much the farmers' tractors sink in the fields.

HOGAN: It will bring a bumper crop of summer wheat.

SUSAN: I had the most delicious veal marsala the other night—in Tony's on Myrtle Street. You could cut it with a fork.

HOGAN: Brother John puts too much salt in the beans.

SUSAN: Practical advice.

HOGAN (*miming his directions*): The best way to get candle wax off clothing is to harden it with a piece of ice.

SUSAN: Suck an ice cube before taking medicine. It deadens the taste buds.

HOGAN: I never knew that. Personal feelings.

SUSAN: Oh . . .

HOGAN: Don't stop to think.

SUSAN: I get confused. I love . . . (*a beat*) the smell of fresh apple butter.

HOGAN: I love you.

(*They look at each other gravely*)

SUSAN: That's not a foolish little thing.

HOGAN (*trying to make light of his declaration*): We are commanded to love all God's creatures. It was a foolish thing to say.

SUSAN: You will have a difficult time as a hermit. There will be no one to talk to—even in sign language. I think you will need companionship.

HOGAN: I need your companionship—on Wednesday for an hour. I'm planning a scandalous day. I'm going to buy a hamburger.

SUSAN (*teasingly*): I won't be an occasion of sin?

HOGAN: A Trappist is well practiced in resisting temptations of the flesh. Even beautiful women.

SUSAN: It would be wrong.

HOGAN: Of all the wrongs in the world, I don't think an hour's talk between a monk and a young woman rates very high on God's scale. (*He touches her hair*)

SUSAN: (*pulls back from him*): Don't. One of the monks might see us.

HOGAN: Let them. They would proclaim me in the Chapter of Faults. Can you see the looks on their faces if I were to stand up and tell them I was in love with a woman, one that's not yet seated at the right hand of God?

(*The lights go up again in the abbot's office*)

MEREDITH: Hogan was a passionate man.

DOM GREGORY: Was he? Why do you think so?

MEREDITH: His writings. What did you think I meant?

DOM GREGORY: I was wondering what you had read.

MEREDITH: I just struggled through "Christianity and Violence." He wrote passionately on the need for peaceful protest.

DOM GREGORY: Monks are men of peace.

MEREDITH: That hasn't always been so. (*She walks over to read the inscription:* Pax Intratibus)

Peace to all those who enter here. Hogan didn't mouth inscriptions on monastery walls. He raged against so-called just wars. He must have been a trial to the authorities in the church. Did you ever quarrel with Hogan?

DOM GREGORY: An abbot is never infallible in the eyes of his monks.

(*Meredith sits back in the high-backed chair and swivels it so that she is invisible to the audience for the remainder of the act. Dom Gregory takes a dish with a small piece of fruitcake out of a desk drawer and puts it on the desktop. He takes a very small piece and slowly chews it, his eyes closed as he judges its taste. Hogan enters*)

HOGAN: You sent for me.

DOM GREGORY (*in a cordial tone*): Father Francis! Have the rest of this piece of fruitcake. Tell me your opinion. (*Hogan hesitates to take the fruit-cake*) It's all right, Brother Augustine is trying a Caribbean recipe. He's using coconut, lime peel, and rum. Taste it! In this circumstance, it would not break the Benedictine rule.

(*Hogan reluctantly takes the remainder of the piece of cake*)

HOGAN: (*eating the cake without enthusiasm*): I'm afraid I'm not a good judge.

DOM GREGORY: Tastes different. I'd like . . .

HOGAN: I've never liked fruitcake.

DOM GREGORY: Oh? (*He shrugs*) It's not why I sent for you.

HOGAN (*expectantly*): Is it about the hermitage?

DOM GREGORY: The monks refer to you as the priest who has a woman.

HOGAN: Some say, I'm "the problem." (*He gives the Trappist sign for problem: an imaginary question mark drawn in the air with his finger*)

DOM GREGORY: Passions trouble all men, even the saints. They must be controlled. If they are not, what is meant by God to be good may become evil. Lust is an overpowering passion.

HOGAN: I know that.

DOM GREGORY: You will break off the relationship then? You will never see her or communicate with her again?

HOGAN: Surely letters.

DOM GREGORY: Not even letters. (*His tone softens. He is, after all, not a cruel or insensitive man*) It's best, Father Francis, for both of you. You'll be amazed at how quickly she'll forget you. And you her.

HOGAN (*vigorously shakes his head*): As one forgets one of Christ's miracles. I would give up an eternity with God for one brief lifetime with her. (*He gives a small, mischievous laugh*) How else can I receive all the sacraments?

DOM GREGORY: Breaking your vow is a sin, Thomas, a grievous sin.

HOGAN: Only God can say that. He does not say it to me.

DOM GREGORY (*shouting as they pass the mixing machines*): Your passions drown out his voice.

HOGAN: When I came to this monastery I was a young man, not long out of Princeton. I was filled with learning and sickened by disgust with the world of men. Centuries of war and greed and cruelty and hatred and avarice, oppression and injustice. All done in the name of God or justice or peace or profit. If you want to understand the social history of man, study hell.

DOM GREGORY: You used the monastery as an escape from the trials of the world. It must have been a disappointment to find that even here, here when we strive so hard for sanctity, men are imperfect.

HOGAN: I learned to love them nevertheless. The love of another human may be pale in comparison with God's love, but it's our first encounter. I know now that there are men and women who overcome evil with good, counter greed with generosity, combat cruelty with kindness, surmount injustice with forbearance, defeat hatred with love. In chapel I thank God that I am like other men, not more holy, not more forgiving, not more worthy of heaven. It's glorious to be a member of the human race. For all the follies of the outside world, I'm ready to go beyond these blessed walls.

DOM GREGORY: Are you? Are you ready to enter the world of business, the world of mass media, the world of high tech, the 9 to 5 day? You are a monk, Thomas, living a life of solitude and contemplation, following a regimen in which little has changed since the year 910. Are you ready for the space age? Wait till you hear its music.

HOGAN: I am ready to face the challenges of that world.

DOM GREGORY: It will destroy you. The world knows you through your writings. A thousand letters come here each month addressed to you, from Buddhist monks, from writers and folk singers and high school students from California. Men come to our doors almost weekly to join the Cistercians because of what they have read in your books.

HOGAN: Are you afraid the order will lose vocations if I rejoin the world?

DOM GREGORY: I am afraid of the loss of only one vocation. You belong here, Thomas. Do not destroy your immortal soul to gain the soft pleasure of a woman.

HOGAN: How easy it is for a priest to give advice on sex. I have done it a hundred times. I have said something similar to some devout retreatant making his tortured confession. Some troubled soul looking to me for holy wisdom. Some openly laughed at me.

DOM GREGORY: Are you laughing, Thomas?

HOGAN: No. Have you ever been in love with a woman?

DOM GREGORY: That question has little bearing here.

HOGAN: If you had, you would know how generous it makes a person. Some men have given up their life for a woman. I can only give up my immortal soul.

DOM GREGORY: You can't give your soul away like a Christmas fruitcake. You can only lose it. The powers of darkness have brought you to the edge of a terrible pit. Pray, pray, Thomas, that you do not fall.

HOGAN (*kneeling*): God has sent Susan Shawnessey into my life. I pray for the courage to keep her.

(*Dom Gregory kneels beside Hogan*)

DOM GREGORY: Pray for wisdom, Father Francis. Pray for wisdom.

(*Both monks pray silently, their heads bowed. After a few moments, Hogan rises, bows to the crucifix on the wall and quietly walks out of the abbot's office. Dom Gregory remains kneeling. Hogan walks up the path leading to the woods, his head bowed. Susan enters carrying a picnic basket which she swings happily. She wears a short summer skirt and a light blouse*)

SUSAN: If there's a hill beyond this, I'm resting.

(*Hogan stops, turns toward Susan, lifts his head and smiles, his delight in seeing her obvious. He seems younger than in the scene with Dom Gregory*)

HOGAN: I see you found the way. Few people take this path, so the growth tends to hid it.

SUSAN: I wish you had warned me. I would have worn jeans. I scratched my legs on some raspberry bushes. (*She lifts her skirt to show the scratches*)

HOGAN: Very pretty.

SUSAN (*laughs and pulls her skirt down*): Monks are not supposed to admire girls' legs.

HOGAN: A woman's body is the most perfect of all God's creations.

SUSAN: That's strictly a male judgment. (*She whirls in delighted happiness, her arms outstretched*) It smells so much fresher than the hospital. The woods are full of orchids.

(*There is the sound of a cardinal singing. Hogan, in the same happy mood, points to the top of one of the trees*)

HOGAN: He's near the top of that old oak. A cardinal. See him! (*He takes her arm and points. She looks for the bird*) I thought I heard him singing before. (*He mimics the bird's song*)

SUSAN (*laughing with pleasure and excitement*): I see him! He's giving us his blessing.

HOGAN (*serious*): That's more than I'd get from his namesake. I've been forbidden to publish "Nonviolence and the Christian Conscience." The hierarchy is afraid it will give the church an unpatriotic image.

SUSAN (*indignant*): They can't forbid a monk to write about peace.

HOGAN: His eminence hasn't forbidden me to write. Just to publish.

(*Susan sits on the log and begins to take items from the picnic basket*)

SUSAN: I brought wine and some of that brie you like so well. And fruit and a loaf of French bread to go with the cheese. They make it fresh in a little Italian bakery on Clinton.

HOGAN (*berates himself*): I could have brought bread from the monastery bakery.

SUSAN: I'm famished.

HOGAN (*sits near her and examines the picnic basket*): My mother had a picnic basket like that.

SUSAN: Oh? The biographies hardly mention . . .

HOGAN: She died when I was eight. Of cancer. It takes an eternity to die that way. When she was dying, she wrote me notes from the hospital, but she never let me in her room, not ever. I used to wonder . . . The picnic basket made me think of it. Sometimes, when I'm alone in my hermit's house . . . I think . . . I think foolish thoughts.

SUSAN: I thought I was the only one who did that.

HOGAN: An icon, I'm not.

SUSAN (*brightly*): I knew you'd have a difficult time as a hermit.

HOGAN: I welcomed loneliness at first. I never realized how starved I would become for companionship, even for Brother Ralph whose breath smells like a sick horse. He kept me humble by loathing my writing. Now look, what a wonderful companion God has brought me.

SUSAN (*growing serious*): Thomas, what will they do if they find me here? Excommunicate me?

HOGAN (*teasing*): Oh, they'll burn you as a witch and the bishop will be summoned to rebless the grounds. (*He mimes giving a blessing and sprinkling holy water*) They'll be platoons of monks armed with aspergillums sprinkling holy water on the trees like rangers at a forest fire.

SUSAN (*thoughtfully*): I shouldn't have come. It will cause you trouble.

HOGAN (*going about the business of opening the bottle of wine*): I'm glad you came. Don't worry about me.

(*Susan sits up straight, shoulders back, and takes a deep breath. She speaks nervously. The words are obviously difficult for her to say*)

SUSAN: Thomas, I talked to my parish priest. I told him.

HOGAN: That you were seeing a monk.

SUSAN: That I was developing a close friendship with a priest. I was careful not to identify you. (*She says the next line hurriedly*) I can't see you again.

HOGAN: Is that what your parish priest told you?

SUSAN: The priest was young. He smelled of after shave lotion. For your penance, ten Hail Marys and never see your monk again.

HOGAN (*pouring the wine into a paper cup Susan holds out to him*): There was nothing to confess.

SUSAN: Nothing? A woman must not come between a priest and God. (*She stands up greatly agitated and begins pacing, her arms around her chest*)

HOGAN: God created women. I don't think he regards them with a jealous eye.

SUSAN: I don't want to be a temptation. I can't help being a woman. If I were a man, we would not cause a scandal and we could talk like two people who are very good friends and are no threat to each other. (*She flings her arms out and stands with the sun behind her outlining her body*) But I am a woman, Thomas. I know the thoughts of men when they look at me. I have the desires of a woman. (*She stands close to him*) I need to be held sometimes. I need permanence. (*Hogan holds his arms out to embrace her. She moves away*) I go to mass every day, but my Catholicism is a cloak. I have the passions of a pagan. Stay away from me.

(*Hogan goes to her and puts his hands on her shoulders*)

HOGAN: I can't. (*He picks up an apple from the picnic basket*) In the monastery we fast most of the year. Our meals are simple, a potato, a slice of bread, a piece of cheese, an apple, but never filling. One is always hungry. (*He takes Susan's hand*) Most of the time we forget our hunger in work, or in contemplation. But there come moments in a day when I put down my saw or hammer or take my eyes off my book of prayer and the desire for food becomes almost unbearable. (*He embraces Susan hungrily*) I resolve not to see you. Yet, an unguarded moment comes, without distraction, and I think, against my will, "I love Susan. I love you."

(*Susan strokes Hogan's hair*)

SUSAN: I don't want to love you. (*She probes his back with her fingertips*) Does it still hurt when I touch it?

HOGAN (*his voice is tense, not because of physical pain, but because of the desires aroused by her touch*): No.

SUSAN (*jerks her hand away*): I'm sorry. It does hurt.

HOGAN: No. (*A beat*) It feels fine.

(*Susan sits. Hogan puts his head in her lap. She massages his back, humming as though she were putting a child to sleep*)

HOGAN: Dom Gregory has ordered me never to see you.

SUSAN: That would be wise.

HOGAN: The love of men and women is seldom wise. I know the wise words to say to you. (*He puts his hand on her bare leg*) Then you come and I have foolish desires. (*He strokes her leg*) There's an ancient belief, not fashionable here, that God is honored by a man and a woman making love. Forget I'm a priest.

SUSAN: That's pretty hard when you're wearing monk's robes.

HOGAN: I'll make it easier. (*He begins removing his black scapular*)

SUSAN: Tell me about hell. Is there really fire there?

HOGAN (*dressed only in his robe, kisses her on the forehead*): Many priests believe there is. There is another theory. Hell is the absence of love for all time.

(*He fondles her with increasing intensity and passion. She responds with intense fervor*)

SUSAN (*doubtfully*): The Bible talks about fire.

HOGAN: To be unloved, even by God. That is the pain of fire. (*He kisses her passionately on the mouth*) If we married, we'd scandalize half the world.

SUSAN: I'm not worried about half the world. Just my family. (*She kisses him hard*)

HOGAN (*kisses her on the nose*): The pope would be angry.

(*Susan playfully runs her index finger down his nose*)

SUSAN: My parish priest would have a fit. (*She giggles*)

HOGAN: Some of my readers would burn my books.

SUSAN: I wouldn't want to be the cause of that.

HOGAN (*kisses her again*): I'd write some more—a fat book on the goodness of love.

SUSAN: I'm frightened, Tom.

HOGAN: Of what people would say?

SUSAN: A little. I can deal with that. I fear I'm competing with the Almighty. I fear the envy of God.

(*Hogan puts his arms around her as if to protect her as the lights dim*)

ACT II

Scene One

When the lights come up again, it is an hour later. Hogan and Susan are in the woods. The blanket is spread open on the ground and the food and utensils lie in the grass. Susan is zipping up her skirt. Hogan is donning his scapular.

SUSAN: Don't look so guilty. You'll have to confess, won't you?

HOGAN: We must ask God's forgiveness.

SUSAN: I don't think I have offended God, Thomas. I don't believe in a vengeful God. He's too busy answering prayers. You know, saving lives and healing the sick.

HOGAN (*considering*): God takes our passions into account.

SUSAN (*kissing him cheerfully*): Then he's forgiven us. We were very passionate.

HOGAN (*sitting down next to her, speaks in a tone of wonder*): I never realized a woman could be so passionate.

SUSAN: I'm human, Tom. Are you disillusioned?

HOGAN: No. Just feeling a little guilty. I have betrayed God.

SUSAN: I don't think God noticed. He's gone off to war to bless the troops. You think too much sometimes. All those years of prayer and contemplation. It makes you gloomy. You should be happy. I am. God doesn't mind.

HOGAN: Perhaps not.

SUSAN (*a brief look of anxiety*): Are you afraid you'll be a father? I mean, that's what they call you, but you could . . .

HOGAN: It would cause a scandal.

SUSAN (*stands and confronts him*): Is that your main concern? It would cause a scandal. The church has withstood greater scandals. This is such a little scandal.

HOGAN: The church has many enemies. The secular media would pervert it into a major disgrace. You can't blame me for . . .

SUSAN: Putting the church first. I suppose it's inevitable.

(*She turns from him and begins repacking the picnic basket, boiling*)

HOGAN (*helping. He tries to placate her*): When we made love it was like the purest form of prayer.

SUSAN: You make it sound like a religious obligation. (*She makes the sign of the cross*) Like I should bless myself before making love.

HOGAN (*laughs*): I doubt if they include that in any sex manual as part of the foreplay.

SUSAN: Oh, Thomas, I'm never sure when you're serious. You're teasing me, aren't you?

HOGAN: Maybe. You give me crazy ideas. (*He takes her hand*) If we were to marry . . .

SUSAN: If! If! I'm not asking you to take any sacred vows. Go on, if.

HOGAN: I couldn't offer you much. I own nothing. My books are the property of the abbey. I have no money. I would be offering you poverty and disgrace.

SUSAN: Oh, Thomas! You'll write more books. Most women would envy me. People around the world know who you are.

HOGAN: A few ancient librarians, bent old men and a couple of women in the book trade. You won't find my poems in the drug store.

(*The abbey bell is heard in the distance*)

SUSAN: I fear only your remorse. You may blame me tomorrow. I've heard men are weaker after sex. It does something to the body, upsets our chemical balance, I think. This is not the time for that kind of talk. I'll make a nine-day novena to Our Lady of Perpetual Help. I'll start tomorrow.

(*The lights fade out.*)

Scene Two

The lights come up on the abbot's office. It is late afternoon on the day following the previous scene. Meredith is alone in the abbot's office. She has a camera in her hand and is taking photographs of the office and its furnishings from various angles.
Dom Gregory enters carrying several books.

MEREDITH: Hogan's presence is everywhere.

DOM GREGORY: Oh? Do you believe in ghosts? Or saints? They both have been known to have miraculously appeared to the living. Neither, I'm afraid, has ever been reported as surfacing in this monastery.

MEREDITH: I mean the selling of Hogan. He's like the peacock at NBC, or Henry Ford at Dearborn. There's a sign by the grotto proclaiming it was his favorite place to meditate. His hermitage is preserved as a shrine. There's even a videotape.

(*Dom Gregory begins putting the books in a certain order in the bookcase. Meredith snaps pictures of him as he goes about his activity*)

DOM GREGORY: It saves us the time of having to answer the same questions of curious visitors who come here. If it would be useful for you, I could arrange a transcript.

MEREDITH: I know the details you tell visitors. They add up to a man who had no shadow. It's too pat. Even saints are capable of sin. Would you say you and Hogan were close?

DOM GREGORY: Our relations were those of brothers.

MEREDITH: "And when they were in the field, Cain attacked his brother Abel and killed him."

DOM GREGORY: Did you memorize Genesis for this interview?

MEREDITH (*laughs*): You just heard the extent of what I know. It seemed appropriate. I'm not much for Bible reading.

DOM GREGORY: That's unfortunate. We do quite a bit of it here.

MEREDITH (*picks up the Bible from the desk*): Most people forget that the Bible was written in ancient languages that no one speaks any more. It seems God spoke only to men.

DOM GREGORY: God spoke to several women. The Virgin Mary . . .

MEREDITH: I was just being bitchy.

DOM GREGORY: Will you show me the article you're writing before it is published?

MEREDITH: No.

DOM GREGORY: I would think it would be responsible to check the accuracy of what you are writing. I'm not asking to censor your . . .

MEREDITH: You'll have to have faith in me. (*She yawns*) Oh, pardon me. I'm not used to bells ringing at two in the morning.

DOM GREGORY: It took me more than a year to get used to these hours even though I often had the night shift in the hospital.

MEREDITH: Why does a physician, a man who graduated at the top of his class at Harvard Medical School, hide in a Trappist monastery? You seldom practice.

DOM GREGORY: This is my family. It wouldn't be ethical to practice here. (*He takes out a ledger and a pen from a desk drawer*) If you have no more questions about Father Francis, I must do the ordering for our bakery. Father Jerome tells me we are running short on raisins.

MEREDITH: Tell me, as a man of science, how can you believe in all the religious myths? God? Don't you have doubts?

DOM GREGORY: As you say, I have a physician's knowledge of anatomy. In my examinations, I have listened to the murmurs and rumblings, the clicks and beats and reverberations of hundreds of human bodies. I have seen them torn and mutilated by edges of glass and steel. I've watched powerless while disease misshaped and shriveled them. A physician can only do so much. Death, in the end, defeats him.

MEREDITH: Is that why you quit medicine? You let death have the battle-field on earth. The hereafter is the domain of clergy. It's safe ground for a priest.

DOM GREGORY: I found I could not give my patients what they wanted most: eternal life in a perpetually youthful body.

MEREDITH: You could have restored people to health, relieved pain and suffering.

DOM GREGORY: Medical knowledge has advanced to the state where we routinely cure diseases which used to allow the old a peaceful death. The old die still, but many more of them die long, agonizing deaths worthy of the Inquisition.

In time, I came to realize that in a society without God, good health, smooth skin and a satisfying sex life had replaced heaven as the goal of most of my patients. For myself, the important things in life cannot be seen or touched. That's why I came here. To be alone with God. (*He puts down his papers and confronts Meredith*) Why did you come?

MEREDITH: You know the reason. I outlined my purposes in my letter to your abbot general.

DOM GREGORY: Oh, yes. This relentless pursuit of a man who has been dead for two decades.

MEREDITH: A violent death. Do you believe the official reports?

DOM GREGORY: No. I don't think it's necessary to speculate . . .

MEREDITH: You helped unleash the hounds when you mailed Hogan's journal to the media.

DOM GREGORY: You're not the first reporter to come here. You've started late in the chase. There have been many since Father Francis's death, especially from the religious press. The trail is well traveled.

MEREDITH: Those doing the searching were looking for a saint. I don't believe in your saints. I prayed to too many in parochial schools—a lot of screwed up people talking to animals, disfiguring themselves, leading armies in God's cause.

DOM GREGORY: I thought you might be a Catholic.

MEREDITH: Bless me, father, it's been twenty years since my last confession. Since then, I've learned a few things about the Catholic Church—the supreme stag party. Canon law 813, women denied the right to serve mass. Canon 1327, women are not allowed to preach unless male clergy are present. Canon two thousand and four, women have no right to put forward a candidate for sainthood.

DOM GREGORY: Not many lay persons can recite canon law. You know a lot about us.

MEREDITH: I've known a few of your priests.

DOM GREGORY: Vespers will be beginning soon. You had more questions?

MEREDITH: Only a couple more. (*She reads from her notebook*) Hogan's published papers on the war in El Salvador were an embarrassment to certain members of the hierarchy. Some Catholic newspapers reminded readers of his communist past.

DOM GREGORY: He was a very young man then. He was tormented by social injustice.

MEREDITH: You must have known he was the subject of an FBI investigation.

DOM GREGORY: I cooperated with it. There was a suspicion, it seems, about any American who received a peace medal. They found little that was damaging.

MEREDITH: There are also those who said he went to El Salvador to aid the communist peasants. A friend in the State Department believes he was targeted by the death squads.

DOM GREGORY: We don't know for certain why Father Francis died. Only God knows. If you had known Father Francis, you would know he was incapable of duplicity.

MEREDITH: Was he? All men lie and cheat, if there is something they want badly enough, particularly if a woman is involved—even men of the cloth.

DOM GREGORY: I've read several things you have written. You believe in homosexual marriage, the freedom to sell pornography, uncensored speech. I can't believe you're scandalized by some foolish indiscretions of a poor monk.

MEREDITH: I believe in human rights, a married clergy, women priests. You should be glad I'm not still a Catholic . . .

DOM GREGORY: You should have been an abbess in the Middle Ages, a few of them commanded bishops.

(*Meredith picks up the large, ornate candlestick near the desk and, holding it like a bishop's staff, strides around the room*)

MEREDITH: I would have loved it, striding in front of the procession, with a crosier in my hand, instead of trailing in the rear, holding flowers.

DOM GREGORY: I see you with a sword in your hand, another Joan of Arc warring against the vow of celibacy. You wouldn't have a personal interest?

(*Meredith puts the candlestick down*)

MEREDITH: What are you suggesting?

DOM GREGORY: The house where you stayed is often filled with pious women seeking retreat. Sometimes their work brings them in close frequent contact with priests deprived of intimate human comfort.

MEREDITH: A relationship with a priest sucks. Everybody forgives him. It's unnatural for a man to live a life of celibacy. His calling is from the Almighty. Even God doesn't forgive the woman.

DOM GREGORY: I had wondered about your anger. Surely, I thought, she can't still resent being denied a schoolboy's dull task of serving a priest on the altar.

MEREDITH: A woman can serve a priest as she serves any man. I don't think my priest ever said mass any place but at the main altar in a major cathedral. He liked to see his name in lights above the confessional.

DOM GREGORY: There are vain and weak men in all occupations. To give up your faith . . . (*He walks to the window*) I sometimes look at the stars in the early morning. You can see them clearly here, away from the lights of the towns and cities. Science can only guess at creation. Perhaps it takes a poet to understand God.

MEREDITH: Hogan was a poet. Did he have a better understanding of God?

DOM GREGORY: You've read many of his books. You know how passionately he expressed his love of God.

MEREDITH: His journal suggests he may have had some doubts in that last year. That would have been after his long hospital stay. Where did you say it was?

(*Dom Gregory looks at her for several moments struggling within himself. At last he answers*)

DOM GREGORY: Albany.

MEREDITH: I suppose it would have been a Catholic hospital.

DOM GREGORY: It was a hospital in Albany.

Scene Three

The lights fade out immediately on the office scene. They come up on Susan weeding with a hoe what was the monastery garden in the earlier scenes. It is now the garden behind her home. It is much the same as earlier, except that the statue of the Virgin Mary is gone and a couple of used and faded lawn chairs take the place of the bench. There is a set of garden tools near one of the chairs. It is five days later.

There are streaks of gray in Susan's hair and she looks worn. Her face shows the twenty years that have passed since her romance with Hogan. She wears a loose-fitting house dress in a flowered print and sandals.

Meredith enters after a few moments.

MEREDITH: Mrs. Raynor?

SUSAN: If you're selling something, you're wasting your time.

MEREDITH: I'm not selling anything.

SUSAN: I hope you didn't wake my husband. He's on the night shift.

MEREDITH: You knew Thomas Hogan.

(Susan looks startled. She stops hoeing and shakes her head)

SUSAN: He died a long time ago.

MEREDITH *(holds her card out)*: I'm from *Quote.* If you're not too busy . . . Sheila Martin sent me here.

SUSAN *(looking at the card)*: How is she?

MEREDITH: She talked a lot about you.

SUSAN *(reserved and suspicious)*: Did she? I bet she talked your ear off. She likes to impress people.

MEREDITH: She told me Hogan nearly left the priesthood because he wanted to marry you.

SUSAN: Is that what she said? *(She kneels down to pull out a weed)*

MEREDITH *(kneels next to Susan and begins helping her weed)*: Let me help you. I had a small garden near Akron when I worked on the *Beacon Journal.* I used to enjoy digging in the dirt.

SUSAN: Sort of a bus driver's holiday.

MEREDITH: Sheila said you had a sense of humor. (*She gives a small laugh*) We're planning a cover story on Hogan. Photos, interviews with famous people who knew him, a eulogy from his Holiness. Everything in good taste.

SUSAN: I'm glad. He should be remembered. He was the conscience of a generation.

MEREDITH: You understand we have to get facts. We would like your impressions, memories. I feel uncomfortable prying into someone's life like this . . .

SUSAN: I can tell when I'm being conned. Patients often try it when they're getting well. A nurse sees quite a bit of life.

MEREDITH: More perhaps than a cloistered monk.

SUSAN: Tom Hogan was no adolescent when he came to the monastery. There had been affairs in college.

MEREDITH: He felt a great deal of guilt about it. Well, he joined an institution that cultivates guilt.

SUSAN: Would you want a man who never felt guilt?

MEREDITH: The public would like to know your part in his life.

SUSAN: His writing . . . it should be the focus. His words are still alive. I reread them often. I fell in love with the words before I met him.

MEREDITH: There's talk of a new biography.

SUSAN: There's been so many. What more can they say?

MEREDITH: No one has written about your part in his life . . .

SUSAN (*stands and resumes hoeing*): It was a small part.

MEREDITH: We're willing to pay—a reasonable amount.

SUSAN: I couldn't . . .

MEREDITH: The public would like to know . . . You'll be admired . . .

SUSAN: What? I'm not important. Tom was someone special, though. His words . . . Did Sheila mention the poems he wrote me?

MEREDITH (*interested, lying*): She said something.

SUSAN: You can't believe everything she says. I don't know why I mentioned them.

MEREDITH: I'd like to see them.

SUSAN: They were very personal.

MEREDITH: I understand how feelings can develop without either one wanting . . . not something we choose.

SUSAN: You want to write about a romance involving a priest.

MEREDITH: I can't make you tell me . . .

SUSAN: I don't think you give a damn about Thomas.

MEREDITH: Half the hospital knew of the affair. If his biographers weren't so intent on making him a saint . . . There are rumors of a secret marriage.

SUSAN: Are you writing a story based on rumors? (*She slams down her hoe and starts to walk off*)

MEREDITH: Maybe you'd rather wait until the tabloids . . . I can see the headlines by the supermarket cash registers. Hogan's Honey!

(*Susan stops and walks back toward Meredith*)

SUSAN: And what headlines would *Quote* . . .

MEREDITH: I'm asking you to trust me.

SUSAN: That's what men say when they want to screw a woman.

MEREDITH (*laughs, breaking the tension between them*): Wonderful! I think we'll be able to reach an understanding. Why don't you think it

over? I'm quite sure if I pushed hard enough, I could get the magazine to
go ten thousand . . . if the poems are published.

SUSAN: I don't want to do something I'm going to regret.

(*Meredith reaches out and reassuringly puts her hand on Susan's arm*)

MEREDITH: You won't regret it. He was a great man. You can help the
public learn that. We have eight million readers.

(*Susan removes Meredith's hand*)

SUSAN: Do you think they'll care?

MEREDITH: I think so.

SUSAN: I don't.

MEREDITH (*shrugs*): In that case . . . OK. I can see I'm being a nuisance.
I'll leave you alone. (*She walks away, then turns*) You can keep hidden the
words of a remarkable man. My God, have you forgotten how hard he
fought all his life to get his words published? (*She begins to exit*) I really
did want to do this story.

(*Susan hoes furiously, as though the hoe is a weapon and she is cutting
down an army of reporters*)

SUSAN (*puts the hoe down slowly*): When you write about Tom, don't
make it sound sordid.

(*The stage lights dim momentarily.*)

Scene Four

*The abbot's office. Two days later. Meredith is pacing the room. She has sev-
eral papers in her hand which she has been reading to Dom Gregory. They
are some of the love poems written by Thomas Hogan to Susan. Dom Gregory is slumped in his chair.*

MEREDITH: Hogan never had a thought or an emotion he didn't put
down on paper. He secreted articles and poems like perspiration. It

wouldn't have been in character if he didn't write a love letter. Even so, you'd think someone in the public spotlight would have been more discreet. (*Reading*) "Your tenderness heats the dead world like a lance of sunlight." (*She shows it to Dom Gregory*) Recognize the handwriting?

DOM GREGORY: That wasn't meant to be read by strangers.

(*Meredith leans forward on Dom Gregory's desk. She is in his face*)

MEREDITH: He should have been choosy about those he wrote to, then. I didn't have to use a gun to get these. She was anxious to step out of the darkness. She told me about the poems. She wanted her share of the spotlight.

DOM GREGORY (*in an angry voice*): It's reprehensible to prey on another's weakness.

MEREDITH: She knew what she was doing. I never had her fooled. You think I'm some kind of shit?

DOM GREGORY: It's not a term I would use.

MEREDITH (*laughs*): Have I hit a nerve? You know, you're wrong about me. Hogan could be my brother. I was a campus radical in college. South Africa, no nukes! Acid rain. The rain forest. I marched. I chanted. I got arrested, the whole bit.

DOM GREGORY: I know. I know you also wrote that piece on Peter Oakes.

MEREDITH (*surprised*): I thought you spent your time in prayer.

DOM GREGORY: A few of us must deal with the world, even in a monastery. (*Dom Gregory rises. He and Meredith circle the room like a pair of cautious boxers. They play with various objects in the room, look at them briefly and set them down*) I thought it would be wise to read some of the things you had written. He was a very private person.

MEREDITH: He was well known in the sports world. He was . . .

DOM GREGORY: Fair game? Other journalists knew he had AIDs. They respected his privacy. The strain on a frail body, the increased pressure, it must have exhausted him.

MEREDITH (*becoming defensive*): He had suicidal tendencies, for God's sake. Don't blame me for his death. He had scars on both wrists.

DOM GREGORY: You have a great capacity for seeking out scandal. You would have been at home during the Inquisition.

MEREDITH: Only if I could have been a monk.

DOM GREGORY: Instead of a journalist. Journalism is sometimes a modern form of the Inquisition. It has a priesthood that sometimes performs a great deal of cruelty for the sake of a greater good. Are Father Francis's letters a matter of public interest?

(*Meredith picks up one of Hogan's books and points to the cover*)

MEREDITH: He was a public figure.

DOM GREGORY: He wanted to be a simple monk. His gifts made him famous. It's much safer in this world to display malice than charity. It's so easy, too. No one can make a fool of you. You're safe from laughter or ridicule because you've never created anything that people can criticize. I'm surprised you're not a drama critic.

MEREDITH: I was. (*She examines the heavy candlestick*) An interesting candlestick.

DOM GREGORY: It came from the Benedictine abbey of Monte Casino. It was on the main altar when it was destroyed by Allied bombing. It's a miracle it survived.

MEREDITH (*puts the candlestick back*): Hogan could have used a miracle. It was convenient that he should die just when he was about to become an embarrassment to the church.

DOM GREGORY: An embarrassment?

MEREDITH: A world famous priest considering marriage.

DOM GREGORY: Is that what the letters say?

MEREDITH: There's talk of it.

DOM GREGORY: Talk? He may have talked of it. He may have written something, I don't doubt it. He received considerable adoration from women. I don't think . . .

MEREDITH: He mentions a novena.

Scene Five

The monastery garden. Susan is praying before the statue of Our Lady. She holds a bouquet of wildflowers. Hogan appears behind her. She crosses herself, rises and turns to him.

HOGAN: Dom Gregory told me you were here.

SUSAN: He fears I'll take you away from here. I'm the evil spirit and I'm a woman. I was afraid to face him. I turned back once. I was nearly halfway here and I drove into a little rest area by the road and turned around. I drove 12 miles back toward Albany, but I knew I had to come. (*She hands him the flowers*) They're for you. I picked them walking from the car.

(*Hogan takes the flowers and puts some in Susan's hair*)

HOGAN: Here's a more attractive background. I'll put the rest on the chapel altar. They'll remind me of you when I say mass.

SUSAN: You would miss saying mass.

HOGAN: It's the most important part of my day. The monastery makes us creatures of habit. Perhaps I should be a Buddhist. They have married monks.

SUSAN: Oh, Thomas, you talk of marrying, but you can't drive a car.

HOGAN: I didn't think that was a requirement.

SUSAN: It's not. It just shows that . . . (*She stops*)

HOGAN: What?

SUSAN: You're not used to doing some things most people take for granted. You're impractical, like my father. He could never keep a job.

HOGAN: The artist.

SUSAN: Illustrator. His paintings never sold. He wasn't successful like you.

HOGAN: He was fortunate. He didn't become well known to strangers.

SUSAN: Did you ever study zoology?

HOGAN: Is that today's subject? Zoology?

SUSAN: That sounds funny, doesn't it? It came out funny. I didn't mean it to. We used to take spring vacations at Myrtle Beach. I had an uncle there. Zoology. You'll see what I mean.

HOGAN: Its a bit obscure right now.

SUSAN: I mean you're like a fiddler crab.

HOGAN: Oh. That explains it.

SUSAN (*laughs*): That is so funny. I'm not good at telling jokes, but that's funny. Things don't come out right when I'm nervous. What I mean is, if you take a fiddler crab away from his little home, if you carry him hundreds of miles, no matter how far you go, he will still function with the tides and daylight hours of his native beach. Here is your native beach. For more than 20 years you've followed its rhythm. The world doesn't dance to the Gregorian chant. (*She kisses him affectionately*) Oh my lovely Thomas, I wish it did.

(*The lights dim*)

Scene Six

(*The abbot's office. Meredith sits at the abbot's desk fiddling with her tape recorder. Dom Gregory paces the floor while he reads from his breviary*)

MEREDITH: I've never had any trouble with this before. I always carry it in my purse. You know the Pope has talked into this?

DOM GREGORY: Does the Pope look as he does in his photographs? I've never seen him in person.

MEREDITH: He looked ordinary close up. From a distance he was more imposing. Popes and cardinals are more impressive when one is focused on infinity.

DOM GREGORY: Infinity is the goal of us all. Father Francis spent a lifetime preparing for it. We are born with two incurable maladies: life, of which we all die, and hope, which says that maybe death is not the end.

MEREDITH (*takes out her notebook*): Hogan was your confessor in El Salvador. You met privately with him a few hours before the shooting. When the investigators talked to you, you hid the details of the conversation under the seal of confession. That was very convenient.

DOM GREGORY: It was I who made the confession. The seal of confession applied to Father Francis.

MEREDITH: Whose lips are forever sealed.

DOM GREGORY: Yes. May God rest his soul.

MEREDITH: Is that what you prayed when the shooting occurred?

DOM GREGORY: I was in my room. The shooting was witnessed by a German Benedictine, Father Braum. He saw four men with some sort of automatic rifles, dressed as civilians . . .

MEREDITH: I read his report. Hogan was walking in the garden, reading St. John of the Cross. He may not even have seen his executioners. The police didn't talk to the Reverend Joseph Lamb.

DOM GREGORY: Reverend Lamb?

MEREDITH: A visiting Methodist.

DOM GREGORY: I remember him vaguely. A small nervous man, jaundiced face. He was an authority on Hindu monasticism. Odd, for a Methodist.

MEREDITH: He saw you coming out of Hogan's room shortly after the death was reported. You had some papers in your hand.

DOM GREGORY: Did the Reverend Lamb offer an idea of what the papers were?

MEREDITH: No. He seemed a very docile person. His name could have been branded on him by God during conception. The papers appeared to be handwritten. There were reports that Hogan had written a letter renouncing his vows.

DOM GREGORY: Is that what you intend to write? There is no such letter.

MEREDITH: Why am I not surprised? You would have destroyed it. It would have made a mockery of his life.

DOM GREGORY: You would like to make it so. You cast out accusations like a man pitching baseballs at a carnival clown. If you should hit the target and drop Bozo in the water and he comes up wet and sputtering in his clown dress, do you think you'll recognize your priest lover?

MEREDITH: Are my throws coming too close to the bullseye? You are sitting on a collapsible seat, my friend. Mankind is rising out of the swamps of superstition and fear of eternal fire.

DOM GREGORY: Out there I see a world of chaos and terror and confusion. At best, you offer only temporary survival. You would limit men and women to a flicker of existence in a perishable universe. Father Francis is in paradise.

MEREDITH: Or hell.

DOM GREGORY: Even hell might be preferable to nothingness.

MEREDITH: Perhaps that is hell. (*A beat*) Let's talk about Hogan. He looks like hell in the photographs taken at the conference.

DOM GREGORY: Father Francis was not well when he left for Central America.

MEREDITH: Not well? Christ!

DOM GREGORY: We honor Christ here.

MEREDITH: Sorry. But he was passing blood. I saw the medical records. Cancer was gnawing away at his prostate. Abstinence may have its price.

DOM GREGORY: He was taking estrogen. It helped some, but it had other effects. Psychological. He lost much of his spark. He talked about the depression of living. His new poems were Lenten. They had the essence of Good Friday.

MEREDITH: I remember one of the poems he wrote in San Salvador. "An unexpected chill comes out of my soul. I breathe the cold winds of darkness."

(*Hogan enters. He looks tired and in pain*)

HOGAN: My head feels like a dark stone in which no light has penetrated. I sleep very little. I awaken before morning, feeling cold.

DOM GREGORY (*puts his hand on Hogan's shoulder*): Enjoy the warm winds of San Salvador while we're here. There is nothing in the Benedictine rules that say a monk cannot enjoy God's sunshine—or an unexpected pleasure.

HOGAN: Unless the unexpected pleasure is a woman's company.

(*He looks for a chair and drops in it, tired*)

DOM GREGORY: I thought your lecture on Marxism and Monasticism went very well. You were touched by the Holy Spirit. It's not often that a monk's speech gets television coverage.

HOGAN: A local station and the Religious News Service. Hardly CNN. Even so, I kept grasping for the right word and missing it. I hope I was understood. The point I was trying to make . . . (*He pauses to let a spasm of pain pass*)

DOM GREGORY (*alarmed*): Are you all right?

HOGAN: Okay now. Sorry. My point was that a monastery is the only true communist society. Each to his own need. We have no possessions of our own. The bright lights from the camera blinded me. I couldn't see the audience. I could only feel its coldness.

(*He wraps his arms around his chest*)

DOM GREGORY: You were mistaken. Its warmth toward you was apparent from the applause—several times.

HOGAN: I wanted to flee into the darkness, but the lights were a physical force pinning me to the lectern.

DOM GREGORY: You sometimes have an appetite for the spotlight.

HOGAN: Was I asked here for a lecture on pride?

DOM GREGORY: No. I want you to hear my confession.

HOGAN: Father Basil is your regular confessor. He is wiser than I.

DOM GREGORY: He, as you know, is not here.

HOGAN: One of the other priests.

DOM GREGORY: You have always been my hair shirt. We are not allowed special friendships, but . . . (*He kneels by Hogan's chair*) I need your absolution. (*He makes the sign of the cross*) Bless me, father . . .

HOGAN (*ill at ease*): I would rather an informal discussion. We are not children herded to church on a Saturday afternoon.

DOM GREGORY: Since my last confession I have been impatient with my brother monks many times.

HOGAN: How often? Once a day?

DOM GREGORY: More. A thousand times. My thoughts stray too far from Christ's love.

HOGAN: Is that all?

DOM GREGORY: No. I have been deceitful to a fellow priest.

HOGAN: Was it a serious matter?

DOM GREGORY: For him, yes, a serious matter.

HOGAN: Perhaps not as much as you thought. Did you profit from your deceit?

DOM GREGORY: It was done to save a soul—as my duty as Christ's shepherd. I was obliged to remove a priest from temptation to commit a grievous sin.

HOGAN: I understand now why you insisted I hear your confession. My invitation to participate in this Central American trip, so far from the Abbey of Our Lady of Champlain . . . You arranged it all?

DOM GREGORY: I had a hand in it, yes. You have a true vocation. You would not be happy in this life or the next outside the priesthood. Thomas, the whole of your adult life has been in the service of Christ and his church.

HOGAN: You went to a lot of trouble unnecessarily.

DOM GREGORY: Then I am doubly sorry for my sin. You have ended the affair?

HOGAN: The affair is over.

DOM GREGORY: May I have your forgiveness? And your absolution?

HOGAN: You may have my forgiveness. (*He places his hand on Dom Gregory's head*)

DOM GREGORY: And your absolution, Father Francis.

(*Hogan begins to make the sign of the cross over the abbot*)

HOGAN: I absolve you of your sins in the name of the Father and . . . (*He drops his hand. Dom Gregory looks at him startled, disbelieving*) Absolution comes from God. I no longer believe in the words. You should have confessed to someone else.

DOM GREGORY (*rises*): Bullshit! I've never met a monk with a stronger faith. One more devoted to Christ and his Mother.

HOGAN: It was the faith of a young man, a child's faith, untested. I had no doubts about God. When I was ordained it was a festival of joy. I could bring Christ himself down from heaven. Now I would gladly give up that great gift to live in sin with a woman I don't know as well as I know the newest postulant back in the abbey.

(*Dom Gregory moves to put his arm around Hogan*)

DOM GREGORY: It's over.

HOGAN: I've been writing her.

DOM GREGORY: You must pray. Only through prayer . . .

HOGAN: My thoughts of her overshadow my prayers to God. I spend my silent hours writing foolish poems.

DOM GREGORY: This is not the Chapter of Faults, Thomas.

HOGAN: The power to love is one of the things that makes us like God.

DOM GREGORY: You have found a woman's love. Think how much more rewarding God's love must be.

HOGAN: If God exists.

DOM GREGORY: You know He exists! Your text on the proofs of God's existence, praised by the world's leading theologians.

HOGAN: Praised by those who believe in an all powerful and merciful God. That God has vanished from the universe. He's a selfish and jealous God.

DOM GREGORY: Remember you're a priest! Father Francis.

HOGAN: My habit is a costume worn by a clown on Halloween. I juggle God's promises of eternity to please the spectators. I never felt loved—except for a few brief hours. God's love wasn't enough after that. (*Agonized*) I cannot give you absolution. I am no longer one of God's priests.

DOM GREGORY: Of course you are. The temporary attentions of a woman cannot compare with God's eternal love. You're making a bad bargain. Thomas, you referred to eternity just now. That is not the language of an unbeliever.

HOGAN: A figure of speech.

(*Dom Gregory puts his hand kindly on Hogan's shoulder. Hogan makes no objection*)

DOM GREGORY: Even some of the great saints had periods of doubt. God sometimes makes suffer those that he loves. Who can understand God?

HOGAN (*shivering*): I feel the coldness of the absence of God. I need warmth.

DOM GREGORY (*he may go to an actual small control panel or go through the action of looking at one*): The air conditioning. It's turned up.

(*He turns the control down to low*)

HOGAN: I should write.

DOM GREGORY: You need to go out into the warm sunshine.

(*Hogan walks to the door*)

HOGAN: I need rest.

DOM GREGORY: I should not have kept you from your bed. Go and rest.

HOGAN: Yes.

DOM GREGORY: And Thomas, read St. John of the Cross. I will pray for you.

HOGAN (*exiting*): Yes. Pray for me.

DOM GREGORY: What more could I have said? Belief is a gift.

MEREDITH: What?

DOM GREGORY: The last time I saw Father Francis, he had been dead for several hours. There was nothing that could have been done, medically.

MEREDITH: He was a trial to you. You might have been glad to see him gone.

DOM GREGORY: No. I loved the man. (*Afraid that Meredith will misinterpret the remark, he adds after a brief pause*) As a . . . (*He is about to say "brother," but checks himself*) As I love one of the lesser saints.

MEREDITH: You can't make a saint out of a man who may have lost his faith in God, can you?

DOM GREGORY: Is that what you plan to say? There is no evidence.

MEREDITH: You've seen to that.

DOM GREGORY: We don't know Father Francis's mind at the last moments of his life. Only God knows.

MEREDITH: I didn't come here to write about a plastic saint, one of your painted statues lining the walls of your churches. A man's sins are a necessary part of his story. Hogan had sexuality. He could lose his head over a woman. He had doubts. He was human, for God's sake! He wasn't that angelic mystic you've beatified in the official biography. There's a big demand for fallen idols right now. It's too bad Hogan can't make the lecture circuit.

DOM GREGORY: We live in an age without saints or heroes in starless cities. Doesn't it get uncomfortable keeping your eyes on the gutter?

MEREDITH: Those who keep their eyes on heaven are more likely to trip. You led me to his love affair.

DOM GREGORY (*shakes his head*): I told you nothing.

MEREDITH: Not directly. When I asked, you wouldn't even tell me the name of the hospital where Hogan met his nurse. You let slip just enough information . . .

DOM GREGORY: I don't think there has ever been a crime committed in this abbey. You could leave your door open and your wallet on the bed exposed to anyone passing by and no one would steal it. There are no acts of violence. We try to tell the truth, as we see it. The commandments are carefully kept.

MEREDITH: I know that. For Christ's sake . . .

DOM GREGORY (*Over her, sternly*): No one here takes the name of God in vain. Our days and nights are spent in a lonely effort to attain spiritual perfection. This is a penitential order. We fast half the year. We deprive ourselves of a full night's sleep. We refrain from casual conversations among ourselves. All for the honor and glory of God.

MEREDITH: I do admire . . .

DOM GREGORY: But we take our bodies and our needs and our desires with us into the abbey. Our sins are petty. Annoyance, when a brother priest's harsh laughter disturbs our contemplation. Anger, when someone forgets to fill the raisin bin. Envy, when a monk's hurried writings bring praise from the Pope himself. Our sins are small, when measured by the world's standards. But they can be as destructive inside this abbey as any despicable human act committed inside the darkened cubicles off 42nd Street. I was *jealous* of Father Francis. I did not want to see him made a saint.

(*Meredith is stunned momentarily with the realization she has been used*)

MEREDITH (*a little in admiration*): Well, that's . . . You used me. You old fox. You clever old son-of-a-bitch.

DOM GREGORY: Father Francis was, by all human measure, a good monk for most of his life. But when I saw the movement to make him a saint grow, I could not look aside.

(*The chapel bell rings*)

DOM GREGORY: The monks are being called to chapel for compline. I should be with them.

MEREDITH: The last prayers of the day. Down the road about 50 miles is a Holiday Inn with cable television, a noisy bar, and a very special friend. My good nights will be far more sociable than your chanted prayers.

(The monks are heard chanting. The sound comes from a distance through heavy doors. It is faint)

DOM GREGORY: Did you get everything you came for?

MEREDITH: What was in the papers you took from Hogan's room?

DOM GREGORY: Nothing of importance. A few poems.

MEREDITH: Important enough for you to snatch as soon as you heard of his death.

DOM GREGORY: They weren't meant for the public. I'm not sure he would have mailed them.

MEREDITH: I suppose they're gone. *(Dom Gregory nods)* You were afraid of scandal.

DOM GREGORY: I don't think Father Francis ever sought the world's glory. He wanted to stop writing, several times. I ordered him to continue. *(He pauses)* Only God makes saints. I think he more easily forgives sins that come from love. I believe Father Francis relied on the mercy of God.

(Meredith begins to walk away. She turns and comes back)

MEREDITH: I'll send you an advance copy of the article.

(She offers her hand to Dom Gregory. He takes it and holds it for a moment)

DOM GREGORY: You are welcome to return—for the moments of silence.

MEREDITH: Stir things up again? How would you like a woman abbot?

DOM GREGORY: You wouldn't be the first.

MEREDITH: I know. Goodbye, father. I'll send an order for a fruitcake. *(She exits. The sound of the monks chanting the last prayer in compline, the "Song of Simeon," is heard. A spotlight reveals Hogan sitting in the garden writing)*

HOGAN: Love walks gently as a lamb to where we once sat in the damp green abbey grass. If you and I could meet again on some cool day like two lost sunbeams.

(*A second spotlight reveals Susan, dressed as she was in her last scene, standing reading a letter*)

SUSAN and HOGAN: If we could come together like two parts of one love song and be two parts of the same secret. If only you and I were possible.

(*The spotlight fades on them and the chanting of the monks grows louder. When the hymn is finished, Dom Gregory turns to the audience and sings in Gregorian chant*)

DOM GREGORY: May the all powerful Lord grant us a restful night and a peaceful death, Amen.

(*Curtain*)

ALAN DAVID PERKINS

Nobody Knows
I'm a Dog

a.net.play

Alan David Perkins was born in Quincy, Massachusetts, reared in Mobile, Alabama, and currently lives in Queens, New York. A classically trained French Horn player and former high school band director, Alan began play-wrighting in 1989 and has completed six one-act plays, fifteen full-length plays and two musicals. His plays have received honors from seventeen national competitions and have been produced throughout the United States, Canada, Taiwan and Peru. "Currently," he said, "I play solo tenor horn for the Imperial Brass in Highland Park, New Jersey, and produce community theatre for the Parkside Players in Forest Hills, New York."

Nobody Knows I'm A Dog won The Open Book/Stage & Screen Book Club's fourth national competition and is presented in its form as submitted. However, Mr. Perkins later revised his script, and that entailed a substantially rewritten final scene, which has considerable merit and is included in this volume in addition to the original ending.

Nobody Knows I'm A Dog was produced by The Open Book in New York at The Producers Club, opening March 11th, 1999, with Angelynn Cerridwen directing the following cast:

THE CHEESE	JOHN PUDDINGTON
NADINE	SARALEE KAYE
PHYLLIS	RUSTY THRASHER
CUTIEPIE	SHENICA-ROCHELLE ODOM
PLATO	BILL BIFULCO
HORNDOG	SENDHIL RAMAMURTHY

CHARACTERS

Plato — Male, teenager. Plato is a geeky, nerdy kid.

Nadine — Female, middle-aged housewife.

Phyllis — Male, 30's. Nondescript actor wannabe. Phyllis is not gay—he's just lonely.

Cheese — Male, 40's. The curmudgeon of the group.

Cutiepie — Female, late 20's, early 30's. Not very attractive.

Horndog — Male, mid-30's. Not too smart, working-class type.

ACT BREAKDOWN

ACT I

Prologue

Scene One: Usenet Newsgroup. All six characters pass messages back and forth to each other. Each message takes place within an indeterminate period of time.

Scene Two: E-mail. The characters pass messages privately to each other. Each message still takes place within an indeterminate period of time.

Scene Three: Back to the Newsgroup

ACT II

Scene One: IRC (Internet Relay chat) channel. It is in real time.

Scene Two: E-mail.

Scene Three: Newsgroup.

INTRODUCTION

The stage should be barren with the exception of six evenly spaced stations with a chair and a table or stand that holds a computer or implied computer. The stations shouldn't be in a straight line across—some of them can be on levels. Even though everybody may not be speaking for a while, they're still in the conversation. When engaging in full discussion, the light should be full—when engaging in private E-mail, they should be in spots. When private conversations take place during Act I, Scene Two, the actors can be in spotlights, otherwise they're all involved.

When delivering lines, the actors should be typing at their computers and looking at their screens (therefore, if the computers are working, their lines could actually scroll up the screen). They *never* interact with each other, though they definitely *should* react.

For the sake of those who aren't familiar with the Internet, this play takes place within three of the facets of the Net that allow communication:

The first is Usenet Newsgroups. Newsgroups are sort of a public forum. People can publicly post messages within a Newsgroup, and everyone is free to respond to them or comment on them.

The second is E-mail. E-mail is just as it sounds; electronic mail. It only goes to the selected recipient.

The third is IRC, or Internet Relay Chat. This is an open "channel" where people can converse in real time. As they type it, their messages go to all of the people tuned into that channel instantaneously.

The Prologue is optional.

PROLOGUE

(*In the darkness we hear the clicking of many computer keyboards*)

HORNDOG: Most women find me irresistible, but you will have to be the judge for yourself. I have a great body because I work very hard at the gym. But, my best feature is my ability to put a smile on your face. Overall, I'm **looking for a relationship**. Feel free to start sending those E-mails any time! I'm waiting.

CUTIEPIE: I just wanted to say that I'm single and I exist. That's about all I feel like saying. E-mail me just to let me know if you exist. That's it. I'm just **looking for a relationship**. No further obligations other than a valid E-mail address.

CHEESE: Personable, professional, single white male in New York City looking for a female of any race between 18 and 40 years old **looking for a relationship**. If you're looking for a nice person, please contact me.

NADINE: To all eligible men in cyberspace: If you're **looking for a relationship**, you've found the right gal! I'll be yours tonight. E-mail me any time.

PLATO: Hello. I'm **looking for a relationship**. High intelligence, low maintenance. Any takers?

(*All lines repeat at the director's discretion*)

ACT I

Scene One

USENET

Spot up on Phyllis. We see that he is a normal-looking male)

PHYLLIS: Hello. I am young, attractive and in search of love, friendship, and stimulating conversation in cyberspace. If you're interested in some hot chat, drop me an E-mail anytime. Philip. (*Spot fades down. Beat. Spot fades back up*) Hello, everybody. I have come to believe that a number of people will manufacture different personas when communicating on the Internet to nourish the person they secretly wish they were. Does anyone have any thoughts on the subject? Signed, Hardbody. (*Spot fades down. Beat. Spot fades back up. Phyllis is a bit frustrated*) Hi! I get the feeling that some of the people on the Internet aren't who they say they are. What do you think? Signed . . . (*beat*) Phyllis.*

(Spots bump up on Horndog and Cheese)

HORNDOG: Hi, Phyllis! Welcome to the Newsgroup!

CHEESE: It will be a pleasure conversing with you, Phyllis.

HORNDOG: Anything I can do, just drop me an E-mail.

CHEESE: I am always at your service, Phyllis.

HORNDOG: What do you do for a living, Phyllis?

CHEESE: What do you look like?

HORNDOG: How old are you?

CHEESE: Could we meet for coffee?

PHYLLIS: My my my. I'm amazed at the responses my posting has received! I'll do my best to answer each one of them privately. But, in the

---

*If the Prologue is used as an underscore, all voices should stop suddenly on the word *Phyllis*.

meantime, I'll give you a little personal information. I'm ... (*ponders*) twenty-eight years old ... blonde ... blue eyes ... (*thinks*) five-foot-five ... a hundred and ... (*thinks*) thirty pounds. I'm currently employed as a ... word processing operator ... (*pause as he backspaces over the words*) paralegal ... (*pause as he backspaces over the words*) secretary ... (*pause as he backspaces over the words*) LEGAL professional. I love ... sports and going to the ... opera. I'm still waiting for some response on my question. Hugs and kisses, Phyllis.

HORNDOG: Oh, Phyllis—I'm in love! Can we meet face to face?

PHYLLIS: NO!

(*Spots down on Horndog and Cheese. Spot fades up slowly on Nadine as she types*)

NADINE: Hello. I'm kind of new at this. I guess you'd call me a "newbie." I never expected it would be so easy to log onto the Internet. In response to Phyllis' comment, I think she may have a point. Still, I feel that no matter how elaborately we manufacture an alter ego or online persona it will never veer too far from who we really are. I think we're unable to maintain even the most intricate facade because eventually our true self comes through. In other words, we're the same no matter who we become. Anyway, I just wanted to say 'hi' and help get the ball rolling. This whole Internet thing is very exciting. Nadine.

(*Pause. Spot stays up on Nadine, but Plato speaks in the dark*)

PLATO (*voice over*): Dear Nadine: There's an ancient Chinese proverb that states that a journey of a thousand miles must begin with a single step. And quoting Josia Gilbert Holland, "Joys divided are increased." Yours, Plato.

(*Pause. Spot up on Horndog*)

HORNDOG: What the hell does that mean?

PLATO (*voice over*): It means I'm happy to make her acquaintance. You have a peculiar handle. Are you proud of being called "Horndog"? Does it accurately represent the real you or is it some ruse to make you appear how you wish you were? Then again, to quote William Hazlitt, "Life is the art of being well deceived."

HORNDOG: Does anyone know what this guy is talking about?

NADINE: Thank you for the response, Plato. It's almost frightening—answering a letter through a computer. I liked your quote by William Hazlitt. I have to say that I agree with it. We're always deceiving somebody. Maybe we're afraid of the truth? Or maybe it's just a guilt trip. Nadine.

(Spot begins to fade up on Plato. We now see that he is in his mid-teens. Before he types he first rifles through a book of quotations that he diligently keeps at his side)

PLATO: Dear Nadine: If you liked that one, how about this one: "We are never deceived; we deceive ourselves." Johann Wolfgang von Goethe.

NADINE: That's very deep. I don't think I've ever thought about it that way. Why do you think this is so? Nadine.

HORNDOG: You know what I think? I think it's good, clean fun. I think people just like to pretend, you know? It's like make-believe. When I was a kid I always wanted to be a fireman. Now I'm a cook, but I still want to be a fireman.

NADINE: Then why isn't your online persona that of a fireman?

HORNDOG: Who says it ain't? Just think about fires and hoses.

PHYLLIS: Horndog! That's disgusting!

HORNDOG: Some people like that, do you?

PHYLLIS: No, I don't.

NADINE: Neither do I.

(Spot up on Cheese)

CHEESE: Dear insipid morons: Now that we've introduced ourselves, how about getting a life. Some of us have more important things to do than exchange "hi's" and "how-do-you-do's." Only in this country can we take an invaluable tool like the Internet and reduce it to a smiley button. Get some lives. The Cheese.

PLATO: "Rudeness is the weak man's imitation of strength." Welcome aboard, Cheese. Yours, Plato.

NADINE: Plato! That isn't very nice. You should apologize.

PLATO: P.G. Wodehouse writes: "It is a good rule in life never to apologize. The right sort of people do not want apologies, and the wrong sort take a mean advantage of them." Which are you, Mr. Cheese? Yours, Plato.

CHEESE: Dear Mr. Plato: It is I who should apologize—not for my rudeness but for assuming that you had a grain of intelligence. You're a loser, Plato—both online and in real life. The Cheese.

CUTIEPIE (*voice over*): Excuse me, Mr. Cheese, but if you dislike everybody here so much, why do you read the postings? Cutiepie.

CHEESE: Dear Ms. Cutiepie, in all humility and cordiality I pose the following questions: Who the hell are you, what do you want and what business is it of yours?

(*Light fades up slowly on Cutiepie. She is not very attractive*)

CUTIEPIE: I'm just a person like you, Mr. Cheese. I want nothing. And it *is* my business since this is a public forum. I think you're being unnecessarily hostile. Cutiepie.

CHEESE: My Dear Ms. Cutiepie: Hostility is never unnecessary. It takes all we can muster as humans *not* to kill each other a thousand times over. And what kind of an image do you wish to project by being called "Cutiepie?"

CUTIEPIE: You don't like it?

CHEESE: Let's just say that it probably reeks of the subject of the discussion. It's like when someone tells you they've fixed you up with a "nice girl." You start to wonder how fat she is.

HORNDOG: So, Cheese, does that mean you're really a rat?

CHEESE: It means, you neanderthal, that I am the master and ruler of my own life and domain. I am King. I am the Big Cheese.

CUTIEPIE: So I can assume you're aged and smell bad?

CHEESE: Ho ho, ha ha. I'm sure you think you're a wit. Too bad you're only half right.

HORNDOG: Hey Cutiepie! Don't let Cheese bother you. I like your name. Hey, how 'bout a profile?

CUTIEPIE: Dear Mr. Horndog: A profile at this time is not possible. Let's just say that I'm female, single, and breathing. Cutiepie.

HORNDOG: Dear Cutiepie: I'll bet you're really a cutie-pie.

CHEESE: Dear Mr. Horndog: Please keep your hormones in check.

HORNDOG: Dear Cheese-head: Who the fuck asked you?!

CHEESE: Ah yes, Mr. Horndog. Your intelligence, or lack thereof, finally surfaces. I think you'll find nothing hidden with Mr. Horndog. Online and off he's probably a boor. Adoringly, The Cheese.

NADINE: Dear Mr. Cheese: I find your being judgmental very disturbing. I really wish you and Mr. Horndog wouldn't bicker. It's very unbecoming. Nadine.

PLATO: Jean Jacques Rousseau writes: "Do not judge, and you will never be mistaken." There's also a Native American proverb: "Don't judge any man until you have walked two moons in his moccasins." Yours, Plato.

NADINE: You're very wise, Plato.

HORNDOG: Dear Nadine: Duh.

CUTIEPIE: Dear Mr. Horndog: I want to assume that your crudeness is an act. For the sake of mankind I hope that you are both sensitive and intelligent. So if you can't say something nice . . .

CHEESE: Oh, God. It's Jiminy Fucking Cricket. Please, Cutiepie, we *are*, after all, adults.

PLATO: "To the mean all becomes mean." Nietzsche.

HORNDOG: Yo' Plato! What's your problem? The man's entitled to his opinion! Who died and made you smart?

NADINE: Dear Plato: I find you quite interesting. Do you mind if I ask your age? Nadine.

PLATO: To quote Katherine Hepburn; "Either you are interesting at any age or you are not. There is nothing particularly interesting about being old—or being young, for that matter." Yours, Plato.

CHEESE: Dear Ms. Nadine: Either you're very young, very naive, or very stupid. Plato is obviously a child. Either that or some horny computer geek with a book of quotations who's never gone out on a date. The Cheese.

HORNDOG: Oh—like you, Cheese?

CHEESE: Dear Mr. Horndog: Please purchase a jar of vaseline and a smut magazine and get yourself a hobby. The Cheese.

CUTIEPIE: Dear Cheese: Why do you pick on poor Plato? Horndog asks for it, but Plato is a nice man.

CHEESE: Dear Ms. Cutiepie: Because Plato is an insipid moron. The Cheese.

NADINE: I don't think Plato is a moron. I think he's rather sweet.

CUTIEPIE: So do I.

PHYLLIS: Me, too.

PLATO: Ladies, ladies, I appreciate your coming to my rescue, but I assure you that it is not necessary. I'm perfectly capable of defending myself against the wrath of our Mr. Cheese.

HORNDOG: Yo' Phyllis, how long have you been lurking?

PHYLLIS: Have I been? I guess I have. Not too long, I suppose.

NADINE: Dear All: Forgive my ignorance. What is "lurking"?

CUTIEPIE: Nadine: Lurking is when you read the conversations but don't participate.

CHEESE: My dear Nadine: Lurking is an act similar to spying. It's the direct sign of a coward.

PLATO: Dear Mr. Cheese: As Mark Twain once said, "The human race is a race of cowards, and I am not only marching in that procession but carrying a banner." I'm sure Miss Phyllis will have plenty to say when she's ready. Yours, Plato.

CUTIEPIE: At least she isn't saying anything stupid. Right, Cheese?

HORNDOG: Yeah, Cheese Man. Leave the girl alone.

CHEESE: Dear Mr. Horndog: Is that a threat? Should I be afraid of you?

HORNDOG: Dear Mr. Cheese: Yes, you should.

CHEESE: Once again, Mr. Horndog, your true nature surfaces. I suspect that in real life you are not in fact the boorish tough-guy you project online. No, in fact, I suspect that you are a coward—a coward who has been picked on his entire life to the extent that he has one dream—to be the furthest thing from his true self: a bully.

HORNDOG: Dear Mr. Cheese: You don't know shit. I think you're an asshole. Bite my ass, motherfucker!

NADINE: Boys! The intellectual level of this conversation has fallen through the floor. We owe it to ourselves to behave like adults. Now, one more outburst and I'll make you go to your rooms.

HORNDOG: Yes, mommy.

CHEESE: Dear Nadine: Judging by the tone of your string of conversations I can now safely assume that you have children. My guess is that you're some middle-aged, bored housewife who's discovered her computer is a source for a little excitement to make up for the void in her ordinarily pointless and hum-drum existence by allowing her to pretend that she is a vixen, and a single one at that. I am right, am I not? The Cheese.

NADINE: Dear Mr. Cheese: Nothing could be further from the truth. I am not a housewife nor am I middle-aged. For all you know I may not even be a woman. But you, my judgmental friend, will never know. Love and kisses, Nadine.

PLATO: Dear Nadine: "One is not born a woman, one becomes one." Simone de Beauvoir.

NADINE: Thank you, Plato. That's very sweet.

HORNDOG: Hey Nadine, don't make me sick.

PHYLLIS: Dear Mr. Horndog: I don't exactly know what your problem is, but you could do with a little sweetness yourself. The fact that you have to hang out on the singles newsgroup on the Internet speaks for itself. We all have our problems and we all have our reasons for hiding behind our computer personas to socialize. But with your attitude you'll wind up doing worse than Mr. Cheese. Lighten up, dude. Try being friendly and a little sensitive to women. Maybe then one of them will go out with you. Remember, you can attract more bees with honey than vinegar. I'm no Plato, but you get the idea. Yours, Phyllis.

CHEESE: What do you mean "doing worse than Mr. Cheese"?

NADINE: Bravo, Phyllis.

CUTIEPIE: That was rather harsh, Phyllis, but necessary. Thank you.

CHEESE: Pardon me while I interrupt your nauseating praise of Ms. Phyllis's actually possessing a spine, but I demand you explain your overtly hostile crack deliberately pointed towards me.

NADINE: This is not about you, Cheese.

HORNDOG: Yeah. Mind your own business, dickhead.

PHYLLIS: Dear Cheese: I feel no explanation is necessary. You wake up with yourself every day and surely you know how unpleasant you are. Frankly, I wish you weren't on the newsgroup.

NADINE: Hear, hear.

HORNDOG: That's the best thing I've heard yet.

PLATO: The Dalai Lama says: "We live very close together. So, our prime purpose in this life is to help others. And if you can't help them, at least don't hurt them."

CHEESE: Does this mean I am being evicted?

CUTIEPIE: No, not at all.

PHYLLIS: Speak for yourself. Take a walk, Cheese.

HORNDOG: The Cheese stands alone.

CHEESE: Fine. I don't need any of you. Consider me offline. Cordially, The Cheese. By the way, the Dalai Lama says: Fuck you all.

(*Lights go down on Cheese*)

HORNDOG: The Cheese is dead! Long live The Cheese!

NADINE: He was a grump. I'm glad he's offline.

CUTIEPIE: I think he was a sad man. We talk about online personas versus our real persona and we never thought about him.

HORNDOG: He was a dick. Good riddance.

CUTIEPIE: Something is making him angry. I feel bad for him.

NADINE: Plato, what do you think?

PLATO: "We never touch but at points." Ralph Waldo Emerson.

(*Blackout*)

Scene Two

(*E-MAIL*)

Lights up on Cutiepie)

CUTIEPIE: Cheese? It's Cutiepie. I hope you don't mind my sending you a private E-mail, but I'm sad that you've left the newsgroup. I don't know why you're always so mad at everybody. If you want to talk to me I'll listen. Cutiepie.

(*Light on Cheese*)

CHEESE: Dear Ms. Cutiepie: I apologize for my brash behavior. I do tend to become consumed by my hostility from time to time. Please let everyone know that it was not personal. The Cheese.

CUTIEPIE: You were always personal. Why don't you like people?

CHEESE: The very notion that I do not like people is absurd. I resent that you even would mention it.

CUTIEPIE: Do you have any friends in real life?

CHEESE: What kind of question is that?

CUTIEPIE: I don't have many friends. I thought maybe you didn't, either.

CHEESE: People are morons. I have trouble talking to them.

CUTIEPIE: People are not morons. But I know that sometimes it's hard to relate. Just because they don't understand you doesn't mean that they're bad.

CHEESE: I would not hesitate to say that you have never met with an undeserved adversary.

CUTIEPIE: I would not hesitate to say that you shouldn't assume anything.

CHEESE: Oh?

(*Lights down on Cutiepie and Cheese and up on Plato and Nadine*)

NADINE: Dear Plato: I wanted to send you a private E-mail because I think that you display a very mature and well-educated wisdom. Frankly, I find that fascinating and a little sexy. For that matter, don't think that I haven't noticed that you never tell about yourself. I'd like to know who you are in real life—your real name, your age, what you do, what you look like . . . It's okay, I don't bite. Nadine.

PLATO: Dear Nadine: William James said "The art of being wise is the art of knowing what to overlook." Yours, Plato.

NADINE: That's very nice, but for once could you not speak in quotes? I'd like to know who you really are? Are you a college professor? Do you have children?

PLATO: "Anybody who hates children and dogs can't be all bad." W.C. Fields.

NADINE: I take it then you don't have children. And please, no quotes.

PLATO: No, I have no children, nor do I like them. They're all selfish and cruel. Children, teenagers in particular, are horrible creatures. Nobody should be allowed to assimilate into society until they're at least twenty-one or a college graduate.

NADINE: If you had one, maybe you would feel different about them.

PLATO: I take it you do? You seem to allude to them frequently.

NADINE: Maybe I do, maybe I don't. Maybe I want them and can't have them. Maybe I have them and don't like them.

PLATO: I assume there's a reason for your ambiguity.

NADINE: So, what do you do? I'll bet you're some kind of English or Philosophy professor.

PLATO: Alas, no. I . . . (*beat*) work with computers. And you?

NADINE: A question! Plato finally asks a question! I . . . (*beat*) am a writer. Yes, I am a writer.

PLATO: Does repeating it make it so? What do you do, Nadine?

NADINE: I said I was a writer.

PLATO: I know, but you and I both know that is not true.

(*Lights down on Nadine and Plato, and up on Horndog and Phyllis*)

HORNDOG: Dear Phyllis: I kept a printout of your profile. You sound totally hot.

PHYLLIS: Thank you, Horndog. Right now I feel a little hot.

HORNDOG: You do! Is there any way we can meet face to face?

PHYLLIS: Are you always this aggressive?

HORNDOG: I'm coming on too strong, aren't I?

PHYLLIS: Yes, you are.

HORNDOG: I'm sorry. I just get so excited when a woman leaves me E-mail. Women don't talk to me too much in real life, and when they do it's usually to get me in bed.

PHYLLIS: Oh. Look, Horndog, I think that's more than I need to know.

HORNDOG: No, no, you don't understand. I'm a good-looking guy! I'm just not gifted in the brain department, so I try to hang around with people who are and they treat me like I'm stupid. Lots of smart people hang out on the Internet, so I figure I'll hang out on the Internet, too! You sound pretty smart. Are you smart?

PHYLLIS: Sometimes I don't think so. Right now I don't think so.

HORNDOG: That's too bad. You sound smart. So, what do you like in a guy? I know it's kind of a personal question, but I got nothing to lose.

PHYLLIS: Oh, my. In a man. I really don't know. It depends on the individual. What do you look for in a woman?

HORNDOG: It depends on the individual. See? I told you that you was smart. What do I look for in a woman? Well, she's gotta be smart—just like you! And she's gotta be good-looking—just like you!

PHYLLIS: Is that it?

HORNDOG: Oh, she's gotta like me. I find that attractive in a woman.

(*Lights go down on Phyllis and Horndog and up on Cheese and Cutiepie*)

CHEESE: I recall a cartoon I once saw in *The New Yorker*. There was a dog typing away at a computer, and the caption had the dog saying, "On the Internet, nobody knows you're a dog."

CUTIEPIE: I like that.

CHEESE: It's very poignant. I think it represents the majority of people on the Net.

CUTIEPIE: People like us.

CHEESE: Perhaps people like us.

CUTIEPIE: You don't think you're attractive?

CHEESE: If I did would I have to resort to the Internet to socialize?

CUTIEPIE: Beauty is in the mind, Cheese. If you don't believe you're beautiful, how will anyone else?

CHEESE: Ah, but that's not true. Here on the Internet, I'm Mel Gibson.

CUTIEPIE: More like Mel Brooks. You make yourself very ugly.

CHEESE: I suppose that it's not the best image that I've projected in my only social outlet.

CUTIEPIE: Then if this is your only social outlet, why are you so mean?

CHEESE: *Because* it *is* my only social outlet.

(*Lights down on Cutiepie and Cheese and up on Nadine and Plato*)

NADINE: You sound very sexy. What are you wearing?

PLATO: Dearest Nadine, please check your spelling. Apparently you inadvertently asked what I was wearing.

NADINE: I was. What are you wearing?

PLATO: Right now?

NADINE: Yes. Tell me what you're wearing right now. You can tell a lot about a man by what he wears.

(*Plato picks up a copy of* GQ *magazine and rifles through it*)

PLATO: Well . . . I'm wearing a freshly pressed Van Heussen white shirt, a Nicole Miller necktie, khaki dockers, and Bass bucks.

NADINE: Hmmm. You sound very classy and very handsome. Do you want to hear what I'm wearing?

PLATO: . . . sure . . .

NADINE: I'm wearing a sheer, black silk teddy with red lace panties and black fishnet stockings. Does that excite you, Plato?

PLATO: . . . yes . . .

NADINE: What would you like to do, Plato?

PLATO: DO?!

(*Lights down on Plato and Nadine and up on Cheese and Cutiepie*)

CHEESE: Since nobody knows you're a dog, do you have dog-like qualities?

CUTIEPIE: I would have to say "yes." I think we all do.

CHEESE: I know that frequently I'm not what people feel comfortable around.

CUTIEPIE: You'll have to do better than that, Cheese. Why would people not feel comfortable around you? Do you make them feel ill at ease?

CHEESE: I fear that I do, but I don't exactly know how I do it. I tend to rub people the wrong way.

CUTIEPIE: But right now it's just you and me. You're not rubbing me the wrong way.

CHEESE: Don't worry. I will.

CUTIEPIE: You will with that attitude. Let's try an experiment. In this experiment, nothing you do or say will rub me the wrong way.

CHEESE: It sounds great in theory. We both know that in reality it won't work.

CUTIEPIE: Do you want it to work? Or are you one of those types who want people to dislike them? You know, when you act badly and treat people poorly, it ruins all of your excuses.

CHEESE: Excuses for what?

CUTIEPIE: Excuses for being alone. It officially becomes your fault.

(*Lights down on Cheese and Cutiepie and up on Phyllis and Horndog*)

PHYLLIS: You can be the most handsome man in the world, but if you come across with an attitude like that, nobody will want to go out with you.

HORNDOG: I don't think I have what most women want.

PHYLLIS: And what's that?

HORNDOG: If I knew, I'd do something about it.

PHYLLIS: And you don't think it's your attitude?

HORNDOG: What's wrong with my attitude?!

PHYLLIS: You come across like a pig.

HORNDOG: But you know better, right?

PHYLLIS: I think you're a pig, too.

HORNDOG: And what makes me a pig?

PHYLLIS: You're too interested in yourself to care about the person you're talking to or their feelings. You focus on superficial things like appearance. You have a terribly inflated ego.

HORNDOG (*in a different, more serious tone*): Does that make you feel threatened?

PHYLLIS: Threatened? In what way?

HORNDOG (*still in a serious tone*): Does it make you feel uncomfortable? Do you now distrust me?

PHYLLIS: Horndog? Are you the same person who began this string? Those questions don't seem like you.

(*Lights down on Phyllis and Horndog and up on Plato and Nadine*)

PLATO: Why, Mrs. Robinson, I do believe you're trying to seduce me.

NADINE: I thought we agreed—no more quotes?

PLATO: Nadine, I think there are some things about me you should know.

NADINE: The only things I want to know is what you'd like to do to me. Would you like to kiss me?

PLATO: Nadine, I can't believe we're having this conversation.

NADINE: Tell me, Plato. Would you like to kiss me?

PLATO: Yes.

NADINE: Then go ahead. Kiss me.

(*Lights down on Nadine only*)

PLATO: Dear Mr. Horndog: I know you and I are not on the best of terms, but I have a problem that I think you can help me with. Situation urgent. Plato.

(*Lights up on Horndog*)

HORNDOG: Yeah, Plato ol' pal! Whas'sup?

PLATO: Thank you for your response. I'm having problems with a woman.

HORNDOG: No shit? Who'da thunk. Tell me bud, what's the problem?

PLATO: I feel as though I'm being seduced.

HORNDOG: Congratulations. Now, what's the problem?

PLATO: That *is* the problem. I'm being seduced online. She keeps telling me what she's wearing and asks what I'm wearing. She wants me to kiss her.

HORNDOG: You lucky bastard. She wants to have cybersex with you.

PLATO: Look, Mr. Horndog, I know for someone of your ilk this may be normal, but I've never . . . I don't know how . . . I'm not sure . . . I just don't know what to do.

HORNDOG: Plato, relax. Let the ol' Horndog help ya. We'll be like that french guy with the big honker—Cyrano the Beeswax. The girl wants you to basically talk dirty to her. Go through the motions without actually being in the same room. Some folks get off on it. When it's good it can get pretty hot.

PLATO: So what do I do being that she wants me to kiss her? I can't very well kiss her through the computer. And it's Cyrano de Bergerac, not Beeswax.

HORNDOG: Describe kissing her. Be poetic—you're good with that shit. Find a steamy novel and recite your favorite passage.

PLATO: It seems so . . . perverse.

HORNDOG: Yeah. It's the best!

(*Lights down on Horndog and back up on Nadine. Plato rifles through his stuff until he finds a romance novel. He searches for a passage and reads lifelessly—as though he's reading a stereo manual*)

PLATO: From the tips of your dainty fingers my lips caress each inch of your creamy skin, rising inch by inch as I reach the nape of your smooth, delicate neck. I can see your lips quiver with antici . . . (*turns page*) . . . passion as I nibble on the lobe of your left ear. Finally, I pull you close as

I press hard with my lips against yours. I can feel the softness of them against mine and the warmth of your breath.

NADINE: Oh! Oh my! Oh, God! Take me, Plato! Take me!

(*Lights down fast on Nadine and up on Horndog again*)

PLATO: Oh my God, Horndog, it worked. She wants me to take her.

HORNDOG: Hot damn! Some guys have all the luck.

PLATO: But it feels so . . . dirty.

HORNDOG: You'll learn to love it when you're a little older.

PLATO: I beg your pardon, Mr. Horndog. What is the insinuation of "when you're a little older"?

HORNDOG: You're a kid, aren't you?

PLATO: I feel you have misjudged me, Mr. Horndog.

HORNDOG: How old are you? Thirteen? Fifteen?

PLATO: Sixteen. How did you find out?

HORNDOG: In your case, it was easy. You try too hard to sound old. Besides, only a kid would have this much trouble with cybersex.

PLATO: Please, Mr. Horndog, don't let anyone know. I'll do anything.

HORNDOG: Your secret is safe with me. Hopefully someday you can return the favor.

PLATO: Thank you. I am forever in your debt. So, what do I do now?

HORNDOG: Stall. It'll get Nadine going.

PLATO: *Nadine?*! How did you know . . . ?!

HORNDOG: I know a lot of things.

(*Lights down on Horndog and up on Nadine*)

PLATO: No. Not yet. I'm not ready.

NADINE: Then allow me to get you ready.

(*Lights down on Nadine and Plato and up on Cheese and Cutiepie*)

CHEESE: So what's your excuse? You seem quite nice. Why do you choose to hide behind an obvious ruse of an online persona?

CUTIEPIE: Between you and me, I'm not too pleasing on the eye.

CHEESE: Now, Cutiepie, if you went by your own given requisites for beauty, I would think that you were quite attractive. It radiates from you.

CUTIEPIE: Why, Mr. Cheese, do I detect actual kindness?

CHEESE: Let's keep this our little secret, shall we?

CUTIEPIE: Do you have a scanner? I'd love to see a picture of you.

CHEESE: I as well would like a picture. I live in New York City. Where are you from?

CUTIEPIE: Boston. That's not too far. Maybe we could visit each other some day.

CHEESE: That would be good. I travel to Boston frequently with my job. I work as a social worker. I do some consulting with a clinic in Boston about every two weeks.

CUTIEPIE: Got your picture. You're a rather handsome rogue. Nicer than what I expected.

CHEESE: I received your photo as well. Horndog is right. You really are a cutiepie.

CUTIEPIE: Please don't tease me.

CHEESE: I would never tease you. I'll be in Boston this weekend. May I take you out to dinner?

CUTIEPIE: Yes.

(*Lights down on Cutiepie and Cheese and up on Phyllis and Horndog*)

PHYLLIS: Dear Mr. Horndog: Though I am flattered by your continuous and seemingly relentless advances, I must now formally ask you to cease and desist from further harassment.

HORNDOG: Are you a lawyer?

PHYLLIS: No, but I work in a law firm, remember?

HORNDOG: Tell me, Phyllis, why would you say you're a woman on a singles newsgroup on the Internet if you didn't want men to talk to you?

PHYLLIS: I never "said" I was a woman. I *am* a woman.

HORNDOG: Lots of times men will pretend to be women because they're not too interesting and nobody talks to them. But if they pretend they're a babe, everyone wants to talk to them. Guys on the Net tend to be pretty horny.

PHYLLIS: Are you insinuating that I'm not who I say I am?

HORNDOG: Baby, nobody is who they say they are.

PHYLLIS: I assure you that I am a woman.

HORNDOG: Fine. I assure you that I'm a parakeet.

PHYLLIS: No, you're not.

HORNDOG: How do you know? Meet me in person and we'll both find out who each other really is.

PHYLLIS: I have to get back to you on this.

(*Blackout*)

Scene Three

USENET

(*Lights up on all except Cheese*)

CUTIEPIE: Hello, everybody. Within the discussion of who we are in real
life as opposed to who we are online, I want you all to know that I had
dinner with Cheese this weekend. Unlike the person he presents online,
he's actually quite sweet and quite charming. We may have judged him
too harshly. Cutiepie.

PHYLLIS: Cheese was a jerk. He behaved like a child. Phyllis.

NADINE: So, tell us about the date! Nadine.

PLATO: I have two for you: Leon Trotsky said, "An ally has to be watched
just like an enemy." Or, as Woody Allen says: "The lion and the calf shall
lie down together but the calf won't get much sleep."

CUTIEPIE: Come on, give the Cheese a chance. We had a delightful time.
He's so nice once you get beyond all the pain. He hasn't had it easy. Being
nasty was just his way of keeping everyone at bay. He didn't want to be hurt.

NADINE: There are better ways to do that. We all have pain, Cutiepie. We
were never deserving of his wrath. Face it, the man was downright rude.

CUTIEPIE: But he's different now. Please let him back.

PLATO: "Life is a slate where all our sins are written; from time to time
we rub the sponge of repentance over it so we can begin sinning again."
George Sand.

HORNDOG: Come on, Plato. Be a guy. Forgive the dude.

PHYLLIS: I say we take a vote.

NADINE: Is the Internet ready for democracy?

PLATO: John Dryden says: "The most may err as grossly as the few." I'm
in. Plato.

PHYLLIS: Fine. All in favor of the Cheese coming back? I vote "yes."

CUTIEPIE: I vote "yes."

HORNDOG: Sure. Why not. Let the dude back.

PLATO: Gandhi said: "The weak can never forgive. Forgiveness is the attribute of the strong." Let the Cheese return.

NADINE: Only if he behaves.

CUTIEPIE: Thank you. Thank you, all of you.

(*Lights back up on Cheese*)

CHEESE: Yes. I'm sorry I was so harsh and judgmental. You all have been quite decent to me and I returned your decency with hostility. I agree that was wrong and I'm sorry. No hard feelings, and I hope that we can all become friends. Sincerely, the Cheese.

PHYLLIS: Wow! Cutiepie, you must have worked wonders on him. He sounds like a new man.

CUTIEPIE: He is a new man, Phyllis. Like all of us, he's alone. That can be tough sometimes.

HORNDOG: Yo! Welcome back, Cheese! I hear that you and Cutiepie are a real item.

CHEESE: An item? Yes, I suppose we would be considered an "item." We had a lovely date, true. She really is a lovely person.

NADINE: Who would have thought it. Congratulations, Cutiepie and Cheese.

CUTIEPIE: Thanks, Nadine. It's a little scary. I really have never dated much. And, as a social worker he only gets to come to Boston every two weeks.

HORNDOG: Hey, I got a great idea! Why don't we all meet on an IRC channel?

NADINE: Again, forgive my ignorance. What is an IRC channel?

PLATO: IRC stands for Internet Relay Chat. It's a part of the Internet where we can actually converse in real time. Someone creates a channel and we all log on to it at the same time, thus allowing us to converse. What you type goes out immediately to all others logged on to that channel.

NADINE: It sounds exciting! Seems a lot better than having to wait a day for responses. I'm in.

CUTIEPIE: IRC? I'd love to have an IRC session!

CHEESE: Name the time and place.

HORNDOG: Yo, Phyllis! We haven't heard from you yet. Are you in or out?

PHYLLIS: Dear Horndog: I'm in. Lord knows why, but I'm in.

NADINE: Dear Phyllis: Don't worry, dear. We're all your friends here.

HORNDOG: How about this Saturday at eleven o'clock Eastern time. That's eight o'clock for the Westcoasters.

NADINE: Plato? Are you in?

PLATO: Saturday is a busy day for me. I might not be able to be there.

CUTIEPIE: Aw, come on Plato! Don't be a party pooper!

NADINE: Plato, if you're not there I'll find you and drag you online by your ears.

HORNDOG: Come on, Plato. You owe me.

PLATO: Fine. Fine. Eleven o'clock Eastern Standard Time. And what shall we call this channel?

NADINE: How about "Plato"?

CUTIEPIE: Great! "Plato" it is! See you all this Saturday night!

PHYLLIS: Great! I'll be there!

CHEESE: We'll be live this Saturday.

NADINE: You won't be sorry, Plato.

HORNDOG: This is gonna be fun. See you there.

(*Lights go down on Horndog only*)

PLATO: Dear Nadine, Cutiepie, Cheese, and Phyllis: I don't know if you've noticed this or not but there's something about Horndog I don't exactly trust. He seems to know more than he lets on. Be wary of any questions he asks and, more importantly, be wary of any accusations he makes. He's told me a few things in private that struck some uncomfortable nerves. Yours, Plato.

PHYLLIS: Dear Plato—carbon copy to Cutiepie, Cheese, and Nadine: I know what you mean. He seems like a jerk but then he starts figuring you out. I don't think he is representing himself honestly.

(*Lights fade out on Phyllis, Cheese, and Cutiepie, but remain upon Plato and Nadine*)

NADINE: Dear Plato: Be on the IRC channel fifteen minutes early.

PLATO: My dear Nadine, I don't know if that will be possible.

NADINE: I said be there fifteen minutes early. No excuses.

PLATO: Yes, ma'am.

(*Blackout*)

ACT II

Scene One

IRC

Lights up on Nadine, who sits quietly, waiting. Eventually the light comes up on Plato

NADINE: It's about time, mister.

PLATO: Hello, Nadine. I hope you are navigating adeptly through the Internet Relay Chat.

NADINE: I think you know why I wanted to chat with you . . . alone.

PLATO: I suspect I do.

NADINE: We have unfinished business, Plato.

PLATO: Nadine, there is something I need to tell you.

NADINE: You can tell me anything, sweetheart.

PLATO: You're making this very difficult.

NADINE: Don't you want me?

PLATO: Yes! Oh God, yes!

NADINE: Then what is it?

PLATO: To quote Thomas Fuller: "Prospect is often better than possession."

NADINE: I find your repartee very sexy, but now I want action.

PLATO: Nadine, we're talking through a computer.

NADINE: Sex has never been safer.

PLATO: You see, that's kind of the point.

NADINE: Oh, I know your type. You prefer it in person. I understand.

PLATO: You've done this before?

NADINE: Me? Sure. Haven't you?

PLATO: Me? Sure. All the time.

NADINE: Then let's get to it, Tiger.

PLATO: Wait.

NADINE (*beat*): Okay, I'm waiting . . .

PLATO: What do you look like?

NADINE: Do you know who Cindy Crawford is?

PLATO: You look like Cindy Crawford?

NADINE: My hair is darker.

PLATO: Excuse the assumption, Nadine, but if you looked like Cindy Crawford I hardly think you'd have a need for conversing in a singles newsgroup over the Internet.

NADINE: I like the mental stimulation. Now stimulate me.

PLATO: What do you really look like?

NADINE: Okay, I don't look like Cindy Crawford.

PLATO: I figured as much.

NADINE: It's more like Elizabeth Hurley.

PLATO: Aw, cut it out.

NADINE: What does it matter? We're two living, breathing souls joined by a phone line. I'm real, Plato. I'm a real woman and you're a real man—and through the miracle of modern science we're actually touching. It doesn't matter what we look like or what we do for a living or our gross annual income. We've stripped all of that away to expose our pure, raw, uninhibited self.

PLATO: It pains me to say this, but I disagree with you totally. It *does* matter what we look like or what we do for a living. If you've never been laughed at and shunned because you were different you're truly missing one of life's greatest heartaches. And what's more, we have *not* stripped all of that away; but buffered and filtered even more significantly than if we met face to face. For all I know you're an old woman, or some middle-aged man getting his jollies off. For all you know I'm some pimply faced kid who can't relate.

NADINE: But you're not. Let go with your expectations, Plato. Use your imagination. Not only can I be anyone I want to be but I can be anyone *you* want me to be. You just have to want it.

PLATO: I want what's real.

NADINE: Sometimes we can't have that. We have to settle for fantasy. What's your fantasy?

PLATO: I have no fantasies.

NADINE: Everyone has fantasies.

PLATO: It's silly.

NADINE: Fantasies are never silly. Tell me.

PLATO: It's my fantasy that I'll fit in and people will like me and actually be interested in what I think and what I have to say.

NADINE: How old are you, Plato?

PLATO (*rifles through his book*): "We turn not older with years, but newer every day." Emily Dickinson.

NADINE: Oh, Christ, you're a child.

PLATO: No.

NADINE: How old are you? Twelve? Thirteen?

PLATO: I assure you, I am no child.

(*Lights up on Horndog*)

HORNDOG: Howdy howdy howdy! Am I interrupting anything?

NADINE: You're ten minutes early, Horndog.

PLATO: Mr. Horndog! Hello! Welcome to the IRC.

HORNDOG: Hey, it's great to meet you two in person—or at least in real time.

PLATO: The feeling is mutual.

NADINE: I don't think I'll be up for the chat tonight.

HORNDOG: Aw, Nadine, babe, don't be a pill! It'll be great!

NADINE: I'm sorry, Horndog. I'm feeling a bit low right now. I don't think I'll be very interesting to talk to.

HORNDOG: Horseshit. Did old man Plato piss you off?

NADINE: I suspect that Plato is no old man.

HORNDOG: Sure he is. Plato and I go way back. At least twenty years. We went to grade school together, right, Plato ol' pal?

PLATO: We certainly did, Horndog.

NADINE: Then my accusation is inaccurate. I apologize, Plato. I hope I haven't ruined any potential.

HORNDOG: Ooooh, Plato! You dirty dog!

PLATO: No. No potential is lost. "Treat people as if they were what they ought to be and you help them to become what they are capable of being." Johann Wolfgang von Goethe.

NADINE: Then what are you afraid of?

HORNDOG: Let me tell you about my old buddy Plato. He's kind of the brainy type. Not good with people. He's great with books and computers but this one-on-one stuff makes him nervous. Right?

PLATO: Yes. Exactly.

NADINE: You poor man. I'm so sorry.

HORNDOG: What ol' Plato needs is someone he can trust. Someone who can bring him out of his shell.

NADINE: Oh, Plato. Do you forgive me?

PLATO (*beat*): Yes.

(*Lights down quickly on Nadine*)

HORNDOG: So, Plato, I guess you owe me again.

PLATO: I guess I do.

HORNDOG: You may get your chance to pay me back—with interest.

PLATO: You make me nervous.

HORNDOG: Don't worry, pal. Just let me feel my way around. I think I've got this all figured out.

PLATO: Got what figured out?

(*Lights back up on Nadine*)

NADINE: Where did you two go?

HORNDOG: Just a little private chat. Plato owes me some money for a football bet he lost.

PLATO: Right. I'll have it wired to you tomorrow.

NADINE: You boys . . .

HORNDOG: So, I wonder if Cutiepie knows yet.

NADINE: Knows what?

HORNDOG: About Cheese. It's obvious.

NADINE: What's obvious?

(*Lights up on Phyllis*)

PHYLLIS: Hi, everybody!

NADINE: Hi, Phyllis!

PLATO: Welcome, Phyllis.

HORNDOG: Hey, Phil! How's it hangin'?!

PHYLLIS: I see that in real time you're still a jerk.

NADINE: Horndog was just telling us about Cutiepie and the Cheese.

PHYLLIS: What about them?

HORNDOG: Nothing. Nothing. Just a hunch.

NADINE: Come on, Horndog. Don't leave us guessing.

HORNDOG: It's still just a hunch. I'm not too sure right now. You'll be the first to know.

(*Lights up on Cutiepie*)

CUTIEPIE: First to know what?

HORNDOG (*covering*): About my new job.

CUTIEPIE: Oh? What is your new job?

HORNDOG: Research. I'll be doing research.

CUTIEPIE: Isn't that fascinating! What kind of research?

HORNDOG: Oh, whatever comes up. I'll be working for a publisher.

PHYLLIS: Correct me if I'm wrong, but doing research takes keen intelligence. I thought you weren't very smart.

HORNDOG: Who said that?

PHYLLIS: You did. You said you like going on the Internet because you want to be smarter by talking with smarter people.

HORNDOG: I guess it worked.

(*Lights up on Cheese*)

CHEESE: Hi, everybody!

NADINE: Hi, Cheese!

PLATO: Welcome, Mr. Cheese.

PHYLLIS: Hi, Cheese.

HORNDOG: Yo! Cheese!

CUTIEPIE: Hi, honey. I thought you'd never get here.

CHEESE: Sorry I'm late. I had some troubles at the office. One of my cases got a little intense.

CUTIEPIE: I'm sorry. So, I guess we're all here!

HORNDOG: So, where are we all logging in from?

CHEESE: New York City.

CUTIEPIE: Boston.

PLATO: Los Angeles.

NADINE: San Francisco. We're not too far from each other.

PHYLLIS: Connecticut.

HORNDOG: New Jersey. But I know something you don' t know, Phyllis.

PHYLLIS: What's that?

HORNDOG: We work in the same neighborhood.

PHYLLIS: How do you know that?

HORNDOG: You said you were a "legal professional." I read that as either secretary or, more likely, word processing operator. Well, I'll bet you dimes to bagels that your law firm is somewhere in midtown Manhattan since that's where the big law firms are that would have a word processing department. I'll even bet you again that we don't work too far from each other. I'm on Madison and 46th.

PHYLLIS: I used to just not like you. Now I don't trust you as well.

PLATO: How do you know these things, Horndog?

HORNDOG: Know what?

NADINE: Yes. It seems you know a lot about us. It also seems you are smarter than you let on. Cheese, you're into this kind of stuff. What's going on here?

CHEESE: It appears that Mr. Horndog, like the rest of us, likes to project an image different from his real self. Perhaps he has something to protect.

HORNDOG: Perhaps you're a shithead.

CHEESE: Ah, the return of the *true* Horndog. Why don't you scratch yourself for us? Or better yet, roll over and play dead.

CUTIEPIE: Cheese, behave.

CHEESE: Sorry. Like I said, it was a tough day. I'm just venting a little.

HORNDOG: Hey, it's cool. No offense taken, Cheese.

NADINE: So, now that we're live, what do we do?

PHYLLIS: We figure out what gives with Horndog.

HORNDOG: What do you mean "what gives?"

PHYLLIS: With all of our talk about not truly representing who we are, we feel you are the worst offender.

HORNDOG: Nice accusation . . . for a guy.

NADINE: What?!

CUTIEPIE: Phyllis is a man?

CHEESE: I'm appalled!

NADINE: That's a lie.

HORNDOG: No, it isn't. Tell 'em I'm right, Philip.

PHYLLIS: I'm not gay.

HORNDOG: I never said you were.

PLATO: "We lie loudest when we lie to ourselves." Eric Hoffer.

PHYLLIS: You don't understand.

NADINE: Then why did you do it?

PHYLLIS: Because nobody answered my postings as "Philip." When I signed on as "Phyllis" people wanted to talk to me. Right, Horndog? Right, Cheese? You two seemed pretty eager to get my attention.

CHEESE: Guilty.

HORNDOG: I suspected from the start. I remember your original post. I'll admit, it did nothing for me.

PHYLLIS: I hope you'll all forgive me.

CUTIEPIE: It's you who should forgive us. You tried to join in as yourself and we didn't give you a chance.

PLATO: Alas, Cutiepie is correct.

NADINE: I feel so foolish.

PHYLLIS: Not as foolish as I do.

HORNDOG: Sorry I blew your cover, Phil. If it means anything, for a minute there I was actually turned on.

CHEESE: Excuse me everyone, but I have to go.

(*Lights bump down suddenly on Cheese*)

CUTIEPIE: Cheese? Cheese, what's the matter? Where did you go?

NADINE: That's odd.

HORNDOG: I guess his wife must'a caught him.

CUTIEPIE: But Cheese isn't married.

HORNDOG: Oops.

CUTIEPIE: But we went out! We met in Boston!

HORNDOG: And he lives in New York—with his wife.

CUTIEPIE: Horndog, I demand to know how you know everything!

NADINE: Yes, come clean!

PHYLLIS: What else do you know?

PLATO: "A little learning is a dangerous thing." Alexander Pope.

HORNDOG: I know Plato is sixteen years old.

PLATO: It's a lie.

HORNDOG: No it isn't. You told me yourself.

NADINE: I feel sick.

HORNDOG: Maybe it's menopausal. Women of your age should be careful.

CUTIEPIE: Okay, what do you know about me?

HORNDOG: Nothing, except that I suspect that you are cute in name only. I don't mean to be rude or anything. Let's just say that you probably don't date much.

CUTIEPIE: Cheese liked me.

HORNDOG: Cheese is married.

(*Lights off on Horndog*)

NADINE: Horndog? Where did he go!

CUTIEPIE: Horndog, you can't do that!

PLATO: He's gone.

PHYLLIS: Who is he?

CUTIEPIE: A very troubled person.

NADINE: Plato? I'm sorry. I didn't know.

PLATO: Neither did I.

NADINE: I feel very dirty.

PLATO: No. You were merely tapping into a hidden side of yourself. It was actually quite beautiful.

NADINE: What's your real name?

PLATO: Billy. Just geeky little Billy Rosenblatt who's too smart for kids his own age, so he attempted to be someone else where he'd have no age.

PHYLLIS: I guess none of us planned on getting busted.

NADINE: Sixteen. I have a daughter your age.

CUTIEPIE: Online I can be as beautiful as I always wanted to be.

NADINE: Cheese thought you were beautiful.

CUTIEPIE: Cheese was no prize. But he was real.

NADINE: Hey, Billy, maybe you'd like to meet my daughter sometime.

PLATO: I don't think so.

NADINE: Why not?

PLATO: I don't get along well with people face-to-face.

CUTIEPIE: I think he's right. I'd rather keep it this way.

NADINE: Hello. My name is Nadine Shumacker. I'm fifty-one years old. I have a sixteen-year-old daughter and a fourteen-year-old son. I've been married to the same man for twenty-one years. I'm bored to tears.

PHYLLIS: Hello. My name is Philip McGary. I'm thirty years old and I still live with my parents. I'm an actor wannabe who works as a word-processing operator in a law firm in New York City until I get that big break. I don't have a lot of friends.

PLATO: Hello. My name is Billy Rosenblatt. I'm sixteen years old. My best friend is my computer. I passed the G.E.D. when I was fourteen. I currently attend California Polytechnic, and I can't relate to anyone human.

CUTIEPIE: Hello. My name is Debbie Berman. I'm twenty-eight years old, and nobody knows I'm a dog.

(*Blackout*)

Scene Two

E-MAIL

(*Lights up on Horndog*)

HORNDOG: Dear Cheese, Cutiepie, Plato, Nadine and especially Phyllis:

I'm sorry I exposed your little game of charades. I had no intention of hurting anybody. I'm not asking for forgiveness. But I feel I at least owe you an explanation.

I work for CyberPress in Manhattan. I write articles and books on the Internet. For the past year I've been researching personalities on the Net—how and why people choose false personas. One of the final stages of my research was to infiltrate a Newsgroup and figure out exactly who participates. I suppose it worked. .

I know you hate me, but you're better off in the long run. You don't need to lie to one another in order to get along. Being yourself is always the best thing to do.

Permit me to introduce myself. My name is Daniel DelMonte. I'm thirty-eight years old. I have a degree in English from Penn State and a degree in Computer Science from NYU. To date I've written four books including a basic DOS manual, a beginners guide to the Internet, where to find love online, and a downloader's guide. My Newsgroup exposé will be my fifth. Maybe you have read my work. They're not bad and they sell nicely enough to where I make a good living.

At the risk of adding salt to the wound, I would like to chronicle our experience in my new book. To avoid any potential humiliation, complete anonymity will be assured.

If it makes anybody feel any better, I've been where you all are. Back when I was an editor at Bantam I'd come home on Friday night, turn on the computer and not leave the room until Monday morning. You would think I had no life, as you probably think you don't now. I learned that was not true. I had a whole family and a scad of friends. My online life was quite rich. My offline life practically didn't exist. It got me through some rough periods and to this day I still correspond with lots of my online friends. But, eventually, I evolved. Yes, even Plato will eventually fit into Real Life. It's not a bad place, and it's not as safe as being online, but it definitely offers some experiences you can't get through a computer.

Cyberspace is a great place. I love my time there. I also love my time outside of it.

So, how did I discover everybody's secrets? Research. I've been online for many years and I can smell a fake a mile away. Plato was easy—no adult would try so hard to sound smart. I gained his trust and eventually he told me the truth. Nadine was also easy. First of all she kept her first name intact. That meant she'd lost some of the adventurous nature of her youth. She would always sound motherly. Eventually it all clicked into place.

Phyllis was also easy. I could tell he was uneasy with the concept of saying he was female because he would frequently lurk. Then I'd ask him questions about men and relationships and I'd get responses that another man would give. Then I remembered his earlier posts.

The Cheese was tough. I knew he was unhappy and I knew he was definitely older. As a matter of fact, Cheese would usually hit on the truth before I would. I guess it's part of his training as a social worker. The hostility threw me off. It wasn't until I witnessed a divorcing friend of mine go off on his wife that I recognized the signs.

Cutiepie would have never chosen the name "Cutiepie" unless she wasn't. She had the most integrity out of the group, knowing all she had to do is be herself and never be seen. Nobody knew she was a dog.

And now you know who I am. Again, I don't ask for your permission or forgiveness, though both would be nice. Either way, I appreciate all of your participation in my little experiment.

Yours, Dan.

(*Fadeout.*)

Scene 3

USENET

(*Lights up on CHEESE, CUTIEPIE, PLATO, NADINE and PHYLLIS.*)

NADINE: The weather in San Franciso is heavenly this time of year. This past weekend I took the kids to the Wharf. If any of you are on the West Coast, you really should go. I told my daughter about Billy. She wants to meet him. Do you think I should arrange a meeting? Philip, how did the audition go? Nadine.

PLATO: My dear friend Nadine: No! Absolutely, unequivocally NOT! I have no desire to meet anyone's daughter under any circumstances for even the largest sum of money. Count me out out out! School sucks. Life sucks. I just upgraded to Celeron. Computer doesn't suck. Billy.

CUTIEPIE: Billy: Think you should hook up with Nadine. You can't keep running away from real people. It's okay until you get your head on straight, but after a while it really becomes unhealthy. By the way, I want everyone to know that I'm coming to New York next week. Philip and I are going to meet face-to-face.

CHEESE: Hi, everyone. My wife and I are working out our problems. Things were getting pretty ugly. I figured that since I dole out counsel and advice for a living it might be a good idea to actually listen to it for a change. I told her about all of you, particularly Debbie. She's uneasy about my socializing online, but I assured her that we're all just friends. Yours, Herbert.

PHYLLIS: Auditions stink. Two call-backs and they go with someone else who looks just like me! I'm considering taking a weekend job waiting tables to supplement my income. What's the theatre scene like on the West Coast? If things don't get any better I'll be bunking with Billy. So Herb, please tell me: Is Debbie as sweet a person face-to-face as she is on-line?

CHEESE: Even nicer. Debbie is one of the most beautiful women I've ever met—inside and out.

NADINE: I'll be in Los Angeles on the fifth. I'm bringing my daughter and plan on hunting down Billy. You can't hide.

PHYLLIS: Attention everybody! I'm back from my adventure in the Big Apple! Debbie a.k.a. Cutiepie and I met and had a wonderful time! I showed her all around New York City—caught a Broadway show—and danced the night away. The Cheese was right, she is truly a beautiful person.

NADINE: Just returned from LA as well. Plato Update: He's a great kid with a ton of potential and no self-confidence. We had a lovely time in Los Angeles—we actually went to Disneyland. My daughter, Barbara, thought he was very cute. Hey, Billy, Barb wants to know if you'll call her. Oh, by the way, I confiscated your book of quotations. You've marked some pretty heavy ones.

PLATO: My dearest friend Nadine. Though your visit was delightful and your daughter was lovely, I wouldn't try to move mountains. Please return my book of quotations. Billy.

CUTIEPIE: Come on, Billy, Call the girl. Deb.

PHYLLIS: I know we don't want to bring it up, but did you all read Horn-dog's letter?

PLATO: I prefer not to discuss it.

PHYLLIS: I've read his books. They're good. As long as he doesn't give my name, I have no problem with letting him use the experience in his new book. I look forward to reading it.

NADINE: I can't forgive him.

CHEESE: Why not?

NADINE: He lied to us!

PLATO: We lied to each other.

PHYLLIS: We lied to ourselves.

NADINE: Oh, God. We've all become holy people. I was having a great time! A little role-playing is healthy!

PLATO: Nadine, you were trying to seduce me.

PHYLLIS: Excuse me? What was that?

CUTIEPIE: Did we miss something?

NADINE: I was having fun! It was harmless fun!

PLATO: It made me very nervous. I do hope you'll have the good sense to keep that fact from Barbara.

NADINE: I'll have to because I think we should have a reunion. How about NYC? My family and I have decided to take this year's vacation there.

CUTIEPIE: That's wonderful, Nadine. Any chance of Plato coming with you?

PLATO: Regarding a trip to the East—unlikely due to funds being extremely limited. Remember, I'm only sixteen—seventeen next week.

CHEESE: Billy: I have a pull-out sofa if you need a place to stay. It would be great to finally meet you.

CUTIEPIE: I think we should take the opportunity to find Horndog and lynch him.

PHYLLIS: Color me there. I know where he works.

PLATO: An excellent suggestion. I feel if we confront him face to face we can all either make our peace with him or punch his lights out right then and there.

CHEESE: That's some very mature thinking, Billy—except for the punching. Though, between you and me, I wouldn't mind taking a swing at him myself.

NADINE: We'll be leaving on the eighteenth. We'll be staying at the Milford in Times Square. Do any of you know it?

CHEESE: The Milford?! Nice hotel, bad location. Do you have your flight itinerary? I could meet you at the airport. Herb.

PHYLLIS: Herb, I'd like to join you. E-mail me your phone number. We can work out details.

NADINE: This is so exciting! All these friends whom I've never met. You've all meant so much to me. You've given me a new life and I'll always be grateful. Love, Nadine. P.S. See you all in a few days!

CUTIEPIE: I have to admit, I'm enjoying conversing with all of you more now as yourselves than as who we weren't—especially Billy and Philip. For this I can forgive Horndog.

PLATO: "Friendship is by its very nature freer of deceit than any other relationship we can know because it is the bond least affected by striving for power, physical pleasure, or material profit, most liberated from any oath of duty or constancy." Francine Du Plessix Gray. I knew that one by heart. Get the sofa ready, Herb.

(*Fadeout*)

Epilogue

USENET

(*Lights are down. We hear a voice-over*)

VOICE-OVER: Hello. I am young, attractive and in search of love, friendship and stimulating conversation in cyberspace.

(*Lights fade up. We see a dog at one of the computer stations*)

VOICE-OVER (*cont'd*): If you're interested in some stimulating conversation, hot chat, or just a unique point of view, drop me an e-mail anytime. Rex.

(*Fadeout*)

Scene Three—*Alternate Ending*

USENET

(*Lights up on Cheese, Cutiepie, Plato, Nadine, and Phyllis*)

NADINE: The weather in San Francisco is heavenly this time of year. This past weekend I took the kids to the Wharf. If any of you are ever on the West Coast, you really should go. I told my daughter about Billy. She has a friend who wants to meet him. Do you think I should arrange a meeting? Philip, how did the audition go? Nadine.

PLATO: My dear friend Nadine: No! Absolutely, unequivocally *not*! I have no desire to meet anyone's friend under any circumstances for even the largest sum of money. Count me out out out! School sucks. Life sucks. I just upgraded to Celeron. Computer doesn't suck. Billy.

CHEESE: Hi, everyone. Unfortunately, my wife filed for divorce today. I was such a fool. For a man who doles out counsel and advice for a living, I'm terrible about listening to it. I think I will be in need of some moral support for the next few months. I hope I can count on all of you. Yours, Herbert.

NADINE: I'm sorry to hear that, dear. We will always be here for you. Nadine.

PHYLLIS: Auditions stink. Two call-backs and they go with someone else who looks just like me! If I'm ever to get my own apartment I may have to take a weekend job waiting tables to supplement my income. What's the theatre scene like on the West Coast? If things don't get any better I'll be bunking with Billy.

PLATO: Dear Philip: Feel free to rent my room, and my parents as well if you like. I've transferred to a dorm at Cal Poly in order to attempt to socialize with other loser computer geeks. My roommate is fourteen years old. I guess there are other boy geniuses in the world.

CUTIEPIE: Dear Everyone: It is with deep regret and great courage that I say what I'm about to say. It's time I went offline. I've been doing a lot of thinking since the whole Horndog incident, and as much as I hate to admit it, he's got a point. I'm more than some pixels on a computer screen, and

I have to thank Cheese a little for that. But pixels are hardly the basis of a relationship—at least the kind I'd like to have and feel I deserve. I'm still mad at you, Cheese, but for the first time someone has helped me feel like less of a dog, if you'll pardon the metaphor. Love to all, Debbie.

NADINE: Goodbye, Cutiepie. We'll all miss you.

PLATO: Goodbye, Debbie.

CHEESE: Goodbye, and, if it helps, I'm sorry. If there's ever anything I can do—as a gesture—let me know.

CUTIEPIE: As a matter of fact, could you recommend a good therapist in the Boston area? I think it's time. Deb.

CHEESE: I know many therapists I can recommend. I will E-mail them to you. All the best, Herb.

(*Lights off on Cutiepie*)

PHYLLIS: So, Herb, tell me—was Debbie really a dog?

CHEESE: Phil: True beauty can come from so many places, not so much in a physical manifestation. The soul contains the real beauty. Keeping that in mind, Debbie was one of the most beautiful women I've ever met. Herb.

PHYLLIS: I know we don't want to bring it up, but did you all read Horndog's letter?

PLATO: I prefer not to discuss it.

NADINE: I can't forgive him.

CHEESE: Why not?

NADINE: He lied to us!

PLATO: We lied to ourselves.

NADINE: Oh, God. We've all become holy people. I was having a great time! A little role-playing is healthy!

PLATO: Nadine, you were trying to seduce me.

PHYLLIS: Excuse me? What was that?

CHEESE: Did we miss this?

NADINE: I was having fun! It was harmless fun!

PLATO: It made me very nervous. A little. Okay, I was . . . flattered. It was still creepy.

PHYLLIS: I've read his books. They're good. As long as he doesn't give my name, I have no problem with letting him use the experience in his new book. I look forward to reading it. Phil.

CHEESE: I think we should try to find Horndog and lynch him.

PLATO: Oh . . . my . . . God. Please disregard any past reference I would have made to being insecure, pathetic, or geeky. I attended an all-night gaming session this weekend. All right, I'm still pathetic and geeky, but not so insecure. Hey, it's a start. I can honestly say I'm receiving an education now at college far beyond anything I would have ever imagined. I'm also learning a lot in the classroom. Yours, Billy.

CHEESE: Update from Divorce Central: My wife found copies of my correspondence with Debbie. Horndog: if you're out there, we have to talk. Your chronicle can save or ruin me.

PHYLLIS: Well, the inevitable has come and I'm trying desperately to move out of my parents' house. If anyone knows of any apartments, let me know. Phil. PS: Did I also mention it must be a *cheap* apartment?

PLATO: Dear friends. It pains me to come to this, but it is now time to bid you all a fond farewell. Between my studies and babysitting my wunderkind roommate, I feel I won't have the time nor the reason to stay around. I'll drop by from time to time, but, as Horndog stated, I think I've finally evolved. I'm off to attend something called a "kegger." Billy.

CHEESE: Farewell, sir, and the best of luck to you. I'm sure you will find your own in an academic setting. And stay away from those frat parties. Your friend, Herb.

PHYLLIS: So, Bill, no pithy closing quote?

PLATO: Alas, no closing quote as my book of quotations has found a new use—keeping my University-issue desk from wobbling. Live long and prosper. Billy.

NADINE: Goodbye, Billy. We'll miss you . . . and . . . I never meant to hurt you.

(*Lights off on Plato*)

CHEESE: Phil: I'm in need of a roommate. Without my wife's half of the rent, I'll be out on the street within a few weeks. Interested? Drop me an E-mail and we can work out the details. By the way, I'm afraid I'll be going the way of Billy. My lawyer suggested that I shouldn't socialize on-line—at least until the divorce is finalized. Therefore, this is the Big Cheese, signing off. You've all been terrific. Thank you for getting me through some tough times. Herbert.

(*Lights off on Cheese*)

PHYLLIS: Hey, guess what? I'm moving in with the Cheese! Who would have thought. Since it's not a good idea to drink around a recovering alcoholic . . . or something like that . . . I'll be logging off, too . . . or at least for a while. Besides, now that I'll be living in New York City, I plan on auditioning for everything I can. It's gotta break sooner or later. I'll always be grateful to you, Herb, Billy, and Debbie for not turning your back on me when Horndog blew the whistle. Love, Philip.

(*Lights off on Phyllis*)

NADINE: Everyone's leaving me! I suppose that's how it all happens. One by one, the fledglings leave the nest.

(*Long pause as she waits for a response. She gets none*)

To all eligible men in cyberspace: If you're looking for a relationship, you've found the right gal! I'll be yours tonight. Any takers?

(*Blackout*)

SKOT DAVIS

Consider the Banana

The following one-act play, a finalist in the sixth National Readers Theatre Competition cosponsored by The Open Book and the Stage & Screen Book Club, was immediately regarded as a likely companion piece to the winning script, *Blood and Ivy*, which appears later in this volume. Skot Davis, author of *Consider the Banana*, is a prolific American playwright currently living in Frankfurt, Germany. His plays have been produced in New York, Los Angeles, Frankfurt, and, in the playwright's words, "the thriving theatrical meccas of Santa Cruz and Salinas, California." He is also a novelist and recipient of a National Society of Arts & Letters Short Fiction Award.

Consider the Banana was produced by The Open Book in New York at The Producers Club, opening December 3rd, 1999, with Marvin Kaye directing the following cast:

RUDY .... RUSTY THRASHER
CAROL .... ALICE KING
TOM .... JOHNNY BLAZE LEAVITT
REBECCA .... JONA TUCK

CHARACTERS

Rudy   Early 30's, a likable middle manager at a large corporation.

Carol   Early 30's, Rudy's wife, an assistant bank manager with a degree in Fine Arts.

Rebecca   20, a Princeton student on a semester abroad in Central America.

Tom   20, a University of Maryland student.

TIME: The present.

SETTING: The Americas.

The stage is divided in two, and the characters on one side are completely unaware of those on the other. The action on both sides, however, is simultaneous and continuous.
  Stage right we see the kitchen/breakfast area of an upscale condominium. The place is well furnished but with little personality. One exit leads outside, the other toward bedrooms and bathroom. There is a small television set on a table or counter, turned off. A wall clock shows about 7:45. Rudy, a North American in his early 30's, stands at the door leading outside. He waves, shuts the door, and goes to the table, sitting down before his mostly finished breakfast. He is dressed in suit pants and dress shirt, his collar unbuttoned and his sleeves rolled up. He picks up a banana, swivels it nervously before his eyes.
  Stage left, we are outside of a small house or hut. Perhaps the leaves of a tropical tree overhang. We see nothing of the interior of the hut, but from within we can hear three or four voices speaking Spanish, perhaps laughter. Tom, a North American, no more than 20 years old, enters from off left wearing cut-off Levi's and a new handmade Guatemalan shirt. He is sweating in the heat, looking around as if unsure of his way.
  Stage right: Rudy sighs, sets down the banana, picks it up again.

RUDY: Consider the banana . . .

(*Stage left: Tom stops just outside the entrance to the hut*)

TOM (*haltingly, to those inside*): ¡Hola! Pardon, estoy buscando, uh, una mujer americana . . . no, pardon, norte americana . . .

VOICE FROM INSIDE HUT (*voice over, friendly*): Base, entre.

(*Stage left: Tom hesitantly enters the hut. Stage right, Rudy speaks as if to a small audience, but he is only distracting himself; the fourth wall is in place*)

RUDY: Yes, consider the banana. America's most popular fruit: more bananas bought and consumed than apples, oranges, or any other kind. Flavorful, bright and sunny yellow, and after all these years still cheap as hell. (Keep supply up, production costs down; that's the formula.) But is all this enough to explain such popularity? Consider this: Reliability. Assuming ripeness, and a lack of mushy spots—which any of us can detect without opening the banana's protective skin—there's no such thing as a bad banana. Bad apples there may be, but that's not my story.

(*Stage right: Rudy sets down the banana, idly stacks his dishes but does not leave his seat. Stage left: Tom backs out of the building, nodding, then looks around uncertainly*)

TOM (*to himself*): C'mon, Becca, where are you? I don't want to miss that first bus. Whenever the hell it is.

(*Tom yawns, shrugs, goes around the corner of the hut and sits down against its wall. He stretches. Stage right: Rudy picks up the banana again*)

RUDY: And yet, are bananas truly the most desired, the most enjoyed fruit, or just the most available? Apples and oranges have seasons, after all, but bananas are always in abundance: day after day, year after year, regular as clockwork. (*Glances at the clock*) Perhaps it's this availability, this easy over-abundance, which is the real reason for the banana's astonishing sales numbers. We eat what's put on our plate. And yet, yesterday afternoon, at the Safeway, the plate—the banana table—was completely empty. In the middle of the day. I think yours truly can truthfully say he had never witnessed such a circumstance before. In fact, this banana, which I now hold and discuss, and thus conveniently delay to eat, this final banana was purchased from an evil-looking man in a trench coat at a price so steep that . . . well, I hardly dare mention it.

(*Stage left: Tom starts to fall asleep against the wall. Stage right: Rudy sets down the banana, sighs*)

RUDY: "I don't want to go to school, Daddy." Well, Kates, today we're even.

(*Stage right: Carol enters, in sweats, brushing her hair vigorously. She is tall, dark-haired, perhaps a year younger than Rudy*)

CAROL: Did I hear the Kiddie Kart honk?

RUDY: Yep. She got off fine. Lipstick on her cheeks and feathers in her hair. Did you know she was supposed to dress up today?

CAROL: She just told me this morning. A skit or something. For the holiday.

RUDY: Holiday for some. Bankers, for instance.

CAROL (*getting coffee for herself*): I have to go in this afternoon to meet with his lordship, the Branch Manager.

RUDY: It never fails to astound me—Columbus Day, Lincoln's Birthday, Armadillo Day—any excuse to hit the golf course, you bankers are there.

CAROL: Rudy, I think I've heard this before.

RUDY: Kids are in school, van drivers are driving vans, decent hardworking West Coast Sales Managers are working their charisma to the bone . . .

CAROL: Speaking of which, you're going to be late.

RUDY: I'm not going to work today. (*Beat*) You know what the first thing Katie said to me this morning was? "Daddy, where's the tomahawk?" Naturally I told her, Sorry, kiddo, we don't got no tomahawk. "We had one in Michigan," she said. "In the garage by the wood."

CAROL: She meant the hatchet.

RUDY: I finally figured that out. Where'd that go, anyway? It definitely would have accented her outfit.

CAROL: It's almost eight.

RUDY: I told you, I'm not going to work today. No, today I'm considering the banana. (*Carol does not grace this with a reply*) Have you ever really considered a banana, I mean really? Look at these lines. Look at this . . . this . . . I mean, you've made sculptures, have you ever seen anything quite like this?

CAROL: So you're not going to work.

RUDY: Actually, I don't have to go. You want to know why? (*Beat*) I'll tell you why. We were supposed to go on a field trip today, but it was cancelled. (*Beat*) You're supposed to ask, "Where were you going to go?"

CAROL: I was thinking more about "when."

RUDY: I'll tell you where: We were going to visit a bank, but they're all closed. (*Carol is not amused. Rudy sighs*) Its D-Day today, that's all.

CAROL: D-Day? (*Realizing*) Oh.

RUDY: Do 'em Day. Doomsday. Downsize Day.

CAROL: That's hard, Rudy. I know.

RUDY (*sighing*): Just part of being a West Coast Sales Manager.

CAROL: Well, it is.

RUDY: Are you crazy? It's horrible, I hate it. I hate doing this to people—

CAROL: You're not doing it.

RUDY: You're right, I'm sitting here avoiding doing it. Consider the hatchet . . .

CAROL: I mean, it's not your decision to downsize, you don't even decide who has to be—

RUDY: No, they give me a list. Decker hands me the gun, and I shoot.

CAROL: Now you're being dramatic.

RUDY: Dramatic? I hate this, Carol. This is their job I'm taking—

CAROL: I know. I've fired people before.

RUDY: One at a time, sure. But this, you don't know what this is like. It's like a cloud over the whole place. Poison gas. (*Beat*)

CAROL: Well, at least you're not on the list.

RUDY: I could be. One day, I could be . . . (*Suddenly slapping the table*) Jesus, what am I doing? This is the wrong attitude. I think I'll go sailing this weekend. You know what? I'm finally going to take the boat out.

CAROL: The boat needs work.

RUDY: I'll work on it Saturday, take it out Sunday. I'll rent a boat, whatever. C'mon, you wanna? Let's go, this weekend.

CAROL: You ought to work on it. It's been sitting there how many months since we got here? A year now. (*Realizing*) It's been a year . . .

RUDY: I know, I know, I should. Why the hell haven't I been out there? First the move, now all this OT.

CAROL: Or just get rid of the damn thing.

RUDY: Are you kidding? What are you talking—

CAROL: It's a big expense, sitting in dry dock month after month.

RUDY: Jesus, honey, that's the *boat*, that's Free As the Wind, what are you talking about, get rid of her?

CAROL: What I'm talking about is that I'm sick of living in a condo when we're both working good jobs—decent jobs, anyway, in my case. I want a house.

RUDY: We'll buy a house. We're going to buy a house. Do you want to buy a little crackerbox—

CAROL: Two stories, backyard with trees, big fireplace.

RUDY: Exactly. That's what I want, too. But for what they're asking around here, we've got to have a huge down. You know that. You work in a bank, for Borg's sake.

(*Carol is looking away*)

CAROL: I miss the woodpile.

RUDY: What?

CAROL (*quietly*): The woodpile. I miss bringing logs inside, when fall starts . . . (*Beat*) Forget it.

RUDY: No, no, that's, uh . . . Wait, yeah, I remember you said once, you liked the way the logs felt in your hands.

CAROL: Did I? No, I think I'm just—

RUDY: Rough bark, smooth wood. You said you liked the textures against your hands.

CAROL: I don't know what I said. If you want to know what I really miss it's fall—or spring—just give me a season. (*Opening the front door*) I mean, feel that. That's not weather, that's monotony. Summer the whole year long, then it rains for six weeks, then it's summer again. (*Carol shuts the door a little too loudly*)

RUDY (*anxiously*): You want a house, we'll buy a house. You want weather, we'll . . . buy that, too.

CAROL: Are you going to work?

(*Rudy sighs*)

RUDY: Wait, you go for me, like that old Flintstones episode, remember? Wilma goes to the quarry while Fred stays home and ruins everything— (*Seeing Carol's look*) Oh well. (*Hands on the table as if to stand*) Yes, I'm go . . . No. (*Beat*) I can't get up.

CAROL: I'm going to the store, before it gets crowded.

RUDY: No, I'm serious, I can't get up.

CAROL: What are you talking about?

RUDY: I mean, I'm sure I could get up . . .

CAROL: Is something wrong?

RUDY: No, there's nothing wrong, I mean, maybe there is.

CAROL: Rudy . . .

RUDY: My legs don't seem to work. I mean, of course there's nothing wrong, I'm healthy as a horse, I just . . . can't get up.

CAROL: Rudy, if you're not okay, I'll call the—

RUDY: I'm sure I'm okay. I must be. I'm not going to see a doctor just because—

CAROL: Because you can't bring yourself to go to work.

RUDY: My legs won't work.

CAROL: So call in sick.

RUDY: I can't call in sick! Not today. Decker would kill me—

CAROL (*overlapping*): Okay, so go in—

RUDY: If I don't go in, who's going to dismantle the company?

CAROL: So go then!

(*Rudy puts his hands on the table again, trying to stand*)

RUDY (*in a small voice*): I can't.

CAROL: Oh, Jesus. Where's my purse?

RUDY: Wait, no! Don't go. I just . . . help me here, Carol.

CAROL: Rudy, I have no idea what the hell is going on with you.

RUDY: Neither do I.

(*Beat. Slowly Carol sits down at the table*)

CAROL: All right, so let's look at this. This is not really so mysterious. You have to go in and fire people today, and you don't want to.

RUDY: I have to. I can't just not go to work.

CAROL: But you don't want to.

RUDY: God, who really wants to go to work?

CAROL: McPherson did, or so you always said.

RUDY: Jim. You have to bring him up. God, I wish he was still around.

CAROL: Well it's not like he's dead.

RUDY: No, but . . . actually, he's not, is he? Somebody stops showing up at the office every day, it's like they could be dead. Poof, just disappeared . . . Jim, why were we talking about Jim?

CAROL: He liked going to work, you said.

RUDY: Jesus, of course he did, he was an inspiration. That's why I'm here. He was the one who—

CAROL: Who dragged you along to this weatherless—

RUDY: —who taught me I had to throw myself into something, who . . . believed in me, whatever.

CAROL: A pity the right people didn't believe in him.

RUDY: It was early retirement.

CAROL: He was put out to pasture.

RUDY: Carol, he wasn't—

CAROL: You said so yourself, when it happened. He didn't have the numbers, so they axed him.

RUDY: Of course he didn't have the numbers, they only gave him ten months, the region was a shambles when he came here—

CAROL: You don't have to justify McPherson to me, Rudy. I'm not your Main Office. Besides, he's already gone.

RUDY: Yeah. (*Quietly*) He's not the only one.

CAROL: What are you talking about?

RUDY: Sammy.

CAROL: Sammy.

RUDY: He left. Last week. I caught him cleaning out his desk during lunch. He wasn't even going to say anything to me—can you believe that?

CAROL: Who's Sammy?

RUDY: Who's Sammy? Sammy's my—Jesus, Carol, I'm always talking about Sammy.

CAROL: If you were always talking about him, I'd know who he was.

RUDY: He's the one I've been taking under my wing, I told you about him: Sammy. Just a couple years out of college, loaded with potential—

CAROL: So why'd he leave?

RUDY: That's what I asked him! I talked with him for hours. Well, at least an hour. This is crazy, I told him, you can't just walk out on your career. Why are you doing this? I asked him did he have another offer. "No," he says. Well then what's the reason, Sammy? Finally he says, "Why should I live in fear?" (*Beat*) Jesus, what are you talking about? I asked him.

CAROL: He was just scared about getting downsized.

RUDY: So he downsizes himself?! But no, listen to this, he swears up and down it's not that. "That's just the latest part," he says. "That just makes it all obvious."

CAROL: Just a crazy kid.

RUDY: I mean, what does that mean, live in fear? Living on the street, flipping burgers for minimum wage, that's what you should be afraid of, I told him. This job you have, management track, this doesn't just grow on trees any more. He wouldn't look at me. He couldn't answer that. "Why should I live in fear?" That's all he could say. How the hell should I know why he should live in fear? I mean, he shouldn't—I tried to tell him: Sammy, this is the world, okay, what matters is how you—I mean the attitude you take. You go in there, every day, with a positive attitude, and you're bound to . . . You can survive anything.

CAROL: Was he on the list?

RUDY: That's what kills me, he wasn't on it! I mean, I don't get the list till I go in this morning, but I'm sure—Decker gave me to believe, and he has no reason to mislead me . . .

CAROL: You told Decker you wanted to keep Sammy?

RUDY: Well, I didn't just go in and baldly say, "I keep Sammy" or "Give me Sammy"—I mean you don't just—these are people you're talking about, Carol.

CAROL: So you told Decker what?

RUDY: I just . . . let it be known that, like any manager, I would have certain preferences as to who I would keep—have on my team, and I mentioned a couple names . . .

CAROL: That's standing up for him?

RUDY: . . . Sammy's included—what? What do you mean that's not standing up for him? Jesus, Carol, I loved that kid, that's what I'm trying to tell you.

CAROL: You could have said a lot more than—

RUDY: More? I told you, I talked to Sammy for hours—

CAROL: Decker. You could have told Decker, "Don't downsize Sammy."

RUDY: I could have told Decker? *I* could have—Carol, you don't *tell* your boss anything. I mean, Jesus, you suggest, you infer, you propose, but you don't—do you tell your boss how it's going to be?

CAROL: I tell my boss what I think he needs to hear. When he needs to hear something, yes, I tell him. (*Beat*)

RUDY: Which is why you're still assistant branch manager at a local bank.

CAROL (*coldly*): I'm sorry? What did you say?

RUDY: Oh shit, listen, Carol, I'm sorry, that's not what—

CAROL: The reason I'm still assistant branch manager—

RUDY (*overlapping*): I know, I'm sorry, I—

CAROL: —is that I left the bank in Detroit where I was about to *become* branch manager, because my husband stuck his tail between his legs and let himself be transferred to godforsaken Silicon Valley!

RUDY: Godforsaken? This is California! Everybody wants to be in California. (*Long beat*) So you didn't want to come?

CAROL: No, I didn't. (*Beat*) You finally figured that out.

RUDY: You're, uh, not going back, are—

CAROL (*exploding*): No, I'm not going back! How the hell could I go back? (*Beat*) I'm sorry. I'm not . . . I'm feeling off today. I should just go to the store.

(*Carol doesn't get up. A long silence. Stage left, Tom starts, then falls back asleep. Stage right, Carol stands*)

CAROL: You'll be fine.

RUDY: Yeah. No problem. (*As Carol goes for her purse*) My legs don't work, but that's just a simple case of losing my protégé and having to lay off a third of my staff.

CAROL: Well. Your choice.

RUDY: My choice? What do you mean, my—

CAROL: California. The transfer, following McPherson. Your road, your choice.

RUDY: Yeah. And now what do I do? (*A look of contempt crosses Carol's face, then:*)

CAROL: Quit, like Sammy.

RUDY: Right.

CAROL (*reading from a list*): Milk, bread, fabric softener—do we need anything else?

RUDY: What?

CAROL: Do we need anything else?

RUDY: This is the last banana.

(*Carol nods, opens the front door*)

RUDY (*quietly*): What if I did?

CAROL: Did what?

RUDY: Just . . . chucked it all, like Sammy. What would you say?

CAROL: I'd say, have fun, enjoy yourself.

RUDY: No. Really?

CAROL: Sure. For two weeks. Then get off your ass and find another job.

(*Carol exits. Rudy lets his forehead fall onto his crossed arms. After a long moment he lifts his head slightly*)

RUDY: My choice . . .

Rudy looks toward the door, and it is clear he is seeing Carol there—perhaps as she just appeared, perhaps as she looked ten years ago.
    Stage left: Tom is still asleep. Enter Rebecca, a young North American woman, same age as Tom. She is dressed in comfortable shorts and blouse, something a little nicer than jeans and a T-shirt, though perhaps slightly pack-rumpled. She is looking sad or anxious. Seeing Tom, she goes to him and squats beside him.

REBECCA: (*gently shaking him*): Hedge, wake up . . . I need a hug.

TOM (*waking*): Huh? . . . Oh, Becca. Hi . . .

REBECCA: Hi.

TOM (*tasting his mouth*): Fell asleep . . . Where you been? I was waiting here . . .

REBECCA: I was talking with a woman who lives here.

TOM: Man, this intensive Spanish stuff must be working for you. I tried to ask these guys . . . (*Indicating the hut*) if they'd seen an American girl— North American, whatever. Anyway I'm not sure if I got it across. What is this place, anyway? Why'd you want to meet here? (*Glancing at his watch*) Though shit, we can't have much time to go in, huh? When's the first bus?

REBECCA: (*vulnerably*): Um, Tom? Hedge . . .

TOM (*letting her into his arms*): Hey, what's wrong? Did something happen? Becca? (*Beat*) C'mon, what's going on? (*Beat*) Hey, you're not about to break it off with me, are you?

REBECCA: No! (*Disengaging herself*) You big idiot.

TOM: Hey, I was just . . . checking.

REBECCA: Everything doesn't always relate directly to you, you know.

TOM: Yeah, well. Occasionally things do.

REBECCA: And if I was going to "break up" with you or whatever, which wouldn't precisely be possible because we're not precisely—

TOM: I know, I know: we're just cajh*, like we agreed—

REBECCA: Anyway, if I was, I'd just . . . tell you.

TOM: Fair enough. That's fine. (*Quietly*) Only don't, okay?

(*Tom opens his arms again with a half-tentative look, and Rebecca lets him hold her again*)

REBECCA: Thanks . . . I'm so glad you're here, Hedge. I always think I can do anything, but sometimes it's . . . I'm just glad you're here.

---

*short for "casual"

TOM: Me, too.

REBECCA: Are you, really?

TOM: Well, you know, I don't wanna stay down here forever, but . . . I'm learning a lot.

REBECCA: Oh boy, yeah.

TOM: And besides, when we leave here, it's back to our separate beds . . . on separate campuses. In separate states . . .

REBECCA: Oh, there's E-mail . . .

TOM (*not listening*): That is, unless you decide to, uh . . .

REBECCA (*disengaging herself again from his arms; with finality*): Tom, if I haven't been clear enough, I'll say it again: I am not transferring to the University of Maryland.

TOM: Fine. (*Beat*) That's real clear.

REBECCA: I mean, you understand why.

TOM: Sure, sure.

REBECCA: I mean—

TOM: I wouldn't want you to have to lower yourself to—

REBECCA: Well, it's not the same. I didn't make that up, there are calibers of schools. And you could have made it to—

TOM: To Princeton, the great, ivy—

REBECCA: Or Georgetown, or Michigan, or whatever, if you'd just—

TOM (*with a laugh*): No! Do not say the words, "if you'd just applied yourself"—

REBECCA: —if you hadn't been so worried about looking like a geek that you deliberately screwed up in class.

TOM: You know, let's talk about something that doesn't relate to me.

REBECCA: Fine.

TOM: Good. For instance, tell me already, what happened just now? With this woman.

REBECCA (*sighing*): Oh. Well, we just started talking, and . . . it's not that big a . . . no, it is a big deal. She told me one of her kids . . . had just died.

TOM (*not untouched*): Oh. Yeah, that must be . . . what, died of what?

REBECCA: I'm . . . not sure I understood her exactly. It almost sounded like it could have been diphtheria.

TOM: Diphtheria?

REBECCA: Yes. Can you believe—

TOM: Uh, is it going around, or—

REBECCA: Tom!

TOM: Well, it's not just me I'm worried about, what if you—

REBECCA: Tom, we can't get diphtheria.

(*Beat*)

TOM: Oh. . . . Yeah, that's one of the childhood shots, isn't it. . . . So then how did her kid . . . Oh.

REBECCA: Yeah. Oh.

TOM: Jeez. (*Beat*) Becca, I never told you this, but I once stole a quarter out of a UNICEF box . . .

REBECCA: Tom, it's not funny. It's horrifying.

TOM: Why do you think I make jokes?

(*Stage right: Rudy, whose head has been down, now looks up, almost smiling*)

RUDY: Poof—disappear . . .

TOM: Listen, Becca, let's just get out of here, okay? Grab our stuff, wait for the bus—

REBECCA: Actually, Tom, I found out there's just the one bus. At five fifteen.

TOM: What? (*After a moment; a half-stifled shout*) Damnit!

REBECCA (*taken aback*): Tom . . . ?

TOM: God *damn* it.

REBECCA: What is wrong?

TOM: I'm fine. No problem.

REBECCA: Well, what is the big problem? So we'll miss classes today. I mean, we couldn't very well have just left yesterday, not when Señora Montes was cooking that meal for us.

TOM: No. No. Course not.

REBECCA: So what's the big deal? (*Indicating the hut*) I wanted you to meet these people, anyway. You won't believe the work they're doing—

TOM: The big deal is, it depresses me here, okay!? One bus a goddamn day. Listen, Becca, I just want to get back to the city, where I can at least pretend I'm not surrounded by . . . unbelievable poverty and misery. (*Through his teeth*) Damnit!

REBECCA: Tom, it's not all . . . misery. I mean, can't you feel the vibrancy, the aliveness of—

TOM: "Hey Tom, you wanna take a weekend trip to this completely impoverished village in the hills?" Sure, Becca, no problem. "Say, Tom, I'm doing a semester abroad, studying Spanish and multicultural brouhaha." Really, Bec? Wow, can I come, too?

(*Beat*)

REBECCA: What are you saying, Tom? You wish you hadn't come? (*No answer from Tom*) But you've been really blossoming here, it seemed like—a whole new perspective.

TOM: Another one. Just what I need.

REBECCA (*to herself, not hearing him*): I should have listened to myself. When you first said you were coming, I thought, Why? Why would Tom come to Central America?

(*Tom stares at her for a beat, then looks away*)

TOM: Actually, why did you come here, Rebecca? You're a pre-med student.

REBECCA: I'm keeping up with Bio and everything else. And I've told you why I wanted to come.

TOM: To piss your father off?

REBECCA: Tom!

TOM: No, I know, I know—because you took a hot political science class last year and now you feel guilty—sorry, now you know you're involved.

REBECCA: Tom, why are you suddenly . . . attacking me? I want to help, you know that.

TOM: Who're we helping here?

REBECCA: It's not about . . . this second. This is the first step—to learn, and understand.

TOM (*looking away*): It's pointless, Bec.

REBECCA: What kind of thing is that to say?

TOM: Just the way I see it.

REBECCA: "It's pointless, anyway . . . ?"

TOM: I didn't say that.

REBECCA: No?

TOM: I didn't say "all." Politics. Politics is pointless.

REBECCA: Tom, did you just skip the last ten years? The Berlin Wall? The Philippines? China, almost—

TOM: Yeah. I'm sure all those . . . revolutions were all great. But how are things in those places now? "Meet the new boss, same as the old boss."

REBECCA: You can't say there hasn't been real change—

TOM: Sure, instead of Lenin or whatever, they've got Ronald McDonald.

REBECCA: All right. Great. So if politics is pointless, how do we change things?

TOM: To me, Bec, it doesn't look like we do.

REBECCA: So we just give up.

TOM: No, I don't know. Maybe.

REBECCA (*angry*): I mean, there's no meaning to anything, right? So why not give up?

TOM: Well, is there? Is there ever? Is there ever one great meaningful thing that comes along that doesn't turn out to be just marketing hype? "Sponsored by United Brands."

REBECCA: That's a great . . . choice, Tom.

TOM: It's not a *choice*, it's just what . . . it all turns out to be.

(*Stage right, Rudy stirs*)

RUDY: Go to work go to work go to work go to work go to work. . . . My choice . . .

REBECCA: That's funny. You probably don't even know . . . they used to be called United Fruit.

TOM: Who?

REBECCA: United Brands.

TOM: Yeah, so . . . ?

REBECCA: Chiquita. They just about ran this whole country.

TOM: Well, a banana republic, who better to run it than a banana company?

REBECCA: Tom, they practically ruined the whole place. And it's still U.S. economic interests that keep it this way.

TOM: Yeah, yeah, the big bad corporations—

REBECCA: Yes! But not just corporations: We benefit. *Us.* The lower the wages down here, the lower the prices up north. Why do you think it stays like this here, do you think the people here choose a system where they can't even afford to—

TOM: No, no, please! No more details! I know, they can't afford to . . . keep their kids alive or go to college or eat pizza but damnit, Rebecca I don't have enough money or time or brilliant plans to make it any better! (*Long beat. Tom does not look at her*) All right, all right, so let if fall, the ax: "You've changed, I've changed, it's been a long time since high school, if I ever even felt anything for you then"—

REBECCA (*quietly*): That's not fair, Tom.

TOM: Okay, it's not . But I know you're over there going, "He's not who I thought he was. We're not the same any more." And maybe not, maybe not. But you don't know everything. Because the thing that's the same, Becca, that's always been the same, is I envy you. Did you know that?

REBECCA: I . . .

TOM: I envy the hell out of you. Because for me—"a whole new perspective," Jesus—for me the world keeps getting bigger all around me, and that just makes the half a clue I'm holding on to that much smaller. But you've always known who you are—I mean, back in seventh grade you were already talking about what you wanted to do, your big dream.

REBECCA: Is that it? Oh, but Tom, you could—

TOM: And it never changed, and it always made sense! And it does. I mean, that's the right track: helping people one on one. That *helps*. No one can say a doctor doesn't help people.

REBECCA: Well, I hope to contribute, to make things a little . . .

TOM: You will. I know you will. I mean, that lady you met, with her kid. *You* really *could* do something down here . . .

REBECCA (*nodding assent*): You're right, I could. (*Off-handedly*) Of course, I'm not going to come work down *here*.

(*Long beat as Rebecca's last line sinks in for both her and Tom*)

RUDY: Wife, house, boat, kid. Flipping burgers . . . Rudy, there's nothing to choose. There just isn't anything else to do.

(*Rudy stands. He takes a step away from the table, then stops, looks down at his legs, flexes them. He shrugs. He begins to roll down his sleeves. Carol enters, heads toward the counter without looking at Rudy. Stage left, Tom takes Rebecca's hand*)

CAROL: I forgot my wallet. I am really not functioning today— (*Seeing Rudy; oddly*) Oh. You're going then?

RUDY: Of course. Yeah, listen, I'm sorry about all that nonsense a few minutes ago.

CAROL: Forget it.

RUDY: Good. Good.

(*Rudy exits toward the bedrooms. Carol picks up her wallet, puts it down. Her shoulders are shaking. She looks around, as if baffled by her own emo-*

tions. Holding back tears, she moves to the breakfast table. She takes a deep breath and sits down)

TOM: Listen, Becca, don't get too down on yourself. I probably infected you with my lame cynicism.

REBECCA: No, Tom. I think you did me a favor. I've got to learn, and understand. (*Half mocking herself*) It's the first step . . .

TOM: Well, maybe yeah.

(*Stage right, Rudy enters carrying jacket and tie; he sets down the jacket*)

RUDY: You're still here. Yeah, forget going to the store. Just kick back. You bankers . . .

CAROL (*her voice quavering*): Rudy, don't.

RUDY: Hey, what's . . . What's up?

CAROL: It goes on like this. (*Looking at Rudy*) Doesn't it?

RUDY: What? Uh . . .

CAROL (*wiping forcefully at her eye*): Forget it. Really, go to work.

RUDY: Are you sure? You're okay?

CAROL: I'm fine.

RUDY: All right.

(*With a shrug, Rudy begins tying his tie*)

TOM: So, can we talk about something related to me?

REBECCA (*with a little smile*): Sure, Tom.

TOM: I'll uh, answer your question finally. Why I came on this semester abroad. You probably know already.

REBECCA: Uh, no, I don't think . . .

(*Stage right, Rudy undoes his first attempt and starts over on his tie*)

TOM: I mean, it's not like I've been completely bullshitting you—I have been trying to learn, to catch your fire on all this, but it's not, uh . . . What I'm trying to say is I didn't come here out of any great—I mean, there's this old Springsteen song. Yeah. Uh, do you remember it? This old one: "I Came for You."

(*Beat. Rebecca slowly gets it. She and Tom kiss. Stage right: Rudy irrevocably finishes tying his tie*)

RUDY: Time to bite the bullet. (*Rudy turns to go, then notices the banana*) Ah.

(*Rudy begins—very slowly, obviously putting off his departure—to peel the banana. Stage left: as Rebecca and Tom end their kiss, we hear Spanish voices spilling from the hut, then laughter*)

TOM: Oh, yeah. (*Indicating the building*) So what is this place, then?

REBECCA: You're really interested?

TOM: Of course not, but we're stuck here till 5:15, so . . . Just kidding, Becca. Actually, having said all that stuff, I think maybe I am kind of interested.

REBECCA: Good. Good, because it's great, what they're doing here.

TOM: Which is?

REBECCA: It's this indigenous group that's—

Off left, we hear a vehicle accelerating, then squealing to a halt)

TOM: What the— (*Tom pulls Rebecca back out of sight*) Just lay low—

(*Two Hispanic soldiers enter from left and go straight into the hut*)

REBECCA: . . . group that's organizing banana workers . . .

RUDY (*done peeling the banana*): Perfect.

(*Two things now happen simultaneously: stage left, we hear a gunshot; stage right, Rudy bites into the banana*)

REBECCA (*in a small voice*): Oh, oh, oh my God . . .

(*Stage left: Rebecca sinks to her knees. Tom stands a little apart, stunned, his arms half raised as if a gun were pointed at him, though it is only he and Rebecca outside the hut. The soldiers emerge from the hut and, without noticing Rebecca and Tom, quickly exit. There is a cry of shock and grief from inside the hut. Stage right: Rudy slowly eats the banana. When done, he puts on his jacket*)

CAROL: You're going?

RUDY: 'Nother day, another dollar. (*Rudy now notices the tears escaping Carol's eyes*) Hey. What, you don't want me to go?

CAROL: I want . . .

(*Stage left: Rebecca has begun to cry, quietly but audibly. At the sound, Tom blinks, slowly lowering his arms*)

RUDY: Hey, you never do this.

(*Stage right: Rudy puts an arm around Carol. Stage left: Tom kneels/falls beside Rebecca. He holds, and is held by, the weeping Rebecca. Stage right: As Carol continues silently to cry, Rudy stands beside her, patting her shoulder, glancing at his watch, looking uncomfortably around the room. Lights fade*)

C E MCCLELLAND

Blood and Ivy
An American Anthem

CE McClelland is a playwright and screenwriter who received his Master's in Theatre from Villanova University. His plays have won numerous awards and have been produced in festivals throughout the U.S., including the Playwrights Studio Theatre Festival in Milwaukee, TADA! in New York City and the New Works Festival in Pittsburgh. His plays, *Time To Go* and *Certain Arrangements*, were respectively published in 1995 and 1998. In 1999, his script, *Birds of a Feather*, was named Best Animation Screenplay at the Santa Clarita International Film Festival in California. He has twice been awarded a theatre fellowship by the Pennsylvania Council on the Arts. He lives near Philadelphia.

His Kent State script, *KSU*, was workshopped in 1997 at the National Readers Theatre Workshop & Conference at the Eugene O'Neill Theater Center in Waterford, Connecticut. Expanded and retitled *Blood and Ivy: An American Anthem*, it won the sixth national readers theatre competition and was produced in New York at The Producers Club, opening December 3rd, 1999, with Marvin Kaye directing the following cast:

ALLISON KRAUSE, 19 . . . . ALICIA HILLER

JEFF MILLER, 20 . . . . RUSTY THRASHER

SANDY SCHEUER, 20 . . . . JONA TUCK

BILL SCHROEDER, 19 . . . . JOHNNY BLAZE LEAVITT

MRS. FLORENCE SCHROEDER . . . . ALICE KING

MRS. SARAH SCHEUER . . . . JANICE JOHNSON

MRS. ELAINE MILLER . . . . MOLLY MCMILLAN

MR. ARTHUR KRAUSE . . . . MARVIN KAYE

CHARACTERS

NOTE: This play is intended as an ensemble piece with nine or more actors playing various roles including:

Bill Schroeder, 19

Florence Schroeder, his mother

Sandy Scheuer, 20

Sarah Scheuer, her mother

Jeff Miller, 20

Elaine Miller, his mother

Allison Krause, 19

Arthur Krause, her father

Reporter(s)

Jerry Rubin

Protestors

Mayor

Governor

Guardsman

Roommate #1 (female)

Roommate #2 (male)

Campus Policeman

Hospital Director

Nurse

Woman #1

Woman #2

Man (letter writers, gossip mongers, jury members)

Senator Howard Metzenbaum

American Legionnaire

Ohio Legionnaire

Trustee

TIME
1970–1990

SETTING
In and around Kent State University

REPORTER: It is 1970, and this year Kent State University celebrates its sixtieth anniversary. From its humble beginnings as a four-year teacher's college with an enrollment of 625, the university has mushroomed into a first-class university with a student body of over 21,000. To celebrate the event, there will be an art exhibit featuring the works of renowned American painters, Andres Segovia will perform in concert, and the Drama Department will present Bertolt Brecht's *The Caucasian Chalk Circle*. Marking the eventful year, the student newspaper has stated in its first editorial for the new year—

STUDENT: We intend to catalogue the events of life on campus in a world that can never be shut out. Everything is relevant, and everything has reverberations. After the headlong rush of mankind to both heaven and hell at the same time during the past ten years, we fervently pray that 1970 will be the true dawning of the Age of Aquarius.

(*Mrs. Florence Schroeder reads a letter from her son, Bill, 19, a handsome, clean-cut-looking boy*)

BILL: Dear Mom—I love it here at Kent State, and I'm glad I decided to transfer from Colorado this year. Now that I'm not working part-time for a while, I am reading, walking, and generally having the real fun of being creative. I was loaned a $200 camera and all the film I can possibly ever use. My friend Bruce and I take photography excursions and he is teaching me the ropes. Bruce is a cinematography major. I go to all the free lectures, concerts, or bull sessions on campus. I'm finally getting some semblance of an education. My accumulative average is now 3.28, and I expect even better grades in the Spring Quarter. Classes this Spring are really great. I'm taking Anthropology 151, Experimental Psychology 341, Abnormal Psychology 411, and Military Science. I'm still doing well in ROTC and am second in my class. Someday I hope to attend graduate school before I go on active duty. Well, here in closing is another one of those twenty minute specials I like to pen. One of these days I'll concentrate and take my time, and win a Pulitzer Prize. Are you ready? Here goes—*There are many wonderful things yet to be done,/The thought of the future dominates any other./I promise to be a better son,/If you'll stay just the same as my mother.* Anyway, thanks for last weekend, and every other weekend, and every other day, and everything. Love, Bill.

(*Mrs. Sarah Scheuer reads a letter from her daughter, Sandy, 20, a pretty girl wearing a sweater and matching skirt*)

SANDY: Dear Mom—It's between classes, so I thought I'd drop you a quick note. Being a Speech Therapy major sure keeps me busy, not to mention my volunteer work at the Speech and Hearing Clinic. It was nice seeing you and grandmom over the weekend. Thanks for bringing me that delicious cake. Some of the boys from Alpha Epsilon Pi helped me to devour it in no time flat. Did I tell you they've adopted me as the fraternity's "little sister"? They're all a lot of fun. I have loads of friends here, but, you know, I'm still looking for that special someone who I can care for and love the rest of my life. But I'm beginning to get worried I won't. Gee, I hope I don't die an old maid. Love, Sandy.

(*Mrs. Elaine Miller reads a letter from her son, Jeff, 20, a hippie-looking, long-haired boy, wearing a fringed shirt, beads, and a headband*)

JEFF: Dear Mom—Well, after four months here, I can definitely state I'm glad I transferred from Michigan State. The frat life there was not for me. Besides, I'm glad to see my old friends from New York and I've met some new ones, too. Of course, like any campus today, there's quite a bit of unrest about the war—demonstrations and all. You can't blame them. Like I told you at Easter, there's no way I'm going to Vietnam and kill people. Which reminds me, I've enclosed a poem I've written about the subject. Hope you like it. Love, Jeff. *"Where Does It End?" In the pastures converted into battlefields, the small metal pellets speed through the air, pausing to claim another victim./A teenager from a small Ohio farm clutches his side in pain and as he feels his life ebbing away, he too asks why—/why is he dying here, thousands of miles from home, giving his life for those who did not even ask his help?/The War Without a Purpose marches on relentlessly/not stopping to mourn for its dead,/content to wait for its end./But all the frightened parents who still have their sons fear that/the end is not in sight.*

(*Mr. Arthur Krause reads a letter from his daughter, Allison, 19, a wise-cracking, fun-loving girl. She is wearing blue jeans, a grey T-shirt inscribed "Kennedy," and an army jacket*)

ALLISON: Dear Dad—I'm still going ahead with my plans to transfer to SUNY-Buffalo next fall, if that's all right with mom and you. Though I adore my English and history teachers here, the honors program, especially in art history, is just not as challenging as I would like. I have my own room in the dorm now, which I like a whole lot better. So does my cat

Yossarian. I'm still heavily involved in the peace mobilization movement. However, I'm not joining the SDS. They're all a bunch of—okay, I'll watch my language—they're all a bunch of finks as far as I'm concerned. I believe in protest but not in violence. Well, I gotta run. Barry and I have a date tonight. I know, so what else is new? He's so cute with his mustache and goatee. Put a plumed hat on his head and he'd look just like one of the Three Musketeers and just as gallant to boot. Talk to you soon—Love, Allison.

REPORTER: On a chilly mid-April day this afternoon, student revolutionary Jerry Rubin addressed a crown of 2,000 on the campus of Kent State. Among other things, he said—

RUBIN: The first part of the Yippie program is to kill your parents. And I mean that literally, because until you're prepared to kill your parents, you're not ready to change the country. Our parents are our first oppressors. I have no respect for the court systems of this country. Being young in America is illegal. We are a generation of obscenities. The most oppressed people in this country are not the blacks, not the poor, but the white middle-class. They don't have anything to rise up and fight against. We will have to invent new laws to break.

REPORTER: In a stunning turn of policy, President Nixon has launched a surprise offensive by U.S. and South Vietnam troops against North Vietnamese and Viet Cong sanctuaries in Cambodia. He declared the assaults were essential to save American lives, continue his Vietnam withdrawal program, and help end the war. Nixon announced his controversial decision to the nation Thursday in a dramatic televised speech in which he acknowledged it might make him a one-term president but argued the stakes were too high for political consideration.

PROTESTORS: *One-Two-Three-Four, We Don't Want Your Fuckin' War!*

REPORTER: In the city of Kent Friday night, hundreds of university students who had been drinking in bull-and-beer spots on North Water Street, swarmed into the warm night, blocking the busy thoroughfare and began chanting—

PROTESTORS: *One-Two-Three-Four, We Don't Want Your Fuckin' War!*

REPORTER: A drunk on a balcony hurled a bottle into the street and suddenly the mood turned ugly. Students smashed car windows, set fires in trash cans, and began to bash storefronts. The police were called and the mayor ordered a curfew, which few students were aware of. Police stormed into bars and forced some 2,000 more students into the street. The police pushed the students back toward the campus, then fired tear gas to disperse them.

(*A phone rings*)

MRS. MILLER: Hello?

JEFF: Hi, Mom!

MRS. MILLER: Jeff, I'm glad you called. Your grandmother just called me. She said she heard a report on the radio there was some kind of trouble there last night.

JEFF: It wasn't much. A bunch of kids went downtown and smashed a few windows, that's all.

MRS. MILLER: Why, for heaven's sake?

JEFF: You know, they're all riled up over Nixon and that Cambodia thing.

MRS. MILLER: You weren't among them, were you?

JEFF: Me? Of course not.

MRS. MILLER: Well, I'm certainly glad to hear that.

JEFF: Besides, I had a date last night.

MRS. MILLER: Oh? Who with?

JEFF: You know that girl I told you about. Well, I gotta go. Just called to see how you were.

MRS. MILLER: I'm fine.

JEFF: Good.

MRS. MILLER: You take care.

JEFF: I will.

MRS. MILLER: And Jeff—

JEFF: Yeah?

MRS. MILLER: Stay out of trouble.

JEFF: I will. You know me, Mom.

REPORTER: Saturday night, protestors attacked a one-story ROTC building at Kent State, smashing windows and tossing lighted railroad flares inside. The building caught fire and when firemen arrived, students threw rocks at them and cut their fire hoses with machetes until police interceded with tear gas. Without bothering to consult Kent State authorities, the mayor of Kent asked for help from the National Guard.

MAYOR: As Mayor of the City of Kent, pursuant to the power invested in me as the chief magisterial office of the City, I do hereby request the assistance of the National Guard to assist the Police Department and local enforcement agencies in restoring law and order in the city of Kent and particularly in the area of Kent State University and its environs. Local law-enforcement agencies can no longer cope with the situation and I instruct you to provide the necessary assistance to restore peace and order to our community. In accordance with Section 5923.23 of the Revised Code of Ohio, I leave the mode and means of execution to your direction.

REPORTER: The governor of Ohio, who is still engaged in a tough campaign for Senate nomination, quickly ordered Guardsmen transferred from points of tension in a Teamster strike elsewhere in Ohio. Within an hour, about 500 Guardsmen, already weary from three nights on duty, arrived with fully loaded M-1 semiautomatic rifles, pistols, and tear gas. Order was restored before midnight.

(Mrs. Schroeder reads a letter from her son Bill)

BILL: Dear Mom—I can't believe it! Last night they actually burned the ROTC building to the ground! I know a lot of students are opposed to the program, but you can't go around burning up things you don't like. Amazing! On a lighter note, here's another twenty-minute special—*I am a child, I last awhile/You can't perceive all the pleasures in my smile./You make the rules, you say what's fair/It's lots of fun to have you there.* Love, Bill.

REPORTER: This morning, the governor of Ohio arrived in Kent and made this statement to reporters:

GOVERNOR: The scene here that the City of Kent is facing is probably the most vicious form of campus-oriented violence yet perpetrated by dissident groups and their allies in the state of Ohio . . . Now it ceases to be a problem of the colleges of Ohio. This now is the problem of the State of Ohio. Now we're going to put a stop to this, for this reason. The same group that we're dealing with here today have only one thing in mind. That is to destroy higher education in Ohio . . . Last night I think we have seen all forms of violence, the worst. And when they start taking over our communities, this is when we're going to use every weapon of the law-enforcement agencies of Ohio to drive them out of Kent. We have the same groups going from one campus to the other, and they use the universities that are supported by the taxpayers of Ohio as a sanctuary. And in this they make definite plans of burning, destroying, and throwing rocks at police and at the National Guard and the Highway Patrol . . . They're worse than the Brown Shirts and the Communist element and also the night riders and the vigilantes. They're the worst type of people we harbor in America . . . It's over with in Ohio. I think we're up against the strongest, well-trained militant group that has ever assembled in America . . . We are going to eradicate the problem . . .

(Mrs. Scheuer reads a greeting card from her daughter Sandy, who has taken off her sweater to reveal a red blouse underneath)

SANDY: Dear Mom and Dad—Happy Anniversary! How long have you two enjoyed wedded bliss now? Can it really be twenty-seven years and still counting? Wow! I hope I'm as lucky as you are when I get married. Thanks, Mom, for bringing me up my spring clothes the other day. I needed them desperately, especially that pretty spring blouse I like so much—you know, the red one. I'm wearing it now. Well, I have to go cook dinner. Jeff Miller and a couple of the guys from the frat are dropping by my apartment later on. What a bunch of moochers, but I love them. Are the lilacs blooming in the back yard? They are here, and they smell heavenly. I hope you have a wonderful day on Monday. All my love to you both, Sandy.

(*A phone rings*)

MR. KRAUSE: Hello?

ALLISON: Hi, Daddy. Hope you didn't mind me reversing the charges.

MR. KRAUSE: That's all right, Allison. I was hoping you'd call. What the—I mean what's going on there at the university?

ALLISON: The pigs have taken over the campus.

MR. KRAUSE (*correcting her*): Allison.

ALLISON: Sorry, Daddy. You know how I feel about the war, now this. Anyway, I guess they're not all pigs. Yesterday, Barry and I were talking to one of the guardsmen. Nice guy, cute smile. No way did he want to be guarding the campus. As we talked, I put a lilac in the barrel of his M-1. Then this officer—now he was a real pig—

MR. KRAUSE (*correcting her again*): Allison.

ALLISON: Anyway, this officer came over and gave the nice guy a hard time for talking with us and yanked the lilac right out of his rifle barrel. But before the SOB could throw it away, I grabbed it from him and said: "Flowers are better than bullets!"

MR. KRAUSE: "Flowers are better than bullets"—sounds like my girl.

ALLISON: Well, mom and you have always taught me to speak my mind. There's going to be a rally here at noon and Barry's going with me. So's Jeff Miller.

MR. KRAUSE: You and Barry are inseparable, aren't you?

ALLISON: Yeah, I guess you could say that.

MR. KRAUSE: Now you be careful.

ALLISON: Don't worry, Daddy, I've got Barry to look after me.

MR. KRAUSE: Bye, Allison.

ALLISON: Bye, Daddy.

(*A phone rings*)

MRS. MILLER: Good morning, Principal's Office, Mrs. Miller speaking.

JEFF: Hi, Mom.

MRS. MILLER: Jeff, what are you doing calling me at work?

JEFF: I was afraid you might have heard about the trouble here over the weekend and I didn't want you to worry.

MRS. MILLER: Are you all right?

JEFF: Sure. Say, did you hear what Agnew said about yours truly?

MRS. MILLER: No, what?

JEFF: He called us anti-war students "bums."

MRS. MILLER: I'm not surprised, coming from him.

JEFF: Mom?

MRS. MILLER: Yes?

JEFF: There's a rally at noon today down by the victory bell, and I'd like to go. Is that all right?

MRS. MILLER: Well, Jeff, I have faith in your good judgment, but do you think the rally will really accomplish anything?

JEFF: Probably not. But the guard has no right to be on our campus. You know, sometimes you've just got to take a stand if you really believe in something. You know what I mean?

MRS. MILLER: Yes, I understand, but please be careful.

JEFF: Don't worry, Mom, I'm not going to get hurt. You know me, I won't get that involved.

GUARDSMAN: Operations Plan, Ohio National Guard, Rules of Engagement: In an action that you are required to take, use only the minimum force necessary. When the Riot Act has been read within hearing, it is unlawful for any group of three or more people to remain unlawfully or riotously assembled and you may use necessary and proper means to disperse or apprehend them. Your use of force should be in this sequence: a) issue a military request to disperse; b) riot formation-show of force; c) simple physical force, if feasible; d) rifle butt and bayonet; and e) chemicals. When all other means have failed or chemicals are not available, you are armed with the rifle and have been issued life—I mean—live ammunition. The following rules apply in the use of firearms: 1) rifles will be carried with a round in the chamber in the safe position. Exercise care and be safety minded at all times; 2) Indiscriminate firing of weapons is forbidden. Only single aimed shot—I mean—shots at confirmed targets will be employed . . .

(*In the darkness, the victory bell clangs*)

GUARDSMAN (*continuing; using a bullhorn*): Evacuate the commons area! You have no right to assemble! I repeat! Evacuate the commons area at once!

ALLISON: *Pigs Off Campus!*

JEFF: *Get Out, You Motherfuckers!*

PROTESTORS: *One-Two-Three-Four, We Don't Want Your Fuckin' War! One-Two-Three-Four, We Don't Want Your Fuckin' War!*

(*Then the sound of shots in the following sequence—one shot, a two-second silence, an eight-second burst of fire, a one-second silence, and then two final shots—thirteen seconds in all. Then silence*)

(Lights up. A phone rings)

ROOMMATE #1: Hello?

MRS. SCHEUER: Hello. This is Mrs. Scheuer, Sandy's mother, calling. Who's this?

ROOMMATE #1 *(nervously)*: This is her roommate, Mrs. Scheuer.

MRS. SCHEUER: I understand there's been some kind of trouble at the university.

ROOMMATE #1: Yes, I'm glad you called. Sandy's been hurt.

MRS. SCHEUER: My God! Where is she?

ROOMMATE #1: I don't know! I don't know! You might try calling the hospital in Ravenna.

MRS. SCHEUER: Yes, I will. Wait a minute!

ROOMMATE #1: Yes?

MRS. SCHEUER: What was my daughter wearing?

ROOMMATE #1: Why, she was wearing that red blouse you brought up a couple of days ago.

(A phone rings)

CAMPUS POLICEMAN: Campus police.

MR. KRAUSE: My name is Arthur Krause, and my daughter Allison attends your university.

CAMPUS POLICEMAN: Yes?

MR. KRAUSE: My brother just called. He said he heard a news bulletin that there had been a disturbance at the university.

CAMPUS POLICEMAN: Don't worry, sir. Everything is okay. Nobody was hurt.

MR. KRAUSE: Are you sure?

CAMPUS POLICEMAN: Of course I'm sure.

(*A phone rings*)

ROOMMATE #2: Hello?

MRS. MILLER: Hello, this is Mrs. Miller.

ROOMMATE #2: Mrs. Miller! This is Jeff's roommate!

MRS. MILLER: I heard about all the commotion on campus—

ROOMMATE #2: Mrs. Miller—

MRS. MILLER: Now Jeff promised me just a couple of hours ago that he would stay out of trouble—

ROOMMATE #2: Mrs. Miller—listen to me!

MRS. MILLER: Yes?

ROOMMATE #2: Mrs. Miller—Jeff is dead!

(*A phone rings*)

HOSPITAL DIRECTOR: Yes?

MRS. SCHEUER: Hello? They keep telling me they're going to switch me to the director of the hospital.

HOSPITAL DIRECTOR: This is he speaking.

MRS. SCHEUER: At last! This is Sarah Scheuer calling.

HOSPITAL DIRECTOR: Yes, how may I help you?

MRS. SCHEUER: I was told my daughter was hurt in the shooting at the university this afternoon.

HOSPITAL DIRECTOR: What was your name again?

MRS. SCHEUER: Scheuer. My daughter's name is Sandra.

HOSPITAL DIRECTOR: I'm sorry. I don't know anything about a Sandra Scheuer.

MRS. SCHEUER: Are you positive?

HOSPITAL DIRECTOR: Yes. Now if you'll excuse me—

MRS. SCHEUER: She was wearing a red blouse.

HOSPITAL DIRECTOR: Did you say a red blouse?

MRS. SCHEUER: Yes, I brought it to her last Saturday.

HOSPITAL DIRECTOR: Mrs. Scheuer, get here as fast as you can!

(*A phone rings*)

MRS. SCHROEDER: Hello?

REPORTER: Is this Mrs. Louise Schroeder, mother of William Schroeder?

MRS. SCHROEDER: Yes.

REPORTER: I'm a reporter—

MRS. SCHROEDER: Yes?

REPORTER: And I was wondering if you have a picture of your son we could use?

MRS. SCHROEDER: A picture? For what reason?

REPORTER: This is Mrs. William Schroeder, isn't it?

MRS. SCHROEDER: Yes, I told you that already. Now what's this all about?

REPORTER: Mrs. Schroeder, you're son is dead, isn't he?

MRS. SCHROEDER: Dead! What are you talking about?

(*A phone rings*)

NURSE: Ravenna Hospital.

MR. KRAUSE: Hello, my name is Arthur Krause. My wife and I were watching the six o'clock news. We could have sworn the reporter said that one of the dead was an Allison Krause. But that could not be right. It must be a mistake. No one notified us. So we're just double-checking to make sure—

NURSE: That's right, Mr. Krause. Your daughter was brought in this afternoon. She was DOA.

(*Pause*)

MAYOR: As Mayor of the City of Kent, I want to congratulate the Ohio National Guard on a job well done.

WOMAN #1: Congratulations to the Guardsmen for the performance of their duties!

WOMAN #2: I, too, stand behind the actions of the National Guard.

WOMAN #1: I am proud to say that I am the wife of a guardsman. My husband is no murderer. He was afraid. He was sure that they were going to be overrun by those kids. He was under orders—that's why he did it. He said so.

MAN: As for the parents of the dead students, I can appreciate their suffering; they probably don't know the truth. A dissident certainly isn't going to write home about his or her demonstration activities. Parents are learning the hard way and others should take heed!

WOMAN #2: If dissenters refuse to obey the final warning before the punishment, hurling taunts, rocks—stones, they say—sticks, brandishing clubs with razor blades imbedded, then the first slap is a mighty sting!

MAN: If the National Guard is forced to face these situations without loaded guns, the silent majority has lost everything.

WOMAN #1: Live ammunition!—well, really, what did those hoodlums expect—spitballs? How much warning is needed, indeed?

MAN: The National Guard made only one mistake—they should have fired sooner and longer!

WOMAN #2: As a mother of a guardsman, I hope the Guard's actions serve as an example for the entire nation!

MAN: When trouble-makers have long hair, use bad language, and go barefoot and even destroy property, they have to be stopped.

WOMAN #1: Hooray! I shout for God and Country, recourse to justice under law, fifes, drums, martial music, parades, and ice cream cones! America, support it or leave it!

WOMAN #2: The Kent State four should have studied more!

WOMAN #1: 4,004 students should have been killed.

MAN: The score is four—and next time more!

WOMAN #2: I agree with what President Nixon said: "When dissent runs to violence, it invites tragedy."

(*Pause. The parents read letters*)

MRS. SCHROEDER: Dear Mr. and Mrs. Schroeder—Certainly nothing can lessen the extent of your tragic loss, but I hope that the heartfelt sympathy of so many across the nation can in some measure ease your pain. Sincerely, Richard M. Nixon.

WOMAN #1: Mrs. Schroeder—There's nothing better than a dead, destructive, riot-making communist, and that's what your son was; if not he would have stayed away like a good American would do. Now you know what a goody-goody son you had. They should all be shot, then we'd have a better USA to live in. Be thankful he is gone; he was just another communist.

MRS. SCHEUER: Dear Mr. and Mrs. Scheuer—As parents of two daughters, Mrs. Nixon and I feel especially keen at the loss of one so young, so happy, so much a source of joy to her friends, and so full of promise of life ahead.

WOMAN #2: Mrs. Miller—I heard you on TV and if I were a policeman I would kill a lot more of these kids. Keep your kids home, then they do not get in trouble. My boys and girls do not get in trouble. Sure looks bad for you parents. Kids belong in your home, entertain them in your home like we still do here. Hope the police and Army kill a lot more kids. It has to be stopped now as it is getting so you can not go out on the street. We do not feel sorry for none of you parents. Keep your kids at home.

WOMAN #1: Mr. Krause—Your daughter was a hippie, a cheap slut, and a potential killer herself. If you had done your duty as a parent in the first place, your daughter would never have been shot.

(*Pause*)

MR. KRAUSE: My daughter is dead, and since she cannot speak for herself, I will. She resented being called a bum because she disagreed with someone else's opinion. Is this dissent a crime? Is this a reason for killing her? Have we come to such a state in this country that a young girl has to be shot because she disagrees deeply with the actions of her government?

(*Pause, then rumors*)

WOMAN #1: It is all very well to feel sympathy for Jeff Miller, whose head was blown off, but I suppose you know he was so filthy that in the ambulance they had to keep the doors propped open so they could breathe.

WOMAN #2: You've heard about the mother who came to the hospital in Ravenna, took one look at the body of her son and cried, "This filthy thing is no son of mine."

WOMAN #1: The two dead girls were so covered with lice that the hospital attendants nearly threw up.

WOMAN #2: You knew that Allison Krause girl was on drugs.

WOMAN #1: It was a mercy she was shot, because she was pregnant.

WOMAN #2: There's no reason to grieve over her death, because she was so ridden with syphilis that she would have been dead in two weeks.

WOMAN #1: When they got her to the hospital they found she was carrying hand grenades.

WOMAN #2: She was the campus whore.

WOMAN #1: They were all hopheads.

WOMAN #2: They were all communists.

MAN: I hear snipers are coming here from out of state to even the score.

WOMAN #1: I hear hundreds of students from Akron are about to overrun our town.

WOMAN #2: I hear police are on the lookout for radicals disguised as National Guardsmen.

MAN: They say they've already put LSD in our water supply.

WOMAN #1: They say the revolution will start here.

(*Pause*)

REPORTER: After five years of wrangling over profound legal questions and court procedures, May 19 has been set as the opening date for a cluster of civil damage suits in the Kent State shooting. Those being sued include the Governor, National Guard officers, and several members of the Ohio National Guard. The plaintiffs, including the wounded students and the parents of those killed, are seeking approximately $40 million in punitive damages. The fourteen suits have taken four years to be heard in a court of law. Previously, unfavorable rulings were handed down by Ohio

District Court, U.S. District Court, and the U.S. Court of Appeals. The reason given was that according to Ohio's Sovereign Immunity Law, the defendants—namely, the Governor and the Guard—could not be sued without their first giving consent to such action. It was only after appealing the decision to the U.S. Supreme Court that the parents and students in an 8–0 ruling were given their day in court. Said Arthur Krause, who initiated the first suit:

MR. KRAUSE: We don't want the damn money; we want the truth. If I had wanted the money, I would have accepted the one-and-a-half-million-dollar bribe I was offered to drop the suit in 1971. We want the facts out about how the four died. We aren't afraid of the truth. We aren't the ones who have been saying, "No comment" for the past several years.

(*Pause*)

REPORTER: After three months of proceedings, the jury, following five days of deliberation, returned a verdict on August 27.

JURY: We the Jury find in favor of all the Defendants and against the Plaintiff Arthur Krause, Administrator of the Estate of Allison B. Krause, deceased. We the Jury find in favor of all the Defendants and against the Plaintiff Elaine B. Miller, Administratrix of the Estate of Jeffrey Glenn Miller, deceased. We the Jury find in favor of all the Defendants and against the Plaintiff Sarah Scheuer, Administratrix of the Estate of Sandra Lee Scheuer, deceased. We the Jury find in favor of all the Defendants and against the Plaintiff Florence Schroeder, Administratrix of the Estate of William Knox Schroeder, deceased.

REPORTER: Upon hearing the verdict, Mrs. Sarah Scheuer, mother of one of the victims, turned to one of the defense attorneys and said:

MRS. SCHEUER: I want you to know I do believe there is a God in heaven. One day when something like this happens to one of your children, maybe then you will understand how I feel.

REPORTER: In a press conference, Arthur Krause said:

MR. KRAUSE: I knew what was going to happen; that justice would not be served, but I wanted to make sure that there was pressure applied. In the beginning the other families were not as believing that nothing would be done; I think they thought I was some sort of radical. But I can tell you that if you don't stand up for your rights they will be taken away from you like they were from Allison and the others. Thanks to these jurors, a murder by the state is correct. Our court battles establish without a doubt one thing. There is no Constitution. There is no Bill of Rights.

(*Pause*)

REPORTER: Dateline Cleveland, January 8, 1979. Days after a new civil trial ordered by an appeals court in the Kent State shooting had begun, an out-of-court settlement was reached by the two parties, bringing to a close nearly ten years of litigation. The Governor, Generals, Command Officers, and the Guardsmen who were defendants in the civil case brought by the parents of the victims have agreed to sign the following statement as part of the settlement:

GOVERNOR: In retrospect, the tragedy of May 4, 1970 should not have occurred. The students may have believed that they were right in continuing their mass protest in response to the Cambodian invasions, even though this protest followed the posting and reading by the University of an order to ban rallies and an order to disperse . . .

GUARDSMAN: Some of the Guardsmen on Blanket Hill, fearful and anxious from prior events, may have believed in their own minds that their lives were in danger. Hindsight suggests that another method would have resolved the confrontation. Better ways must be found to deal with such confrontations.

GOVERNOR and GUARDSMAN: We devoutly wish that a means had been found to avoid the May 4 events culminating in the Guard shootings and the irreversible deaths and injuries. We deeply regret those events and are profoundly saddened by the deaths of four students and the wounding of nine others which resulted. We hope that the agreements to end this litigation will help to assuage the tragic memories regarding that sad day.

REPORTER: The parents of the students killed at Kent State have issued the following statement:

MRS. SCHEUER: A settlement of the Kent State civil suit has been reached out of court.

MRS. SCHROEDER: And for this we are grateful.

PARENTS: We, as families of the victims wish to interpret what we believe to be the significance of this settlement.

MRS. MILLER: The state of Ohio, although protected by the doctrine of sovereign immunity and consequently not legally responsible in a technical sense, has now recognized its responsibility by paying a substantial amount of money in damage—$675,000—for the injuries and deaths caused by the shooting.

SANDY: $15,000 for the life of Sandra Lee Scheuer.

ALLISON: $15,000 for the life of Allison B. Krause.

JEFF: $15,000 for the life of Jeffrey Glenn Miller.

BILL: $15,000 for the life of William Knox Schroeder.

MR. KRAUSE: Most of this money will help obtain sufficient financial support for one of the victims of the shooting that he may have a modicum of security as he spends the rest of his life in a wheelchair.

MRS. SCHEUER: State officials, National Guard command officers, and guardsmen have signed a statement submitted to the families of the victims of the shooting which not only expresses regret and sorrow—eight years belatedly—but also recognizes that another method than the use of loaded combat rifles could have resolved the confrontation at Kent State University. The statement also asserts that better ways must be found for future confrontations which may take place.

MRS. SCHROEDER: The Scranton Commission which investigated campus disorders in the summer of 1970 said that the Kent State shooting was—

MRS. MILLER: "Unnecessary."

MR. KRAUSE: "Unwarranted."

MRS. SCHEUER: "And inexcusable."

MRS. SCHROEDER: The signed statement of the officials and the guardsmen at least now agrees that the shooting and killing was unnecessary, and now at last, the State of Ohio has assumed responsibility for the act.

PARENTS: We recognize that many others related to the May 4, 1970 event have also suffered during the past eight years—including:

MRS. MILLER: Kent State University students.

MR. KRAUSE: Faculty.

MRS. SCHEUER: And administrators.

MRS. SCHROEDER: As well as Ohio National Guardsmen and their families.

PARENTS: Indeed, we believe that some of the guardsmen on Blanket Hill on that fateful day also became victims of the Ohio National Guard policy which sent them into a potential citizen confrontation with loaded combat rifles. We did not want those individual guardsmen to be personally liable for the actions of others and the policy of a government agency under whose orders they served.

MRS. MILLER: We believe that citizens and law enforcement must, in the words of the signed statement of the settlement, find better ways.

MR. KRAUSE: We appeal for those better ways to be used not only on campuses but in cities and communities across the land.

MRS. SCHEUER: We plead for a federal law which will compel the consideration and use of those better ways.

PARENTS: We are simply average citizens who have attempted to be loyal to our country and constructive and responsible in our actions, but we have not had an average experience. We have learned through tragic events that loyalty to our nation and its principles sometimes requires resistance to our government and its policies.

MRS. MILLER: A lesson many young people, including the children of some of us, had learned earlier.

MRS. SCHEUER: That has been our struggle and for others this struggle goes on.

PARENTS: We will try to support them.

MR. KRAUSE: For Allison.

MRS. SCHEUER: For Sandra.

MRS. MILLER: For Jeffrey.

MRS. SCHROEDER: And for William.

PARENTS: For peace and justice.

(*Pause*)

REPORTER: A ceremony, commemorating the fifteenth anniversary of the National Guard shootings, was held on the campus of Kent State University. Florence Schroeder, mother of one the students killed, said:

MRS. SCHROEDER: There is pain, but I try to remember the joys Bill brought our lives. Still, spring brings with it remembering, and a great deal of love and longing for him. Finally, after nine years, the funeral is over now. I can let him go.

REPORTER: Mrs. Sarah Scheuer, another parent of a slain student, said:

MRS. SCHEUER: My daughter was a special person who was not involved in any of the demonstrations, yet in the press she was called a Communist. We left Germany to guarantee that our daughters could live in a country with freedom. It doesn't make sense now ten years later. The pain will always be there. I have some advice to all parents of college students: Listen to your kids and remember what happened at Kent State. Since our Sandy died there have been changes in the rules on soldiers and guns on campus. That doesn't make it hurt any less, but hopefully it means Kent State won't happen again.

REPORTER: Senator Howard Metzenbaum, a featured speaker at the commemoration said:

SENATOR METZENBAUM: I am pleased there are plans to build a memorial on this site. There is a right to dissent in a democracy, and it is not enough to allow dissent. We must demand it.

REPORTER: But some members of the American Legion hope to halt construction plans for a memorial to the Kent State students killed or wounded by the National Guard in 1970. According to the Legion's resolution committee:

AMERICAN LEGIONNAIRE: The construction of this memorial would be an insult to the patriotic veterans who served their country honorably and well.

REPORTER: The American Legion of Ohio condemned a proposed memorial to the students killed and wounded at Kent State as—

OHIO LEGIONNAIRE: An insult to patriotic Vietnam veterans.

REPORTER: The 1300 delegates, representing 142,000 member veterans, described the four students who were killed as—

OHIO LEGIONNAIRE: Felons.

REPORTER: And denounced the memorial at the Legion's state convention in Cleveland as—

OHIO LEGIONNAIRE: A memorial to terrorism.

(*Pause*)

REPORTER: Attempts to honor the 13 students, injured or killed in the 1970 Kent State shootings, have been repeatedly thwarted. In 1978 university trustees rejected a memorial sculpture with a Biblical theme— Abraham and Isaac as—

TRUSTEE: Inappropriate.

REPORTER: At Kent State University, problems continue to plague attempts to build a memorial to the 13 students injured or killed by National Guardsmen in 1970. Although the the university held a ground breaking ceremony in the winter of 1989, no action has been taken in the construction of the memorial. The May 4th Task Force, a group devoted to the memory of the event, has taken steps to block construction of a scaled-down monument. The university was prepared to raise $1.3 million dollars toward its completion. However, in November of 1988, the Kent Board of Trustees voted to disregard the original design of 13 marble disks set in granite squares, representing the 13 slain and injured students, and plan a new memorial which would cost $100,000 or less. (*Pause*) Twenty years to the day, a memorial will be dedicated tomorrow morning at Kent State University commemorating the four students killed and the nine students wounded when Ohio National Guardsmen fired indiscriminately into a crowd of protestors and bystanders.

(*Sandy, Allison, Bill and Jeff sit on or lean against four pink granite slabs spread evenly across a bare stage. They stare into space for a few moments then Sandy begins to sing softly*)

SANDY (*to the tune of "The Old One Hundred"*):

> By the rude bridge that arched the flood,
> Their flag to April's breeze unfurled,
> Here once the embattled farmers stood,
> And fired the shot heard round the world.

(*Allison jumps up*)

ALLISON: You've got it all wrong, Sandy. You mean embattled Guard, don't you? And they didn't stand here. They stood over there—on that hill—above where we—

SANDY: I know, Allison. I—

(*Bill jumps off a slab*)

BILL: And it was May, not April.

SANDY: I know that, too, Bill.

(*Jeff gets up*)

JEFF: And there was more than one shot.

SANDY: Thanks for telling me what I already know, Jeff.

ALLISON: Sixty-seven to be exact.

SANDY: Will you guys give me a break? I was just using a little poetic license, that's all. What's wrong with that?

BILL: Nothing, I guess.

SANDY: Geez, thanks for nothing.

(*Pause. Jeff looks around*)

JEFF: Man, the old place sure hasn't changed that much, has it?

ALLISON: There's a new building over there, Jeff.

JEFF: Where?

SANDY: Over there. Above the parking lot—where we—

JEFF: Oh, yeah, I see it. Looks like an addition to the gym or something.

(*Pause*)

ALLISON: So, what do you guys, think?

SANDY: What about?

ALLISON: Our new digs—our shrine—our memorial—or whatever the hell they like to call it.

SANDY: It's—it's nice.

JEFF: It's kind of skimpy, if you ask me.

BILL: God, you're never satisfied.

ALLISON: Wait, the boy has got a point. The memorial is kind of small. Not at all what I expected.

JEFF: And why did they put it here?

ALLISON: Yeah. It would have made more sense to put it on *the* hill.

JEFF: Where *the* embattled Guard stood. Sorry, Sandy.

(*Sandy waves him off*)

ALLISON: Exactly. Or better still on the parking lot—where we—

JEFF: Yeah. And whoever thought of pink stone for Chrissakes?

ALLISON: You mean pink-o, don't you?

BILL: Speak for yourself; I was just watching.

SANDY: And I was just passing by on my way to class.

ALLISON: Remember, Sandy, they also get shot who stand and watch.

(*Jeff examines the slabs*)

JEFF: Hey, look, our names ain't even on these slabs. How the hell am I supposed to tell which one is mine?

ALLISON: Which one would you like, Jeff?

JEFF: Hell, I don't know.

BILL: How about the one on the left—the far left?

JEFF: Very funny, man. Right-of-center-all-American-boy makes joke. I guess we know which slab belongs to you.

SANDY: Now don't you two go at it again. Not tonight. Tonight is—well, it's very special.

BILL: Yeah, she's right.

(*Pause*)

ALLISON: Do you think the old crowd will show up tomorrow for the dedication?

SANDY: Yeah, same old crowd.

JEFF: You mean everybody except that girl. I never see that girl any more.

SANDY: What girl?

JEFF: You know.

ALLISON: Oh, I know who you mean.

(*Allison half-kneels and flings her arms out, a horrified look on her face*)

ALLISON (*continuing*): You mean this one.

JEFF: Yeah, that's the one. She stood over me when—you know. Anyway, she never comes here any more.

(*Allison gets up*)

ALLISON: Why should she? She wasn't even a co-ed, for Chrissakes.

JEFF: I don't care. I still miss her.

SANDY: Hey, have you guys noticed how old everybody's getting?

ALLISON: Yeah, and we haven't aged a bit. I wonder why that is.

SANDY: I miss my folks.

BILL: So do I.

ALLISON: Me, too.

JEFF: Yeah.

(*Pause*)

BILL: The styles sure have changed.

JEFF: Yeah, man, you would fit right in with your Ivy League look and short hair.

BILL: Hey, I had to keep my hair short. I was in ROT-C, remember?

JEFF: Yeah, well we're all a little rot-sy right now, man, if you get my drift.

SANDY: Come on, you guys.

JEFF: Look, I was merely pointing out that for once Slick over there was ahead of his time, that's all.

BILL: Like you were ahead of yours?

JEFF: I thought I could make a difference.

BILL: You made a difference all right. Look at us—look at all of us!

ALLISON: Okay, that's enough!

(*On the side of the stage, parents and friends light candles*)

SANDY: Hey, you guys, look over there on the hill. They've lit the candles.

ALLISON: The vigil's begun.

BILL: They're going down to the parking lot—where we—

JEFF: Yeah.

SANDY: You know, it's nice they remember us like that every year.

BILL: I guess there are things people just never forget.

JEFF: Yeah, man, like where you were when Kennedy got shot.

ALLISON: Not to mention where you were when you got shot.

JEFF: Yeah, right.

SANDY: Tomorrow they're going to bring those candles up here for the dedication.

(*For a few moments they stare wistfully at the candles*)

SANDY (*continuing, turning*): Look, the lilacs are in bloom.

BILL: Just like that day.

ALLISON: And there's smoke in the air.

JEFF: Just like that day.

SANDY: On the hill—

ALLISON: On the parking lot—

BILL: Where we—

JEFF: Yeah.

(*A mist begins to drift across the stage. The sound of protestors. From behind a slab, Jeff grabs a black flag attached to a sawed-off broomstick and begins waving it in the air. Allison joins him. Bill and Sandy watch from the sidelines. Jeff and Allison join in with the protestors' shouts*)

JEFF and ALLISON: *One-Two-Three-Four, We Don't Want Your Fuckin' War! One-Two-Three-Four, We Don't Want Your Fuckin' War!*

ALLISON: *Pigs Off Campus!*

JEFF: Get Out, You Motherfuckers!

JEFF and ALLISON: One-Two-Three-Four-

(*The first shot*)

SANDY: My God, they're shooting into the crowd!

BILL: Ah, don't worry, they're only shooting blanks.

(*A prolonged eight seconds of gunfire. Jeff drops his flag and grabs his face*)

JEFF: Christ, they're killing us!

(*He falls to his knees and then lies prone on the ground. Allison is hit and grabs her left side*)

ALLISON: Yesterday I put flowers in their guns; today they give me bullets in return!

(*Allison falls to the ground as Sandy is hit and clutches her neck*)

SANDY: *What like a bullet can undeceive!*

(*Sandy drops to the ground and lies still. Bill grabs his back*)

BILL: My God, fellas, I'm supposed to be on your side!

(*Bill falls to the ground. He and Allison call out in pain*)

ALLISON: I'm hit! I'm hit!

BILL: Somebody call an ambulance!

ALLISON: Please! Please!

(*Then Allison and Bill lie still like the others. Two final shots then silence. Then, after a few moments, all four look up slowly*)

BILL and JEFF: Some say we got what we deserved.

JEFF: They called us radicals.

BILL: Subversives.

JEFF: Terrorists.

ALLISON and SANDY: They said we were whores.

SANDY: Covered with lice.

ALLISON: Riddled with syphilis.

ENSEMBLE: They say we deserved to die.

JEFF: "Unnecessary!"

ALLISON: "Unwarranted!"

BILL: "Inexcusable!"

SANDY: One!

BILL: Two!

ALLISON: Three!

JEFF: Four!

(*Their chant rises to a crescendo*)

ENSEMBLE: One-two-three-four, the score is four and next time more!
One-two-three-four, *The Score Is Four And Next Time More!* (*Then softly*)
One-two-three-four, the score is four—and next time—more!

SANDY: One.

BILL: Two.

ALLISON: Three.

JEFF: Four.

(*Then silence. They lie on the ground staring blankly into space*)

SANDY (*singing*):

> "On this green bank, by this soft stream,
> We set today a votive stone;

That memory may their deed redeem,
When, like our sires, our sons are gone."

(The lights fade on performers, remain momentarily on slabs, then fade out completely)

ACKNOWLEDGEMENTS

This play is based on letters, speeches, poems, news reports, etc., found in the following sources: *Kent State* by James A. Michener, *The Kent State Coverup* by Joseph Kelner & James Munves, *MAYDAY: Kent State* by J. Gregory Payne, *Time*, the Associated Press, *The Canton Repository*.

The verses sung by Sandy are from Ralph Waldo Emerson's "Concord Hymn" (Sung at the Completion of the Battle Monument, July 4, 1837).

The line "What like a bullet can undeceive" is from "Shiloh: A Requiem" (April, 1862) by Herman Melville.

AL SJOERDSMA, JR.

The 82nd Shepherds' Play

Al Sjoerdsma, Jr. is a prolific playwright from Ann Arbor, Michigan. A graduate of the University of Michigan, with a B.A. and an M.A. in English, he is the author of over twenty plays. He has served as playwright-in-residence at the Canterbury Stage Company, of Ann Arbor, and at the Performance Network in the same city. He received a Hopwood Award in Major Playwrighting from the University of Michigan, was an Annie Award nominee courtesy of the Washtenaw Council for the Arts, and was a member of the Playwrights' Lab at film actor Jeff Daniels's Purple Rose Theatre in Chelsea, Michigan. His play, *Love Among the Aurochs*, won the Y.E.S. Festival of Northern Kentucky University and was performed in 1997. *Progress* was performed the following year at the Cleveland Public Theatre's New Play Festival and in 2000, at the City Theatre in Miami; another script, *Gandhi Goes Fishing*, was produced in 1999 in Miami and also at Milwaukee Rep.

The 82nd Shepherds' Play won The Open Book/Stage & Screen Book Club's sixth National Readers Theatre Playwrighting Competition, and was produced in New York at The Producers Club, opening on April 28th, 2000, with Angelynn Cerridwen directing the following cast:

MOTHER GILCHRIST .... ANGELYNN CERRIDWEN
CAROLE GILCHRIST .... ALICE KING
CLAY MCCORMICK .... DAN TEACHOUT
BILLY NERO .... KIPLEY WENTZ

PLAYWRIGHT'S NOTE

The 82nd Shepherds' Play is inspired by *The Second Shepherds' Play*, an anonymously authored part of the medieval "Townely" or "Wakefield Cycle" of plays, most likely written and produced sometime between 1360 and 1410.

In *The Second Shepherds' Play*, three shepherds guard their flock on a chilly night. Along comes a poor man named Mak, an acquaintance to the shepherds who, after having a chat with the trio, works a spell on them as they sleep, steals a sheep and brings it home to his wife Gill to be used for a future meal. The shepherds eventually discover the theft and make for Mak and Gill's home, but the devious couple conceal the crime by wrapping the sheep in swaddling clothes and pretending it is their newly born child; creating a horned anti-Christ figure in the bargain. The shepherds unravel the deception and punish Mak by tossing him in a sheet, whereupon they are contacted by an angel who informs them of the birth of the Christ child. (This, after they have been anachronistically Christian throughout.) The shepherds journey to Bethlehem and receive the joyous tidings from mother Mary.

This play is the latest version of the Shepherds' Play as seen, revised, altered, expanded, distorted, and modernized through six hundred years and eighty other hypothetical versions.

In addition, *The 82nd Shepherds' Play* is also the fifth part of the Waynesville series, a group of plays taking place in an imaginary Southwestern town. For those unfamiliar with the four previous tales, be assured that this story stands completely on its own. For those familiar with the other plays, it may be interesting to know that Billy Nero's previous appearance in *The Land of Lost Skies* takes place between scenes two and three of Act I of *The 82nd Shepherds' Play*.

CHARACTERS

Although the play's events take place over twenty-five years, the characters show no effects of the passage of time. Instead of thinking of the play as beginning in, say, 1999 and ending in 2024, think of it as progressing forward but passing through the present over and over again. In other words, no one appears to age, the fashions stay the same, the outside world doesn't change. The ages listed below are for the characters at the start of the play and are for characterization rather than casting purposes. Sixtyish Mother Gilchrist, for example, can be played by an actress in her twenties without age make-up of any kind.

Mother Gilchrist is in her sixties. Her appearance varies wildly depending on her mood. When she is feeling old and useless, she appears tired, washed out, helpless, and weak. When she is feeling vivacious, she appears young and very attractive. It is clear that, in her youth, she was a strong, attractive, and desirable woman.

Carole Gilchrist is Mother Gilchrist's daughter. She is about 30 years old at the start of the play. Carole is almost schoolgirlish at the start. Beautiful and intelligent; clearly living below her abilities.

Clay McCormick is also 30 years old. He is tall, strong, unassuming, somewhat clumsy, and insecure.

Billy Nero is about 30–35 years old. Billy was, at one time, a very handsome and dashing-looking man but he is showing the effects of years of alcohol consumption. He is still a magnetic figure, still very attractive in spite of his dissipation; he has blue eyes.

Clay McCormick, Jr. Clay and Carole's son, is played by the same person who plays Billy Nero.

Mary McCormick, Clay and Carole's daughter, is played by the same person who plays Mother Gilchrist.

PLEASE NOTE: The fact that Clay Jr. is played by Billy and that Mary is played by Mother Gilchrist should be kept concealed from the audience until the characters' appearances.

Mother, Carole, and Clay have Southwestern accents. Billy, for the most part, does not have an accent, though he stumbles into it now and again. Clay Junior speaks like Billy. Mary has no Southwest accent at all.

ACT I

The set is the living room of the home of Carole Gilchrist and her mother. There is a couch center stage with coffee table and end tables. Stage right is Mother's armchair with an accompanying ottoman. There is a closet upstage left and an electrical socket in the upstage wall. Stage left is the hallway that leads to the unseen front door. Stage right is a stairway with a landing.

On either side of the main set are areas that can be illuminated by spots. These areas are used for the preludes to each scene and feature sketchy settings. Usually just a small table and chair. Note that the preludes do not always conform to the time frame designated at the start of each scene.

Scene One—Now

Prelude: *In stage right spot. A small bar table with chair. Billy Nero sits at the table. He sleeps with his head on the table. He has a pad of paper and pen, along with a drink. Lots of empty glasses on the table around him. He wakes up, looks around, then looks at his pad of paper, writes a bit, sips his drink, looks at his pad, stands up with pad in hand, clears his throat, strikes a pose as if to begin an oratory, looks closely at what he has written, sits down, crosses out what he has just written, finishes his drink, and starts to fall asleep again.*

Crossfade to the main set where Mother is asleep in her armchair. She is dressed in her robe with slippers on. She has a glass in her hand that looks very much like the glasses that surrounded Billy Nero at the bar. Her arm and the glass rest on the arm of the chair. There is water, which was once ice, in her glass. She wakes with a start, as if having a nightmare, and feels very stiff all over.

MOTHER: God. (*Getting her bearings*) It's so cold. Carole dear. Sweetheart? (*She rubs her hands, leaving the glass on the arm of the chair*) My poor fingers are freezing. Carole? Honey? (*Trying to stretch*) Oh. I'm so stiff.

(*Carole Gilchrist enters. She is in a slip*)

CAROLE: Did you say somethin', mama?

MOTHER: I fell asleep.

CAROLE: Yes, you did.

MOTHER: It's so cold in here, sweetheart. Can't we turn a little heat on? I'm just freezin'!

CAROLE: Honey, it's not a bit cold in here. And it's downright warm outside. We don't want to turn the heat on.

MOTHER: Feel my fingers if it's not cold in here. (*Beat*) Feel! (*Carole feels*) Well?

CAROLE: They're cold.

MOTHER: Of course they're cold. Because I'm old. I don't care how "downright warm" it is outside. When you get to be my age, your fires just naturally start to burn down. Why do you think they call it "ashes to ashes" anyhow? Because the fire burns out and you're embers. You lose your heat. Carole honey, I swear to God . . .

BOTH (*simultaneously*): I think the graveyard won't be any colder than I am right now!

MOTHER: Well, it won't! (*She laughs*)

(*Carole picks up the glass*)

CAROLE: I think you can blame your cold hands on this glass of ice you were holdin' when you fell asleep.

MOTHER: That's not ice, dear. It's water.

CAROLE: Shore. Now. Once your hot little hand melted it all up.

MOTHER: Now, honey, please. That was always just water. Nothin' more than just water. (*Carole sniffs the glass. From her reaction, we can see it had whiskey in it. Mother stretches*) Lord. I don't know how I always manage to get so stiff.

CAROLE: Might have somethin' to do with fallin' asleep in this chair every night.

MOTHER: Might. (*Beat*) What time is it?

CAROLE: Past eleven.

MOTHER: I thought you were going out on the town tonight.

CAROLE: I am.

MOTHER: Better hurry up. You're not even ready.

CAROLE: I've been ready all night. Now I've decided to be unready.

MOTHER: Ah-huh.

CAROLE: Billy is a little bit late.

MOTHER: I see.

CAROLE: Most likely he got busy.

MOTHER: I'm sure that is quite true.

CAROLE: Poetry is single-minded business.

MOTHER: Thirsty business.

CAROLE: Don't be like that.

(*Lights up, like a switch is flipped, on stage right area showing Billy at his table, drinking. They stay on just for a short time, like the lights triggered in carnival spook houses that display the exhibit and then switch off again*)

MOTHER: Me? I was peacefully sleeping.

CAROLE: I don't want to hear it. So, he drinks. So what? He drinks. (*Brandishes glass*) This wasn't filled with colored water.

MOTHER: That was barely a sip, Carole.

CAROLE: That's all any drinkin' is, is a series of sips.

MOTHER: Ah-huh.

CAROLE: Okay, so he does more than sip. He hides bottles around town. Carries two flasks. He falls down. Sometimes he sleeps on the sidewalks. I'm sick of it, too. But what can you do? He's an artist.

MOTHER: He's a Nero. And it's only because he's a Nero that folks let him get away with it. If that other young man who's been pursuing you tried to sleep on the sidewalk, the town would take care of him in a hurry.

CAROLE: The only way Clay McCormick would try to sleep on the sidewalk . . .

MOTHER: Is if you were there sleeping next to him?

CAROLE (*embarrassed*): I'm not interested in continuin' this kind of discussion.

MOTHER: Well, God know *I* don't want to talk about it. I just think it's a damn shame that my beautiful daughter has to wait around for some date who's gettin' drunk somewhere, time goin' by, gettin' older by the minute, just because his name happens to be Billy Nero.

CAROLE: You make it sound like I'm a hundred years old.

MOTHER: Ah-huh.

CAROLE: I'm only twenty-nine.

MOTHER: And workin' as a check-out clerk in that grocery store. If that doesn't punch your clock into middle-age in a hurry, I don't know what will.

CAROLE: I got plenty of time.

MOTHER: Tick-tock. Tick-tock.

CAROLE: Oh, stop it. You know he's an artist. You know artists can't settle down right from the outset. Once he *does* settle down, once he realizes he needs someone, I'm going to be right there ready for him.

MOTHER: Waiting to marry him.

CAROLE: Uh-huh.

MOTHER: Has he asked you?

CAROLE: Not yet.

MOTHER (*positive*): He won't.

CAROLE: You don't know that.

MOTHER: I know money separates. I know the Neros. I know Lucius won't let his son marry Joe Gilchrist's daughter.

CAROLE: In spite of the fact that the two were close friends when they were young?

MOTHER: Not "in spite of." Because of. *Because* they were close friends before Lucius struck it rich. *Because* Joe and me ended up working in Lucius' oil fields. What do you think? Lucius is going to let you get a hold of all of Billy's money?

CAROLE: It doesn't have anything to do with money.

MOTHER: You're a child, Carole, a child. I don't care how old you are.

CAROLE: Why do you say that?

MOTHER: Well, if it's got nothing to do with money, what does it have to do with?

CAROLE (*nervous laugh*): What a question!

MOTHER: You're not pregnant, are you?

CAROLE (*amused*): From Billy? No, mama.

MOTHER: Well, there must be some reason you put up with the drinkin' and the no-shows and all the other dirty tricks he pulls on you. All it does is make you miserable.

CAROLE: I love him.

MOTHER (*looks at her*): I don't believe you.

CAROLE (*surprised*): Mama!

MOTHER: Well, I don't! Listen to yourself. "He's an artist." "Poetry is single-minded business." That's not the music of love, Carole. That's the old jukebox tune of a starry-eyed schoolgirl crush. You'll be over that in a year or two.

CAROLE: What do you know?

MOTHER: More than you think.

CAROLE: In other words . . . what? I should go out with dull ol' Clay Mc-Cormick?

MOTHER: You could do worse.

CAROLE: I've got troubles enough.

MOTHER: He's reliable.

CAROLE: Reliably dull.

MOTHER: He likes you.

CAROLE: I know.

MOTHER: He tries so hard.

CAROLE: He's wasting his time.

MOTHER: He's earthy.

CAROLE: What does that mean? When you kiss him, he leaves behind a little dirty smudge?

MOTHER: You can't have a name like Clay and not be earthy.

CAROLE: I love Billy.

MOTHER: Oh, honey, you know . . . I doubt it.

CAROLE (*tears start to fall during this speech*): I do! It's true. It's awful and it's true. He makes me feel so weak. Just like him. He's weak. He's selfish. But I need him, anyway. Isn't that love? To not give up when you know you should. To accept a hundred pains for one little pleasure? Like tonight, here I am again tonight. Just waitin' and waitin'. Puttin' on clothes, takin' off clothes. Fixin' my face, tearin' it apart. Knowin' there's no reason for it, knowin' he won't show himself, knowin' my rival isn't even another girl, just a dark booth in the back of the Cinnamon Club. Doin' it all, anyway. That's love, wouldn't you call it, Mama? Don't you think that's love?

MOTHER (*comforting Carole*): It's not love, sweetheart, but it's something. The question is, what is going to be done about it?

CAROLE: Done?

MOTHER: Shore. Something's gotta be done.

CAROLE: What?

MOTHER (*thinking*): Something. (*Decision*) Why don't you go and get yourself fixed up? He may show up yet.

CAROLE: No. You're right. I'm actin' like a schoolgirl. He's not coming tonight.

MOTHER: Stranger things have happened . . . somewhere.

CAROLE: I don't see the point.

MOTHER: Go on! Believing in it is the point. Give mama a kiss.

CAROLE: All right. (*Kisses her on cheek*) But I'm only going to have to take it all off again.

(*Carole exits upstairs*)

MOTHER: God. Wouldn't you know it? I believe her. I finally believe her. She's just like me. Damn all the Neros anyhow. (*Beat*) Well, if it's goin' to be that way, might's well see what I can do to help.

(*She goes to the closet and gets a sweater, then exits out front door. There is a moment of no one on stage, then Carole comes downstairs. She is now in a sexy dress but hasn't bothered with fixing her make-up*)

CAROLE: That's all he gets is the dress. He can just go to hell if he expects any more than the dress. (*She notices that she is alone*) Mama? (*Calls up the stairs*) Mama? (*She wanders around a bit, checks the closet door. There is a knock at the front door. Carole is immediately overwhelmed like a love struck teenager. She puts her hand to her heart*) Oh my. Oh my. Mama. He's here. Mama, he's come. (*Another knock*) Oh. Oh, I can't answer it. Mama, answer the door. Mama? (*Another knock*) Oh. (*Yells*) Come in! Come in!

(*Clay McCormick enters, very hesitant and shy*)

CLAY: Evening, Carole. I hope I'm not disturbin'.

CAROLE (*very disappointed*): Oh. Hello, Clay.

CLAY: I know it's late but I was travelin' back to town from my work and I saw your light was on, so . . . (*He looks at her dress*) you shore look lovely. I guess you must be busy dressed all up like that, huh?

CAROLE: Yes. No. I was dressed up for the person that was knocking at the door just now.

CLAY: Well, that was me.

CAROLE: I mean, the knock before you.

CLAY: Oh.

CAROLE: Did you knock only once?

CLAY: No, I knocked . . . I don't know. What? Three times?

CAROLE: I think I heard four.

CLAY: Could have been four.

CAROLE: Could be the first knock was someone else and the other three were yours.

CLAY: Could be.

CAROLE: So, he might have just left.

CLAY: Might have.

(*Carole bolts for the front door. Clay stays behind and watches her. After a moment, she comes back, lugging a vacuum cleaner and small satchel*)

CAROLE: I waited too long. He knocked and nobody came so he turned around and left.

CLAY: I'm sorry to hear that, Carole. But, if it will make you feel any better, I think that every knock you heard was probably pretty much just me.

CAROLE (*sighs*): I think so, too. (*Lights up briefly on stage right bar table. Billy is still sitting there but now Mother is standing above him, talking to him. Lights off. Back on main stage, Carole brandishes vacuum*) I found this on the porch outside.

CLAY: Oh, that's mine.

CAROLE: What's it doin' out there?

CLAY: Oh, you know. Thought I'd show it to you. This is my new job! (*Takes it from her*) Here. A little demonstration. It's not too late, is it? It won't take long. It's nothin' but a vacuum cleaner.

CAROLE: Shore. Why not? (*She sits on the couch*)

CLAY: Actually, forget what I just said. It's *not* nothin' but a vacuum cleaner. It's a hand-held industrial-strength air-filtration system. It has ten times the sucking power of your regular vacuum cleaner. It represents light years of scientific research in the field.

CAROLE: I'll bet.

CLAY: Made from a durable blend of neoprene and nylon, this space age wonder is practically indestructible. I could pound it on your coffee table there for two hours straight and it wouldn't even pick up a scratch.

CAROLE: Don't try it. Okay?

CLAY: On top of that, this little baby is so lightweight you could rock it to sleep in your arms, so quiet it could rock *you* to sleep in *its* arms and so powerful it can suck a golf ball through a pinhole the size of a . . . uh, pin. I memorized all that from the sales manual. You want to hear the full sales pitch?

CAROLE: Shore.

CLAY (*doing the pitch*): Good morning, ma'am. Am I addressing the lady of the house?

CAROLE: Fast forward the full sales pitch.

CLAY: Yes, ma'am. Um . . . (*He pulls out a bag of dust from the satchel*) Observe.

CAROLE: What is it?

CLAY: What do you think?

CAROLE: A bag of dust.

CLAY: Not just any dust. Specially designed, industrial-strength, heavy-duty, nuclear powered, radioactive dust custom-designed in our laboratories, guaranteed to be two hundred percent tougher than any dust you are likely to encounter in your own home.

CAROLE: Nuclear powered?

CLAY: Well, not really, Carole, but it sounds good, don'tcha think?

CAROLE: Two hundred percent tougher?

CLAY: Never mind that. A demonstration.

(*He starts pouring the dust on a spot on the rug stage left of the couch*)

CAROLE: Clay McCormick. You'd better know exactly what you're doin'.

CLAY: Well, of course I know what I'm doin'. What do you take me for? (*An expression crosses his face, unseen by Carole . . . a fervent prayer that it all works. He holds up electric plug from vacuum*) Outlet? (*Carole points to it. Clay walks over and plugs vacuum in, as he talks*) This little beauty is not only going to pick up that dust, it's going to pick up all the dust that your regular vacuum couldn't get. This one piece of floor is going to be so clean, it'll make the rest of the rug look like a filthy pit. A simple push of the button here . . . (*Clay keeps talking through the demonstration but we can't hear a word that he says because the machine is **very loud**. He runs it over the spot he has dirtied and is still talking as he turns the machine off*) showing you the power of modern science at work. (*He looks down at the dirty spot. It has not been cleaned. Carole looks down at it, too*) Er . . .

CAROLE: I thought you said it was quiet.

CLAY: Usually it's quiet. When it's loud, that's when you know it really works.

CAROLE: But it didn't work.

CLAY (*testy*): I can see that. (*Calmer*) I've been demonstrating all day. Maybe the bag is full.

CAROLE: If it's not going to work, it could at least have the courtesy to be quiet.

CLAY: The only way it's *completely* quiet is if you don't turn it on in the first place.

CAROLE: It'd do the same amount of work.

(*Clay starts tugging on the spot where the dust bag is kept. It appears to be stuck*)

CLAY: You can't expect it to work if the dust bag is full. It's a simple matter of removing this . . . (*tugs*) . . . uh . . . spill-proof attachment. Did I tell you about the spill-proof attachment? (*Tugs*) Uh . . .

CAROLE: Careful.

CLAY (*testy again*): I'm careful. Don't it look like I'm being careful? (*He pulls the bag out but it comes out with too much force and spills all over him. He falls backward and sits on the floor with a thud*) Told you the goddamn bag was full. (*Carole can't help herself. She laughs. Clay likes it. Smiles as he speaks*) Oh, now I'm funny. Well, we'll just see how funny I am after the hand-held, industrial strength air-filtration system cleans up everything here in sight.

CAROLE: If it wouldn't hold it all before, how's it goin' to hold it all this time around?

CLAY: Well . . . because this time, half of the dust has already worked its way into my pants, that's how.

CAROLE: Oh God. Your pants. Let me get something for them. I'll be right back. (*She exits into kitchen. Clay gets up, starts brushing dust off of himself and rubbing it into the rug with his foot. Offstage*) I'm bringing a wet cloth.

CLAY (*rubbing dirt into rug*): Fine.

(*Carole enters with rag that is soaking wet. She hands it to him. He starts using it on his pants, realizes how wet it is, and stops. He wrings it out a bit. A lot of water comes out of it. He looks at her*)

CAROLE: I didn't have time to wring it out.

(*Eye contact between the two. Carole, embarrassed, breaks it by looking away*)

CLAY: Carole . . .

CAROLE: What?

CLAY: This is a good job. Compared to all the other jobs I've had, this is a good one. The best. I'm makin' money.

CAROLE: I'm shore you are.

CLAY: Remember back in high school when we used to go out on dates?

CAROLE: You and me never went out together on dates.

CLAY: Well, we danced at the school dances, didn't we?

CAROLE: Maybe once or twice.

CLAY: Was that all it was? Once or twice? Maybe it seemed like more 'cause every time I danced with someone, I would pretend I was dancin' with you.

CAROLE: Well, you can't call that *my* fault.

CLAY: I didn't think of it as a fault atall! (*Beat*) Don't you like me even a little bit?

CAROLE: Of course I do, Clay. You're sweet.

CLAY: Just not as sweet as Billy Nero, is that it?

CAROLE: Don't let's bring Billy's name into this, all right?

CLAY: Well, I can't help but bring his name into this, Carole. Ever since I've known you, he's been right there.

CAROLE (*takes vacuum*): Show me how to use this, Clay. Do I push this little button right here?

CLAY: Though the way he ignores you most of the time, I don't know why you bother to care for him. I mean, Carole, after all . . . (*Carole turns on the vacuum. Clay keeps talking but we can't hear a word he says. Carole runs the vacuum over the dirty spot. She turns the vacuum off*) is that too much to ask? (*They both look down at the spot. It is as dirty as ever*) Damn! Let me see that. (*She passes vacuum to him. He turns it on briefly, runs it over the spot, turns if off, then angrily starts rubbing the dirt in with his foot*)

CAROLE: Don't do that, Clay!

(*Clay picks up the vacuum and shakes it. Billy Nero and Mother enter through front door. Billy is drunk*)

CLAY (*shaking vacuum*): You hunk of junk! Why don't you work?

BILLY: I ask mine the same thing all the time.

CAROLE (*like a schoolgirl again*): Oh. Billy. You came.

MOTHER: He was on his way here when I happened to run into him.

CAROLE: *You* ran into him? What were *you* doin' out?

MOTHER: Takin' a walk.

BILLY (*to Carole*): Tonight I started writing you a poem.

CAROLE (*very flattered*): Have you really? May I hear it?

BILLY (*clears throat; declaims*): Cottonwood snowflakes somersault in summer air. (*Pause*)

CAROLE: Yes?

BILLY: That's it. (*Beat*) I only just now started.

CAROLE: It's beautiful.

BILLY: The second line's going to be the best one yet. (*He plops himself down on the couch, holds his hands up like a spyglass and looks at everyone*) Ooof.

CAROLE: Have you been drinkin'?

BILLY: Uh-huh. (*Looks at Carole and Clay*) You keeping busy?

CAROLE: It's not what it looks to be.

BILLY: Oh, I don't care about that. I'm glad to see you with company. Seeing as I got too stupid and preoccupied to visit tonight. Until your mother . . .

MOTHER (*hastily finishes the sentence*): . . . bumped into him on his way here on the street.

CAROLE: On the street? You didn't get that mud all over your slippers by walkin' in the street. What'd you do, take the short-cut to town to drag him from the Cinnamon Club? What were you thinkin', Mama, out dressed like that? I thought you said before you were freezin'?

MOTHER: The walk warmed me up.

CAROLE (*sighs*): Come on. Let's clean you up before you catch your very death. (*To men*) Excuse us a moment. Billy, please don't go anywhere. I'll be right back.

(*Carole and Mother exit upstairs*)

CLAY (*frustrated; mocking, imitating*): "I've started writing you a poem." (*Exaggerated starry-eyed, hands together, breathless*) "Have you really?" (*Back to Billy imitation*) "The second line's going to be the best one yet."

BILLY (*ignores this, pulls out a flask*): Have you ever wondered what it's like to step out in front of a truck?

CLAY: Is that some sort of threat, Nero?

BILLY: No. (*Drinks. Offers flask*) Want some?

CLAY (*harsh*): No. (*Softer*) Thanks.

BILLY: If you change your mind, let me know. (*Drinks*) What's with the pants?

CLAY: What do you mean?

BILLY: Looks like you got filled full of love and couldn't hold back.

CLAY: Screw you.

BILLY (*shrugs, drinks*): What's with the sweeper?

CLAY: It's my new job. I sell them.

BILLY (*truly interested*): Do you really? Have many have you sold?

CLAY: I just started. (*Beat*) Maybe two or three.

BILLY: I'd like to sell sweepers for a living. Door to door. Right? Door to door.

CLAY: Oh, fine. Go ahead and make fun. Think you're such a bigshot.

BILLY: I'm not making fun. I mean it. Door to door, right? (*Acting out*) "Hello, ma'am. Are you the lady of the house?"

CLAY (*joins in*): "Nice home you have here."

BILLY (*continuing*): "Did you decorate it yourself? You did? Well, it has the look of a professional. Is that what you do for a living? No? Well, you certainly have the eye of a designer. Still, did you know that your concept, your whole well-thought-out comprehensive vision is being undermined by unseen activity happening right at your very feet?"

CLAY (*into it*): Good, good.

BILLY: "It is, ma'am. I assure you it is. Because dust settles, ma'am. Dust settles no matter what you try to do to prevent it. And the only place it has to go . . . is down."

CLAY: "Dust settles." I like that. Maybe you *should* be doin' this for a livin'.

BILLY: Unfortunately, I already have a job. It requires sitting around the house behind a big protective fence and saying, "Yes, daddy. No, daddy."

CLAY: That's a hard job to quit.

BILLY: Doesn't stop me from trying. (*Beat*) Imagine you decided to step out in front of a speeding truck. Suddenly there's a ton of unstoppable mindless metal bearing down on you with no place for you to run. I've always heard people say, when you get in situations like that, time seems to slow down, you can take in everything. But I bet it doesn't. I bet things move fast, like getting yourself caught in an avalanche. Movement. Sound. Snow. Weight. All around you. Overwhelming you. Pulverizing you. No time to think. But imagine you could stop time in that one instant. There. There's a group of people on the sidewalk all staring at you.

There's a woman screaming. There's someone actually laughing. Ashamed of it but laughing. Everyone's pointing. A cloud is starting to pass over the sun. What does it all feel like? Real death is coming. Not that goddamn play death that you feel when you put a gun in your mouth and fight your own muscles on the trigger. This is sure death. No escape. Full realization. What does that feel like?

CLAY (*overwhelmed*): Um . . . bad?

BILLY: Does it? (*Holds out flask*) Want some?

(*Clay takes the flask and takes a couple of big swigs. He realizes that he has overstepped the invitation*)

CLAY (*offers it back*): Sorry.

BILLY: No, no. Keep it. I've got another . . . somewhere. (*He searches pockets for the other flask as he talks*) I bet it feels right. I bet it all fits. Like coming to a sudden shock ending in a page-turner of a novel.

CLAY: I bet it hurts.

BILLY (*agrees*): Pain ruins everything. No doubt about that. But that second before it hit. If I could only capture that second in my mind, even if there's no time to write it down, I could be a *real* goddamn poet instead of the hack writer of crap that I've turned out to be. (*An expression on his face like he's captured that second, then it fades as he finds the flask. Pulls it out with a flourish*) Ah!

CLAY: All these years I've heard Carole say that your poems are the loveliest things.

BILLY (*opening flask*): Carole has always been very sweet to me about that.

CLAY: I wouldn't mind hearing one.

BILLY: Now *you're* making fun of *me*.

CLAY: No, I mean it. (*Beat*) Try me. (*Slight pause*)

BILLY: All right. (*Takes a swig, clears his throat, self-conscious, and recites*)

"There's a whisper in the wind; a soft breath.
If you stop thinking, you hear it.
If you stop hearing it, it's death.
Like an aroma that touches you, half-remembered, aroused.
Like a dream that flickers through you, half in sleep and drowsed.
It speaks to you when you're busy, distracts your purpose, storytells,
Reminds you of things forgotten, pulls your stray thoughts to it and jells."

(*Slight pause*)

It needs some work.

CLAY: No. It's good. I think I like it. (*Billy shrugs*) What's the whisper in the wind?

BILLY: That voice you get in your head, that doesn't sound like you, but's still part of you.

CLAY: Why, if you stop hearing it, is it death?

BILLY: If we're lucky, it finally falls silent when we're dead.

CLAY (*shivers*): Don't talk like that. Talk like that always gives me the willies.

BILLY: Well then, hell, have yourself a drink.

(*Clay and Billy both drink*)

CLAY: I didn't quite tell you the truth before. When I said the number of vacuum cleaners I've sold. It's none.

BILLY (*looks at Clay through his hands like telescope*): I'll buy one.

CLAY: Get out of here.

BILLY: I mean it. You just sold your first vacuum. Let's drink to it.

(*They each hold out their flasks and clink them together*)

CLAY: I don't get it. I mean, aren't we rivals?

BILLY: For what?

CLAY: For Carole.

BILLY: You really care about Carole.

CLAY: Since high school. But I can't replace you. She loves you.

BILLY: You think so?

CLAY: You know that voice in the head you were talkin' about? Mine says "Carole, Carole, Carole." That's all it ever says. (*Beat*) I'd do anything for her.

BILLY: I wish I could be like you.

CLAY: Like me?

BILLY: I'd like to think of Carole just exactly like you do. I'd love to worship her. I'd like to do nothing but pay attention to her. But I can't. Hell, I can't even go half a day without drinking when I want to.

CLAY: Well, I can't sell a vacuum cleaner.

BILLY: You just sold one.

(*Carole enters, looking flustered*)

CAROLE: I'm sorry. Billy, I'm sorry. I don't know what she was doin'. I put her to bed. (*She puts herself into Billy's arms, puts her head on his shoulder, and stays there. Clay gets very uncomfortable*) You feel good.

CLAY: Okay, well . . . (*Beat*) I got a full day in front of me tomorrow.

CAROLE (*remembers him*): Oh. Clay. Thanks so much for stopping by. (*She looks up and sees flask in Clay's hand*) Clay McCormick, are you drinkin'?

(*Clay looks at her, looks at the flask in his hand, looks at her*)

CLAY: (*embarrassed*): Yes.

CAROLE (*giggles*): That's the most life I've ever seen out of you. You should be ashamed of yourself.

CLAY (*big smile*): I am.

BILLY: I've never seen him more ashamed in my life.

(*A beat. Then Billy laughs, Clay laughs. Carole looks at both of them, surprised but pleased*)

CAROLE: Well, I must say, it's nice to see the two of you getting on so well. I admit that when I got Mama up to her room, I thought of the two of you together and I thought, "Oh my God, what in the world have I done." (*To Clay*) Thanks for being so nice to Billy tonight. (*She kisses Clay on the cheek. Clay is overwhelmed by this*) Good night.

CLAY (*flustered, very happy*): Good night. Thank you. I mean, you're welcome. Good night. (*He grabs up his vacuum and hauls it to the door with excited manic energy. He starts to leave but the vacuum is still plugged in. It tugs at him. He realizes it and unplugs it*) Good night. (*He exits. There is the sound of a crash, of Clay and his vacuum falling down the stairs. He speaks offstage*) I'm all right. Don't worry. Thank you. Good night. You're welcome. Good night.

BILLY: He's a good boy.

CAROLE: You got him drunk!

BILLY: Hell, he's not drunk.

CAROLE: He fell down the stairs!

BILLY: That's only 'cause that voice in his head gave out a big ol' rebel yell.

CAROLE: Meanin' what? Oh, never mind. Don't bother tellin' me. (*Beat*) Where have you been? I haven't seen you in ten days.

BILLY: I know it.

CAROLE: It wasn't so long ago, you couldn't wait to get over here. You used to take me to all those out-of-the-way cafes and such. Used to take me dancin'. It's been so long since you took me dancin', Billy. Now, when you're supposed to take me out, I'm lucky if you bother to show up. You go so much time without seeing me, I have to wonder if you even still care about me atall.

BILLY: Carole, I see you every day.

CAROLE: Where?

BILLY: At the grocery.

CAROLE: When?

BILLY: I watch you through the window. Yesterday, I watched you four times.

CAROLE: And you didn't come in?

BILLY: I didn't want to bother you when you're working.

CAROLE: You watch me when I'm workin'? I must just look awful.

BILLY: You don't look awful. There's nothing so beautiful as a woman who's working. The two most beautiful women in this town are you and Sally at the diner when the two of you are working. Women who don't work are just painted toys. Lap dogs. Give me sweaty hair hanging in the eyes with grease in the air over eye shadow and perfume any day.

CAROLE (*angry*): Well, how lovely for you! Did you ever stop to think that maybe I'd like to see you all those times you saw me?

BILLY: I wasn't in any condition for you to see me.

CAROLE: And don't you think that makes me just as much a toy up on some damn shelf even though I'm a sweaty one rather than a painted one?

BILLY: I didn't mean it to.

CAROLE: Well, fine, Billy. I thought we loved each other. Am I wrong? Tell me I'm wrong. People who love each other don't spy on each other through windows. Do they? (*Beat*) Maybe I've just been wasting my time. I mean, waiting for you to ask me to marry you. Are you ever going to ask me to marry you?

BILLY: I think I'd like to if I could trust myself to.

CAROLE: What does *that* mean? Clay McCormick would ask me in a second. In a *second*. Given the chance. You know he would. Maybe I should accept him.

BILLY: Maybe you should.

CAROLE: You don't mean that.

BILLY: Clay McCormick has plenty of things going for him. If I was a woman, I would marry Clay McCormick. If I was a different type of man, I would marry Clay McCormick.

CAROLE: I don't know why you're being so mean. I'm not asking you to propose this instant. I'm asking if you're ever goin' to propose to me atall. (*No answer*) Billy?

BILLY: Um?

CAROLE: I don't care about the money. Tell your daddy I don't care about the money.

BILLY: You think I care about the money? Fuck the money! You can have the money.

CAROLE: I don't want it.

BILLY: Neither do I.

CAROLE: Well, fine!

BILLY: Thanks so much for your permission!

CAROLE: Oh, you're so impossible. I hate you. I think I *will* marry Clay McCormick.

BILLY (*contrite; affected by her sadness*): Carole? (*Beat*) I'm sorry. (*Puts his hand on her shoulder. She shakes it off*) Would you like to go dancing?

CAROLE: Where?

BILLY: Right here. (*He takes her in his arms*)

CAROLE: There's no music.

BILLY: I'll make us some. (*They dance slowly, tight against each other. Billy hums a bit, then sings "I Got it Bad and That Ain't Good"*)

> "Never treats me sweet and gentle,
> The way he should.
> I got it bad and that ain't good."

CAROLE (*tight against him*): Ain't *that* the truth.

BILLY (*singing*):

> "My poor heart is sentimental,
> Not made of wood.
> I got it bad and that ain't good."

(*Carole leans up and kisses him. The kiss lasts for a good long while and is only ended when Billy suddenly breaks into a coughing fit. He pulls away from Carole, uses the back of the couch to hold himself up and coughs. Carole watches helplessly until the coughs subside*)

CAROLE: Are you all right?

BILLY: I'm fine. I'm fine. My stomach's a little upset.

CAROLE: Come with me. (*She takes him by the arm and starts to lead him up the stairs*)

BILLY: Where?

CAROLE: Shhh. To bed.

BILLY: I can't.

CAROLE: Yes.

BILLY: I can't. I can't. Carole, I can't.

CAROLE: Shh. Yes, you can. (*Beat*) You can.

(*They exit up the stairs. A moment later, Mother comes out on the landing of the stairs, dressed in robe and slippers. She comes downstairs, finds her glass, finds Billy's flask, pours some of Billy's liquor into her glass, sips, and wanders the room. She stops at the spot where Clay spilled dirt on the rug and, almost unconsciously, rubs at the spot with her foot, walks over to her chair, sits and shivers with cold. She closes her eyes and drifts off to sleep.*)

Scene Two—Eight Months Later

Prelude: *In stage left spot, Clay stands holding his vacuum cleaner, talking to an unseen customer. He is in rare form; confident, persuasive, and charming.*

CLAY: Did you decorate it yourself? You did? Well, it has the look of a professional. Is that what you do for a living? No? Well, you certainly have the eye of a designer. Still, did you know that your concept, your whole well-thought out comprehensive vision is being undermined by unseen activity happening right at your feet?

(*Crossfade to the main set where Mother is still asleep in her chair. Billy is on the couch, drinking directly from a bottle of Scotch. mother wakes up, looks at him, looks at her watch*)

MOTHER: It's five in the mornin'.

BILLY: I appreciate you letting me stay.

MOTHER: But you never sleep, far as I can tell. That can't be good for you.

BILLY: No, ma'am. It's not.

(*Pause. Billy drinks*)

MOTHER: It's so quiet. We might be the only two people awake in the whole town. Almost makes you feel responsible for them.

BILLY (*quoting*): "We see strange sights while others sleep."

MOTHER: Like standing guard.

BILLY: I'm more like avoiding the guard by becoming the guard. Like the wolf in sheep's clothing. Or the devil with powers to assume a pleasing shape.

(*He puts fingers up by his head signifying horns*)

MOTHER: I agree with the pleasing shape, hon, but I don't know about the rest of it. You're more like the sheep in *wolf's* clothing, seems to me.

BILLY (*still has fingers up*): What about the horns?

MOTHER: Wolves don't have horns.

BILLY: No, but goats do. That's what they call you when you blow the big game. That's a good description of me.

MOTHER: That name only sticks if you regret whatever it is you did to earn it.

BILLY: I do.

MOTHER: Enough to go back in time and change it? (*No answer*) I didn't think so. You're just like your father.

BILLY: Knew my father pretty well, did you, Mrs. Gilchrist?

MOTHER: Oh, yes. Worked for him at his oil fields. More than that. (*She holds up thumb and forefinger very close together*) I came this close to bein' your mother.

BILLY: But you aren't.

MOTHER (*laughs*): No, I aren't.

BILLY (*joking*): So, I guess I don't have to worry about Carole being my sister, then.

MOTHER: I said *you* weren't my son, I didn't say Carole wasn't *his* daughter.

BILLY (*brought up short*): Is she?

MOTHER: Course not. But I scared you for a second, didn't I?

BILLY: I've long since stopped being scared about anything.

MOTHER: Ah-huh.

BILLY: It wouldn't have made any difference. It's not what I wanted, anyhow.

MOTHER: I see. Just like your father. He never wanted any of the things he wanted, either.

BILLY: How do you mean?

MOTHER: Lucius Nero wanted to be a country and western singer, did you know that?

BILLY: No.

MOTHER: He wrote sad songs about broken marriages and finding strange underclothes in the laundry bin. Wanted to go to the Grand Ol' Opry and wear high-buttoned shirts all covered in rhinestones. Trade licks with Roy Acuff. Travel the country. Spend every night making love with me.

BILLY: I would not call that a description of my father.

MOTHER: I know. But that was him. That's what he wanted.

BILLY: What did *you* want?

MOTHER: Oh . . . him, I guess. Not that I expected him. This was before he struck oil but he still seemed like a rich man to me. I was just trailer-trash. You never expected much when you were trailer-trash. Course, I was damn good-lookin' trailer-trash.

BILLY: How good-looking were you?

MOTHER: Better looking than Carole. Mothers are always better looking than their daughters. That's why we all lose our looks when we get old, you know. Otherwise the young ones would never stand an even chance.

BILLY: Do you think he loved you?

MOTHER: Oh, shore. That was the problem.

BILLY: How so?

MOTHER: The minute Lucius wanted anything, he started to worry what it would feel like if he didn't get it. The only way to stop that feeling from happenin' was to decide you didn't want it in the first place. And he definitely wanted me.

BILLY: That's nothing at all like me. When I want something, I want it.

MOTHER: But do you go and get it? (*No answer*) My husband Joe went and got it. But he didn't appreciate it. I used to think if I could combine Lucius and Joe into one person, I'd really have something. But then he'd just spend all day having fights with himself and Joe's looks would only ruin Lucius'.

BILLY: My father's looks?

MOTHER: Oh, he was a good-lookin' man. A good-lookin' man. You look almost exactly like him.

BILLY: Old Lucius?

MOTHER: He wasn't so old then. You could be him maybe thirty years ago.

BILLY: That doesn't make me look forward to my future.

MOTHER: Why not? That doesn't mean you have to end up like him. Time does different things to different people. (*Billy starts nodding off to sleep*) You can go use a bed, Billy.

BILLY: I'm fine.

MOTHER: Go use Carole's bed. She won't mind.

BILLY: Uh-uh. The last time I was there, I threw up in it.

MOTHER: You couldn't have turned her against you any better if you tried.

BILLY: I told her that night my stomach was upset.

MOTHER: I've always wondered. *Did* you try?

BILLY: What?

MOTHER: To turn her against you. *Did* you try?

(Offstage, there are sounds of giggling and shushing. The happy voices of Carole and Clay, trying to find the key, trying to keep quiet. "Don't wake her." Where's the key?" "Okay, ready?" and other such ad-libs as this. The door opens. Clay comes in, carrying Carole across the threshold. Clay holds Carole such that he can't see much of anything)

CLAY: Ta-daaa!

CAROLE *(giggling)*: Quiet, Clay. You'll wake her!

MOTHER: I'm awake already, dear . . .

CAROLE: Mama! What are you doing up?

CLAY: What's goin' on?

CAROLE: Mama's already up.

(Clay maneuvers so he can see Mother)

CLAY: Oh hi, Mrs. Gilchrist. Isn't it a little early to be up?

MOTHER: Aren't you a little early gettin' back? You were supposed to be gone 'til the day after tomorrow.

CAROLE: We got homesick.

CLAY: Wanted to sleep in our own bed.

(*He nuzzles, tickles Carole. She acts like she wants to get away from it but she clearly loves it*)

CAROLE: Stop it!

CLAY (*nuzzling*): Grrrr!

CAROLE (*laughing*): Stop it. Clay McCormick, you stop it!

(*He stops. She sighs*)

CLAY: Carole started to worry that you might be gettin' lonely.

MOTHER: Oh, I'm not lonely.

(*She glances over at Billy, Carole follows her gaze and sees him. Immediately, her manner changes. She is self-conscious and no longer happy in Clay's arms*)

CAROLE: Oh my. Clay! Put me down.

CLAY (*oblivious*): What?

(*She swats him in the back*)

CAROLE: Put me down!

(*Clay puts her down. She smooths out her clothes*)

BILLY: Hello, Carole.

CAROLE: Hello, Billy.

(*Clay finally realizes that Billy is there. He is not happy*)

CLAY (*nods at him, stern*): Nero.

BILLY: Clay. (*Holds out hand to shake*) Congratulations.

CLAY (*wary, shakes hands*): Thank you.

BILLY: Carole. Congratulations.

(*He gives her a chaste kiss on her cheek*)

CAROLE: Thank you.

BILLY: So . . . I hear you've been selling vacuum cleaners, Clay.

CLAY: Yessir. Air-filtration systems. That's true. Using the same speech you used when we sat and talked about it that night.

BILLY: Works for you?

CLAY (*nods*): Couldn't be better. Been plannin' to thank you.

BILLY: Glad to hear it. (*Awkward pause*) Well, it's almost time to get my breakfast at the diner.

MOTHER: You're not goin' to leave me, Billy, are ya?

BILLY: I thought, with Carole and Clay already back . . .

CAROLE: You don't have to leave on our account. Oh! Clay. Our bags are still outside. Could you go and bring our bags in?

CLAY: Shore thing.

(*Clay exits*)

CAROLE (*waits until Clay is gone*): Billy, I just wanted to say I'm sorry the way I threw you out that night when you got sick and how I wouldn't let you see me after that. I know it looks like I married Clay out of spite but I didn't. Okay, I admit I went out with him that first time out of spite but after that spite didn't enter into it. I swear it didn't. It was a serious decision. I thought about it long and hard. (*Clay enters with bags and hears the end of this*) But I wanted to let you know, in spite of it, that I *do* still love you.

(The others become aware that Clay is in the room. They all look embar-rassed, not knowing what to do or say)

CLAY *(forced normality)*: Right. I'll put the bags in our room, okay, honey-bun?

CAROLE: I'll be right up to join you, Clay Bear.

CLAY: There's no hurry. You can spend time with Billy if you want.

CAROLE: Oh no. Don't worry. I'm comin' right up. *(Carole looks long-ingly at Billy. Then, as if making the final choice in this matter, she heads for the stairs)* 'Scuse us. *(She exits up the stairs)*

BILLY: You know, they say a bullet enters your brain so fast, you don't even have time to think before you're in another world. You hear a sound . . . it could be thunder . . . could be a mosquito . . . something from else-where . . . like you never had your finger on the trigger at all.

MOTHER: I'm going up, too. Can I get you anything?

BILLY: No, I'm leaving myself. Getting breakfast.

MOTHER: You know, Billy, you should never regret what you wouldn't do differently. You would have never asked her yourself, would you? *(Billy doesn't answer. He puts his hands up to his eye, like a spyglass, and looks at her)* Just like your father.

(She exits. Billy waits until he is certain she is gone, then he hits himself harshly, alternating hands, around his chest and shoulders)

BILLY: Stupid sonofabitch! Stupid sonofabitch! Dumb, dumb, dumb, dumb, dumb!

Scene Three—Ten Months Later

Prelude: *A chair stage right. Billy enters carrying a handgun. He sits in the chair, makes himself comfortable, gets a good grip on the gun, breathes in deeply, and puts the barrel of the gun in his mouth. He holds his breath, giv-ing off little frightened grunts. His hands tremble and his finger tightens on* *the trigger. But he can't do it. With a loud exhalation of breath, he brings the gun down to his lap. He is both disgusted with himself and relieved. He pants with passing fear.*

   Crossfade to the main set to a tableux of Mother asleep in her chair, and Carole plugging in the vacuum cleaner, her back to the audience. Billy sets the gun down on the chair and walks into the set. He collapses on the couch, asleep. The scene starts. Carole turns on the vacuum and turns to the audience, showing that she is nearly nine months pregnant. She vacuums over the spot where the dust was spilled. It doesn't seem to work. She holds the vacuum end up to her hand to feel if it works. Then, she takes it over and tries it on Billy's head. He keeps sleeping, brushes it away as if it's a mosquito. Carole persists and Billy wakes up. Carole turns off the vacuum.

CAROLE: If this thing worked as advertised, your head would be in the dust bag now.

BILLY: Might be just the experience I'm looking for. What time is it?

CAROLE: After noon. (*Billy sits up with a struggle and holds his head*) Another hard drinkin' night last night?

BILLY: So hard it's easy.

CAROLE: Seems like you've given up even on your poetry these days.

BILLY: I'm still working on that love poem I was writing for you. I thought I even had a few new lines to add to that first one . . . but they didn't turn out to be any good.

CAROLE: That's sweet, Billy, but you don't have to write that poem for me any more.

BILLY: Why not?

CAROLE: Because I'm married, that's why not. Because I'm going to have a baby.

BILLY: So?

CAROLE: So, I don't think it's appropriate. I don't think it's so good that you sleep every night here on the couch, either, do you?

BILLY: I've been specially invited by your mother.

CAROLE: I know. But still. Maybe you shouldn't.

(*Clay enters through front door. He is in a foul mood*)

CLAY: Does everybody in this damn county have a vacuum cleaner they can't bear to part with instead of buying the hand-held, supersonic air filtrator 500?

BILLY: I'll buy one.

CLAY: You don't want another one. I already sold you two.

CAROLE: No luck today?

CLAY: Why would anybody rather hang onto their brokedown ol' Hoover that's just pushin' the dirt around when they could have this space-age little wonder for four easy payments of $39.95?

CAROLE: They're comfortable with what they got, I guess.

CLAY: How can they be when those ol' beaters don't work? This baby *works*. Don't it? (*Beat*)

CAROLE: Shore.

CLAY: Suck a golf ball through a pinhole.

BILLY: But it won't suck up a whiskey-soaked head.

CLAY: What's that supposed to mean?

BILLY: Carole used it to try to suck up my head.

CLAY: Is that all you two do all day? Try to suck each other? (*Billy stifles a laugh*) It ain't funny, Billy. What do you think it's doin' to you . . . nothing to do all day . . . no job to get to in the mornin'?

BILLY: I got plenty of money.

CLAY: I'm not talkin' about money. I'm talkin' about peace of mind. Sense of worth. You want to sleep on this couch till you're eighty?

CAROLE: I already told him he can't spend every night here any more.

CLAY: Why can't he?

CAROLE: You want him to?

CLAY: If he's got no place else to go.

CAROLE: He's got a twenty-room mansion! He's got enough money to buy a house of his own! (*She grabs her stomach*) Oh! He kicked.

CLAY: He did?

CAROLE: Oh! He kicked again! Hurry. Come here! Feel him! Feel him!

(*She takes Clay's hands and puts them on her stomach*)

CLAY: I don't feel anything.

CAROLE: There! He kicked again! He's kicking! Don't you feel him?

CLAY: I don't feel anything.

CAROLE (*pulls Clay's hands away*): That's it. He's stopped.

BILLY (*as if conversation was never interrupted*): I don't think any peace of mind would come from me trying to get a job. No one would hire me, anyway. Carole's right. I've got enough money to buy anything I want and everybody knows it.

CLAY: Maybe so, but you need to pursue something.

BILLY: I'm too busy *being* pursued to pursue something. You ever had that feeling? That something is following you, right there behind you, dogging you step by step? There's a soft growl just behind your left ear. Some sort of tickle, a little muggy breathing on your neck. Could be it's nothing. Could be a dry breeze carrying with it the echo of a far-distant growl. You want to turn around and grab it but you're too afraid it's waiting for you to turn so it can surprise you and grab *you*. So, you never turn to look and you never know if it's really there.

CLAY: But what if it *is* just the dry breeze after all?

CAROLE: I wish you'd take this kind of talk outside. I don't want you to wake up Mama.

MOTHER (*eyes stay closed*): I'm awake.

CAROLE: There. You see? Didn't I tell you?

MOTHER: No, I haven't been sleeping. Not with the vacuum goin'. Just resting.

(*Carole puts her finger over her lips to get the others to keep quiet*)

CAROLE: All right, Mama.

MOTHER: It's cold. I think the graveyard won't be any colder than I am right now.

CAROLE: All right, Mama.

(*Slight pause*)

CLAY (*decides to get to it*): Well, I'm going to get a little something to eat and then have a lie-down before I go out and get back in the workin' world. (*To Carole*) Join me in bed, sweetie?

CAROLE (*pats her belly*): Too pregnant.

BILLY: Too drunk.

MOTHER: Too old.

CLAY: Okay, then.

(*He exits into kitchen*)

BILLY: I don't see you at the check-out line any more.

CAROLE: I'm on maternity leave.

BILLY: The baby isn't even born yet.

CAROLE: Any day now.

BILLY: I miss seeing you. Women working are beautiful but *pregnant* women working are about as beautiful as you can get.

CAROLE: I will never understand you. Maybe if I'd got pregnant before-hand you'd have gotten around to askin' me to marry you. Maybe if I'd knocked a few teeth out and rubbed dirt on my face, we'd have eloped right there on the spot. (*She sits on the couch to relieve her back. The baby kicks*) Oh. There he kicked again. Want to feel him?

BILLY: Okay.

CAROLE: Put your hand here. (*She puts Billy's hand on her stomach. He sits on the couch to do it. Clay comes out of the kitchen, munching on a sandwich. Neither of them see him*) Feel him?

BILLY (*surprised and impressed*): Yeah. Yeah! I think I hear something, too.

CAROLE: He moves around sometimes. (*She steers his head down to her belly*) Listen. You hear anything?

BILLY: Uh-huh.

CAROLE: What is it?

BILLY: I think he's trying to tell me the second line of my poem.

CAROLE (*smile*): I bet he could. (*She lets him lie there for a few moments*) Okay, up. (*He doesn't move*) Billy? (*Beat*) You can get up. (*Billy snores. He is sound asleep*) Oh, for . . . Just like old times. (*She shakes him*) Billy. (*Beat*) Billy. (*Then, a jolt in her belly*) Oh. (*A contraction*) OH! Oh, oh, oh, oh. Clay! I think the baby's comin'! Clay! Clay! Clay! Clay! The baby's coming!!!!!

(*Clay watches, munching on his sandwich, but does not move. Mother opens her eyes but she doesn't move, either. Billy keeps sleeping.*)

Scene Four—Three Weeks Later

Prelude: *In stage left spot. The table at the Cinnamon Club. There is a pen, a piece of paper, and two drinks on the table. Billy sits down, picks up the pen and starts writing. He is inspired, writing quickly. Mother enters behind him, leans over and kisses him on the cheek as he writes. He stands up, holds her chair for her. She sits, then he sits. He hands her one of the drinks, does a bit more writing, then stands up again with paper in hand. He reads to Mother.*

BILLY: Cottonwood snowflakes somersault in summer air.

(She gives him her rapt attention. Crossfade to the main set where Carole is on the couch, no longer pregnant. Her baby is in her hands. The baby is played by a doll. She speaks playfully to him)

CAROLE: "Hello, sweetie. Mama's here, sweetie."

(Clay comes through the kitchen and stops to tickle the baby under the chin)

CLAY: Cootchy, cootchy, cootchy, coo.

CAROLE: You keep that up, you'll put a permanent divot in his chin.

CLAY: It'll be good for him. Girls like a good divot in the chin.

CAROLE: Not *this* girl.

CLAY: Hell, you're the mother. You don't count when you're talkin' 'bout *girls*.

CAROLE: Can't I count for at least the first month of his life?

CLAY: Okay, fair enough. You got one more week to go. (*Tickles again*) Hey, Clay. You're Clay, Junior. Did you know that? You're named after your daddy. Did you know that? Do you like bein' Clay Junior or would you rather have your own name all to yourself? You can't decide? Well, you don't have to decide. Your daddy decided for you.

CAROLE: Don't know why you insisted on naming him Clay, Junior. I thought you hated your name.

CLAY: It's all right.

CAROLE: You liked it well enough to give it to somebody else.

CLAY: Hell, Carole, if *my* daddy had cared enough to want to name me after himself, I'd have been as proud as can be and *his* name was Wilmont. It's not the name itself that's important. It's the knowing that someone was proud enough of you to name you with their own name, which is the most precious thing they've got. Proud enough to tell the world that this is their very own son. That's what it's all about.

CAROLE: Well, then, does the proud papa want to hold his proud son?

CLAY: You bet. (*She passes the baby to him. He tickles it under the chin*) Cootchy, cootchy. Look at him watchin' me. Isn't that cute? He's watchin' his daddy. Look at those big bright blue eyes.

CAROLE: Aren't they beautiful?

CLAY: They are the bluest things I've very seen. Look at them. How'd he ever get eyes that blue?

CAROLE: Babies are like that.

CLAY: *Your* eyes aren't blue.

CAROLE (*joking*): Don't rub it in.

CLAY: Neither are mine.

CAROLE: I still love you, though.

CLAY: How come *his* are?

CAROLE: It happens sometimes.

CLAY: When the parents don't have 'em?

CAROLE: Uh-huh. Sometimes the blue don't even stay. It turns as he gets older.

CLAY: Turns to what?

CAROLE: Some other color.

CLAY: Since when?

CAROLE: It happens.

CLAY: Really?

CAROLE: Really.

(*Clay looks at her, then at the baby*)

CLAY: Look at that nose on him.

CAROLE: What about it?

CLAY: It's familiar.

CAROLE: Clay, he's three weeks old. That nose is about the size of a tic-tac.

CLAY: It's not *my* nose.

CAROLE: Stop it, please. This is *your* son.

CLAY (*defensive*): I know it.

CAROLE: All right, then. (*She hands him a baby bottle*) Here. Why don't you feed him?

(*He takes the bottle, tilts it up to the baby's mouth, looks, takes it away, tilts it up again*)

CLAY (*joking*): Hey, you put a bottle to his lips, you know who he looks like?

CAROLE: Who?

CLAY (*looks again, not joking now*): Goddamnit. He does look an awful lot like him at that.

CAROLE: What are you talkin' about?

CLAY: Look at him. Looks like a baby goat sucking away at that bottle. There's only one other person in the world that *I* know of who can suck at a bottle like that.

CAROLE: Oh, for God's sake, will you stop it?

CLAY: Don't tell me that nose isn't familiar. That's a Billy Nero nose if I've ever seen it.

CAROLE: That tiny little thing?

CLAY: Tiny? Are you kidding? Looks like a goddamn snout.

CAROLE: Clay, listen to me, will you listen to me?

CLAY (*still looking at baby*): What?

CAROLE: This *can't* be Billy's son. It can only be *your* son. I am married to *you.*

CLAY: I know it.

CAROLE: I know you've been worried about Billy and me but there's no need. I am married to you. Not to Billy. To *you*. You're the only one I'd be with. Understand?

CLAY: Yes.

CAROLE: I mean it.

CLAY: I know you do.

CAROLE: Then cut it out before I start to feel insulted.

CLAY: I'm sorry. I don't know what I was sayin'. Just worries. Stupid pointless worries. (*Beat*) I love you.

CAROLE: I love you, too.

(*Clay kisses her*)

CLAY: Wanta take the baby?

CAROLE: Uh-hmmm. It's time I put him down for his nap. (*She takes the baby*) Come on, sweetheart. Come on, little Clay. Mommy's goin' to have you take a nap. (*Carole exits*)

CLAY (*scoffs*): My son. If that little blue-eyed goat is my son, I swear to God I'll eat 'im.

(*Fade to black*)

ACT II

Scene One—One Month Later

Prelude: *In stage right spot. Billy in his chair at home, holding his gun. He looks at it, looks away, looks at it. Then, summoning up his nerve, he takes a deep breath, puts the gun in his mouth and holds it there.*

Crossfade to the main set where Carole is standing, Mother is in her chair, and baby is in a bassinet. Carole and Mother are arguing.

CAROLE: I don't like it.

MOTHER: You've made that abundantly clear, dear.

CAROLE: It's not healthy.

MOTHER: If you say so.

CAROLE: I *do* say so. What are you two tryin' to prove?

MOTHER: I understand if you're jealous.

CAROLE: I'm not jealous!

MOTHER: Course you aren't. You only would have married him if he'd asked you.

CAROLE: Well, I beg your pardon, but a lot's changed since then. And what makes you so high-and-mighty about the whole thing, anyway? *You* aren't goin' to marry him.

MOTHER: How do *you* know?

CAROLE: *Are* you goin' to marry him?

MOTHER: Of course not. We just go out together. Doesn't that make you relieved?

CAROLE: Frankly, it does. I haven't had any idea how far the two of you were intendin' to take this.

MOTHER: Why do you care?

CAROLE: Because the two of you are not good for each other and you know it. It's all just playtime, anyway. You're pretending that he's his own father and he's pretending that you're really me.

MOTHER: Don't fool yourself, Carole. We know who each other is all right.

CAROLE: Plus he's started you drinkin'.

MOTHER: Ah-huh.

CAROLE: He has!

MOTHER: Sweetheart, I was already doing that.

CAROLE: Not like this.

MOTHER: No, before I drank because I felt sad, old, and alone. Now I drink because I'm feelin' young and havin' fun.

CAROLE: Spare me.

MOTHER: I spare you every night I go out to the Cinnamon Club. Spare you the sight of your poor old mother out on the town, dinin', dancin', having fun with the richest man in town like I once could have been while you're at home just like I was thirty-some years ago with a child and a stick-in-the-mud husband who's too tired from work to go anywhere.

CAROLE: I can't see for the life of me how all this started to happen. You used to sit around like you were at death's door. I could hardly get you out of that chair. Now, you're hardly ever in it.

MOTHER: Well, you wouldn't let Billy stay over. I had to meet him some-place else.

(*A knock on the door*)

CAROLE: Oh, Lord. Who's that now?

MOTHER: Billy.

CAROLE: What's *he* doin' here?

MOTHER: I invited him over.

CAROLE: And he came over, just like that?

MOTHER: Well, he's got no reason to be late with me. (*Another knock*) Will you answer the door for me, sweetheart?

CAROLE: All right. I give up. (*She answers the door. Billy is there, very drunk*) Billy.

BILLY: Carole.

CAROLE: You're stinkin' drunk.

BILLY: I'm afraid I am. (*To Mother*) Mrs. Gilchrist. Sorry I'm late.

CAROLE: Oh, so you're late. Exactly how late are you?

BILLY: I don't know. About . . . (*Slight pause*)

MOTHER: Three hours.

CAROLE: Three hours! I thought he had no reason to be late with you, Mama.

MOTHER: The difference is, *I* don't mind when he's late.

BILLY: I wonder if you could take me over to see the baby?

CAROLE: The baby?

MOTHER: I invited him to see the baby.

CAROLE: You did?

MOTHER: The boy is two months old and hasn't had a visit from his Uncle Billy. He didn't want to come even now. I had to practically force him to come.

CAROLE: He doesn't have to come if he doesn't want to come.

MOTHER: He thinks he's not welcome here any longer.

CAROLE: He's not welcome to spend all day and night on the couch. He's welcome to come and visit the baby.

BILLY: So, it's all right if I see him, then?

CAROLE: Of course.

MOTHER (*up and very frisky, she leads Billy*): Over here, Billy. There's the little gentleman.

(*Billy looks for a bit*)

BILLY: He's cute. Looks like Clay.

MOTHER (*lifts baby up*): Come here, little fella. That's a good boy. (*Beat*) Put out your arms, Billy. You're goin' to hold him.

CAROLE: I'm not sure that's such a good idea.

MOTHER: Why not?

CAROLE: Because he's drunk.

BILLY: I'm always drunk.

MOTHER: That's true, Carole. He's got a point there. (*To Billy*) Put out your arms.

BILLY: I don't know how to do it.

MOTHER: Everybody knows how to do it, Billy. It's a instinct. (*She puts baby in Billy's arms. He is very stiff, unnatural. Carole is not pleased about it*) There. Don't that feel natural?

CAROLE: Mama, may I please speak to you over here for a minute?

(*She drags Mother over to other side of the room*)

MOTHER (*while going with Carole*): Rock him a little, Billy. That's it.

(*During Mother/Carole talk, Billy starts rocking baby, loses control of baby, and bobbles him, almost dropping him*)

CAROLE: What is the point of this whole sorry exercise?

MOTHER: I don't know what you mean, dear.

CAROLE: Why is this drunk man in *my* house holdin' *my* baby?

MOTHER: I thought you'd appreciate it. Wasn't so long ago, you'd have given anything to have Billy Nero in the house taking care of your baby.

CAROLE: Not any more. (*She looks over. Billy has just gotten things under control. As soon as she turns away, he starts fumbling again*) Everything okay?

BILLY: Fine. Fine.

MOTHER: Thirty years ago, if I could have had Lucius Nero visit me and hold *you* as a baby, it would have made all the difference to me in the world.

CAROLE: Mama, this is not Lucius Nero.

MOTHER: And this is not your house, either. Not yet, in spite of all you've been sayin'.

CAROLE: You want me to move out?

MOTHER: No. Course not. I'm just tired of bein' treated like I'm already dead. I'm not dead. I know it looked like I was for a while there but I'm not. And I'm not just Carole's mother, either. Not just the one who gets pushed aside while everyone else pays attention to you. Billy's brought me out of all that. He talks to me and pays attention to me because I'm me. We are good for each other. I inspire him. He's even done some things for me that he never could do for you. Something so lovely, so wonderful . . .

(*Billy has gotten control of the baby again*)

BILLY: Now, now. We promised we weren't ever going to mention that.

(*Carole looks over at him. When she looks away, he tries to switch the baby's head over to his other arm and fumbles again. It gets so bad that, at the end, the baby is hanging down head-first, with Billy desperately hanging onto the baby's feet*)

MOTHER: He's right. He's right. We promised.

CAROLE: What did you promise?

MOTHER: The point is, without Billy, I might as well have been dead. I wasn't good for anything else.

CAROLE: That's not true, Mama.

MOTHER: What did you think I was good for? Nothing. Shivering and complaining. I said it so often you'd say it with me at the same time.

BOTH (*simultaneously, with Carole saying it as if finally understanding Mother's point*): "I think the graveyard won't be any colder than I am right now."

MOTHER: Your own mama talkin' 'bout bein' cold in the graveyard and you don't even blink. You sing along! What does that tell me about what you think I am?

CAROLE: Oh, honey, I'm so sorry. I never meant it like that. (*She hugs her mother*) Of course you can go out and have fun. Of course you can have Billy come over and visit the baby. God knows I don't want you sittin' around waitin' to die. But you must know it never pays to depend on the likes of Billy Nero. He may have all the best intentions in the world, he may even want to make you happy, but the minute your back is turned, he's just as likely to do something that will completely break your heart. (*She turns and looks at him. Billy is struggling with the baby, holding onto him by his feet. Carole is immediately outraged. She leaps into action*) Are you crazy!!!!???

BILLY: Hang on. I've almost got it worked out.

(*Carole grabs her baby back and slaps Billy in the face*)

CAROLE: What is *wrong* with you?!

BILLY: I'm drunk.

MOTHER: It's no secret, sweetheart.

BILLY: I'm not so sure it's a good idea letting a well-known drunk handle your baby, do you?

CAROLE (*comforting baby*): Oh, shut up.

MOTHER: He's right. That's probably the sad reality.

CAROLE: Both of you, shut up. Don't talk to me about reality. I'm the only one who's ever concerned with reality. The rest of you . . . you're livin' in some . . . goddamn . . . (*she is too angry to speak*) oooohhhhh!

(*She storms out through front door, taking the baby with her*)

BILLY: That could have gone better.

(*He bends over, hands on knees*)

MOTHER: Are you goin' to be sick?

BILLY: No. Lately, I . . . I can't seem to get my breath. Lungs are all pickled or something. (*Laughs*) Put me in a jar, I'll last forever. Like radioactive waste. (*He gets wobbly*) Shit. Whole house is shaking.

MOTHER: Sit down. Breathe deep. (*He sits on couch, head back. Mother stands behind him, stroking his hair with her hand*) Better?

BILLY: Little bit.

MOTHER: I don't know what got into you, anyway, comin' over as loaded as this.

BILLY: Couldn't help it. Got some bad news.

MOTHER: What news?

BILLY: I'm engaged.

MOTHER: You are? To who?

BILLY: My very own lapdog. Bleached blonde and skinny. Overly pampered. Yapping often and endlessly.

MOTHER: I see.

BILLY (*looks at her through his "spyglass"*): Daddy wants an heir. Heir of the lapdog that bit him. (*Laughs, which causes his head to hurt. He grabs his head*) Ow! Daddy *insists* that I marry. Doesn't want me to come around here any more.

MOTHER: That man.

BILLY (*starts to sag*): Feels like all the blood is pooling on one side of my head.

MOTHER: What's her name?

BILLY (*waves it off*): Amanda Something-or-other. Big bewildered eyes. Nose so small it looks like it's pointed inward. Thinks money existed before people. Thinks it's a Newtonian law. Just there to breed the next line of Neros. As if I want any little hamsters in diapers. (*Beat*) Damn, but I feel heavy.

(*He slides off the couch right onto the floor, unconscious. Mother runs over to him*)

MOTHER: Billy! Are you all right? Can you hear me? Can you sit up? Oh! I'll get help! I'll call an ambulance. Don't move! I'll be right back!

(*She runs into kitchen. Billy comes to and sits up with his back against the bottom of the couch. Soon after, Carole enters from the front door, holding the baby. She sees Billy sitting there and stops at the entrance, looking at him. The baby starts to cry*)

BILLY (*does not look around*): Shhhh! Don't cry, baby. Beautiful baby. Uncle Billy is here. Uncle Billy is here. Shhhh. Don't cry. Shhhh. Don't cry.

Scene Two—Eight Years Later

Prelude: In stage left spot. Clay is behind the wheel of his car. The car is represented by a chair and, perhaps, a steering wheel.

CLAY (*practicing*): Still, did you know that your concept, your compre . . . well-thought . . . your whole well-thought out vision is being undermanned by unseen . . . under*mined* by unseen comprehensive . . . (*Gives up*) son of a bitch. (*He pulls out the flask previously given to him by Billy and drinks*) Son of a bitch. (*Beat. He sings*) "Show me the way to go home."

(*Crossfade to the main set where Billy, also holding a flask, sits on the couch and drinks*)

BILLY (*picks up the song from Clay*): "I'm tired and I want to go to sleep."

(*Clay joins Billy on the set*)

BOTH (*singing*): "I had a little drink about an hour ago."

BILLY (*looking at flask*): Shit, was that already an hour ago?

(*Clay, drunk, laughs. Billy laughs. The laughs subside and they get somber*)

CLAY: I can't sell shit any more.

BILLY: Why not?

CLAY: I can't remember how to do it.

BILLY: Sure you can.

CLAY: No. The patter. I don't remember the patter.

BILLY: You remember it.

CLAY: No.

BILLY: You just don't concentrate, is all.

CLAY: What do you mean by that?

BILLY: What?

CLAY: What's the story with that?

BILLY: With concentrating?

CLAY: Yeah.

BILLY: I don't know. I wasn't concentrating. (*They laugh*) Your mind is too full of distractions.

CLAY: Yours is not?

BILLY: My mind is focused . . . stream-lined . . . pure. Two hundred proof.

CLAY: I don't know how we survive, I swear to God I don't. Not on my salary and commissions. Commissions. What commissions? Even with Carole promoted to manager, we got to be spendin' more than we're able to bring in.

BILLY: Carole's no longer working at the check-out line?

CLAY: Those days are gone.

BILLY: Too bad. (*Holds up flask*) To the days at the check-out line.

(*They clink flasks and drink*)

CLAY: To the check-out line. (*Beat*) What's this about the check-out line?

BILLY: I loved Carole at the check-out line. (*Beat*) I loved Carole everywhere.

CLAY: Me, too. (*Holds up flask*) To loving Carole everywhere. (*They clink flasks and drink*) I've never been able to take care of her the way that you would have.

BILLY: I never took care of her at all.

CLAY: I'm almost startin' to think I'm never goin' to sell another vacuum cleaner.

BILLY: I'll buy one.

CLAY: I've sold you three in the last four months, Billy.

BILLY: I could always use another.

CLAY: If they're broke, you should use your warranty.

BILLY: They're not broke.

CLAY: Then why buy another one?

BILLY: Well . . . it a pretty big house. (*Clay laughs, almost spitting out his drink. Billy chuckles with him. The laugh subsides*) I mean it.

CLAY: It's charity. I don't want your charity.

BILLY: It's not charity.

CLAY: Well, what is it, then? Child support? Cause if it's child support, you can go fuck yourself. (*Beat*) Sorry.

BILLY: Forget it. (*Holds up flask*) To fucking yourself.

CLAY: To fucking yourself.

(*They clink flasks and drink*)

BILLY: It's the only kind of fucking I ever do.

CLAY: Don't give me that.

BILLY: Ask Carole. Ask Amanda.

CLAY: Ask 'em what?

BILLY: Ask Amanda what it was like being married to me. Five years. Came and went so fast, I've had binges that felt like they lasted longer.

CLAY: Probably have.

(*They both laugh a bit*)

BILLY: She was no prize. You should have been with her in bed. It was like she had no damn bones at all. Lying on her was like sleeping on a waterbed.

CLAY (*holds up flask*): To sleeping on a waterbed.

(*They clink flasks and drink*)

BILLY: Of course, it's all my fault, really. The old man was furious. The whole reason for the marriage was to have kids. We weren't going to have kids in a million years.

CLAY: Did you try? (*Silence from Billy. Clay polishes off his flask. He holds it out, mouth down, to let the last dribble onto the floor*) I'm out. (*Billy holds a finger up, as in "watch this." He leans under the couch, feels underneath, almost falls over, comes up with a fifth of some liquor, hands it to Clay*) I guess it's true what they say. You *do* have booze hidden all over town.

BILLY: That place wouldn't have worked if anyone had bothered to use the vacuum cleaner.

CLAY (*holds out bottle*): To vacuum cleaners.

BILLY: To all sorts of vacuums.

(*They clink and drink*)

CLAY: Clay, Junior is afraid of the vacuum cleaner. Not just the noise, neither. The very sight of it scares him to death. How do you like that? The one thing in life most identified with his daddy and it makes him cry. What do you think of that?

BILLY (*shrugs*): Little kids cry.

CLAY: He's not so little. He's eight years old.

BILLY: Is he?

CLAY: He still don't look a bit like me.

BILLY: He looks *exactly* like you.

CLAY: I think he looks like you.

BILLY: That's all in your mind.

CLAY: Oh, that's all in my mind, is it? Well, let me tell you something else. All these years gone by, his eyes never turned. They never turned even one little bit. Still the bluest damn blue I've ever seen.

BILLY: Let me tell *you* something, Clay. There are no horns on you. And there are no horns on your goddamn child.

CLAY: Horns? What the hell's *that* supposed to mean?

BILLY: Just that that boy is not the goddamn devil's son.

CLAY: Hell, I know he's not the devil's son. But is he yours?

BILLY: No.

CLAY: Don't lie to me, Billy. Tell me the truth. I won't care. I promise. It's been eight years. It won't change anything. I swear to you. He's yours, isn't he?

BILLY: He *can't* be, Clay.

CLAY: You don't have to protect her, you know? I swear to God you don't have to protect her. Just tell me the truth. *Please.* I need to know.

(*Carole enters on the landing of the stairs. She is, once again, very pregnant*)

CAROLE: Are you two sad sacks still at it? Billy, why don't you go home before the two of you wake up Mama and little Clay? Sweetie, come up to bed.

(*She exits*)

CLAY: Carole's pregnant again.

BILLY: It's about time you two had another. (*Holds flask out*) To another.

CLAY: Another. (*They clink and drink*) It's not like we weren't trying before. Couldn't make it go. When it happened, I halfway got to thinking that you and she must have just gotten together again.

BILLY: You don't have to worry about that.

CLAY: You do still love her, though.

BILLY: I've always loved her.

CLAY: Then I *do* still have to worry about it.

BILLY: Not for too much longer, I think. (*Sighs*) I can't do anything these days. I can't even write a poem.

CLAY: Shore you can.

BILLY: I can't remember how to do it. Carole's mother once told me that my daddy never wanted whatever it was that he wanted. That anytime he wanted something, he'd make sure that he threw it away, instead. I thought I was different, but I think I turned out exactly the same way. Only I must have wanted a lot more than he ever did, because I've thrown just about everything away.

CLAY: No, you haven't.

BILLY: You know something? Every evening I go home and put a gun to my head. Then I sit back to see if I'm going to pull the trigger. Used to be, every time I put the barrel down, it surprised me. Still alive. How the hell could that be? Now, it's been so many years, it's almost like a game. It's almost too late. I think, if I actually did it now, I'd be the most surprised person on the planet.

CLAY: That doesn't surprise me.

BILLY: What doesn't?

CLAY: That you'd be surprised. I'd be surprised if you weren't surprised seeing as you're surprised that your surprise over the surprise of not pullin' the trigger is no longer a surprise. Surprised?

BILLY (*baffled, holds up flask*): To surprise.

CLAY: To surprise.

(*They clink and drink. Carole comes out again*)

CAROLE: Billy Nero, go on home!

BILLY (*to Clay*): I gotta go on home. (*Stands wobbly*) You're a lucky man, Clay McCormick. I wish to God that I was you. (*Turns to Carole*) Carole. Come down for a kiss goodnight?

CAROLE (*hesitant*): In *this* condition?

BILLY: You look great.

CAROLE: I look huge.

BILLY: You look good enough to be working the check-out lane. (*She comes down the stairs. He pulls an envelope out of his pocket and slips it into the pocket of Carole's robe as he gives her a kiss. Clay doesn't notice, but Carole does*) Tonight your husband told me that he doesn't want charity. I don't blame him for a minute. But if you start to think like that too much, then every kindness that is done you starts to look like charity. Even this kiss could start to look like charity. (*He kisses her*) Instead of what it is. A kindness to the giver who doesn't have anyone else to give it to. Goodnight.

(*Billy heads for door. On the way, he stops at the dust patch on the rug and rubs it absentmindedly with his shoe, then he exits*)

CLAY: What was *that* all about?

CAROLE: I don't know. It's late. Why don't you take yourself up to bed?

CLAY: Might's well. (*He gets up, goes halfway up the stairs, turns*) Aren't you comin'?

CAROLE: In a minute.

(*Clay exits. Once he's gone, Carole pulls out the envelope and opens it. It is filled with a letter, forms, bank statements. She begins to read.*)

Scene Three—Eight Years Later

Prelude: *In stage right spot. Billy in his chair with the gun in his hand. He composes himself, takes the deep breath, puts the gun up to his mouth, strains, and drops the gun with an exhalation of breath. He sits that way for a second or two. Then, almost nonchalantly, barely thinking about it, swiftly, as if he has finally caught that moment, that second before impact in his mind, he raises the gun back up to his mouth and pulls the trigger. A loud gunshot is heard and Billy and his chair fall over backward. Hold on Billy's body lying on the floor, then crossfade to the main set where Carole is dusting and Clay is sitting, working on some papers. Carole is no longer pregnant. Clay has a flask from which he repeatedly drinks.*

CAROLE (*storytelling, casual*): So, anyway, here's this little man givin' a hard time to my cashiers just simply because he's got one lousy coupon that has "no expiration date" written on it. He wants his fifty cents off. I offer to allow him to purchase another brand, I'll give him fifty cents off of the equivalent item, but the product for which he has a coupon is not . . . being . . . made . . . any more. The company is out of business. None of this interests him. He wants the product on the coupon, as if writing "no expiration date" somehow assures immortality. I told him I could stamp "no expiration date" on his goddamn forehead if I wanted, it's still not gonna keep God from snatchin' him when his appointed time has come. He went away mad. (*Beat*) You can stare at that all day, hon. It won't change any of the figures.

CLAY: I can't figure out why we don't just starve.

CAROLE: You act like that's a *bad* thing.

CLAY: It don't balance. It never does balance. It's not even close.

CAROLE: It can't be as wrong as all that.

CLAY: It's worse. How much you bringin' in as a manager down at that grocery store? And then, look at me. I'm hangin' on by my fingertips at work. If I don't hold my end up, I'm goin' to get fired.

CAROLE: They can't fire you. You got twenty years seniority.

CLAY: Twenty years of bein' a salesman. No desk job. No promotion. Barely selling anything. Makin' less money today than I made my first year at the business. (*Looks at papers*) We should be flat broke.

CAROLE: We have a few . . . savings.

CLAY: What savings? If Billy Nero was still alive, I'd suspect him of charity but . . . (*Realization*) by God, it *is* Billy Nero, isn't it?

CAROLE: How can it be?

CLAY: Damned if I know. We weren't in the will. Even if we'd been in the will, old Lucius would have found a way to change it. Then how?

CAROLE: You won't like it.

CLAY: I already don't like it.

CAROLE: Billy started up a savings account for us about six months or so before he died. He slipped all the information in my pocket with a note that last time we saw him before his suicide. Had some things for me to sign. I went to the bank and signed them. Couple of weeks later, he's dead.

CLAY: A savings account for you?

CAROLE: For me and little Clay.

CLAY: Not me?

CAROLE: You didn't want charity.

CLAY: But *you* accepted it?

CAROLE: I came close to refusing it. Then I thought about what he said that night. About the gift bein' more for the giver. He wanted to help us, Clay.

CLAY: What for? Did he think I was a *complete* failure at supportin' us or did he want to leave a nest egg for his son?

CAROLE: No, he wanted to help us for his own sake. My gift to him was to take the money he was offering.

CLAY: How much was in it?

CAROLE (*a hesitant beat*): Five hundred thousand.

CLAY (*almost speechless*): Five hundred thousand! He must have thought I was heading for bankruptcy.

CAROLE: I told you you wouldn't like it.

CLAY: That I'm competing for my family with a wealthy ghost? What's there to like about it?

CAROLE: You know, I am so damn tired of this argument.

CLAY: I'm still competing with him for your love. You know I am.

CAROLE: How can you say that?

CLAY: Look at the way you've been in the eight years since we heard about Billy's death. I hardly seen you cry about it atall. Once at the news, once at the funeral, then never. There's been so little emotion out of you, you just *have* to still love him. Why would you conceal it otherwise?

CAROLE: Oh, I didn't cry enough! That's a good one. I didn't cry enough. If I'd cried every day, you'd have said *that* proves I still love him. Whatever I end up doin' proves whatever you expect.

CLAY: I *expect* you to be honest. Look at your mother. Look how torn up she still is. I half expect her to . . .

CAROLE: Mama. Where *is* Mama, anyway?

(*From front door, Mother enters with Clay, Junior. Clay, Junior is played by the same actor who played Billy Nero. Mother looks shrunken, older, de-*

feated. Other than that, the tableau looks the same as the moment in Act I, Scene One when Mother entered, mud on her slippers, with Billy Nero)

JUNIOR: Here.

CAROLE: Thank goodness. Where did you find her?

JUNIOR: Just wandering around. Taking the short-cut to the Cinnamon Club, I guess.

CAROLE: Mama, you have got to stop doin' this! Where did you think you were goin'?

MOTHER (*disoriented*): I was goin' to see Billy.

CAROLE: You know Billy's dead, Mama.

MOTHER: I know. I know. But, for a bit there I was sure he was waitin' for me. I was so sure we had ourselves a little date. (*Looks at Junior*) And then, for a minute, I was sure that I'd found him like before.

(She goes to her chair and sits)

CAROLE: Oh, Mama! Look at your shoes! You're trackin' mud all over the floor. (*She goes to her mother and takes her slippers off*) Clay, can you get me the vacuum, please?

JUNIOR: Me?

CAROLE: Not you. Your father. Clay, Senior.

CLAY: Wait a minute. Why can't *he* get the vacuum? (*To Junior*) What the hell is so tough about getting the vacuum? Think you're too good for it? You with your savings account and your blue eyes?

CAROLE: Never mind, both of you. *I'll* get it.

(Carole goes to closet)

MOTHER: Come sit here by me, Billy.

JUNIOR: Grandma, I'm not Billy. I'm Clay, Junior.

MOTHER: I know, sweetheart. Billy's dead. Went home one day and shot himself. Never even told me goodbye. (*Grief wells up*) He was my only friend. We were so perfect together. Did you know he wrote me a poem? He did. He wrote me a poem. (*To Junior*) Didn't you?

JUNIOR: Who, me? I'm not writing it for anyone in particular.

(*Everyone stops. Carole has the vacuum in hand*)

MOTHER (*back in right mind*): Not you, Junior.

JUNIOR: Oh. I thought you knew that I was . . . (*Beat*)

CLAY (*to Junior*): You writing a poem?

JUNIOR: Well . . . (*looks at everyone*) just a little one.

CLAY (*to Carole*): He's writing a poem.

CAROLE: So?

CLAY: So? Look at him! Look at him! He looks just like him!

CAROLE: Will you stop this, please? He looks like you! He's *always* looked like you!

CLAY (*motioning at Mother*): She calls him Billy.

CAROLE: Lately, she calls everyone Billy, she calls *me* Billy.

JUNIOR: What's wrong with writing a poem?

(*Clay slaps Junior in the face*)

CLAY: Shut up!

JUNIOR: Jesus, dad!

(*Clay slaps him again*)

CLAY: Don't you dare call me that.

(_Carole steps in between them_)

CAROLE: You keep away from him.

CLAY: Don't tell me what to do.

CAROLE: He's a sixteen-year-old boy. Your own son.

CLAY: Don't tell me this is my son. This isn't my son!

(_Suddenly, Clay goes into a rage. He repeatedly, frantically, tries to reach around Carole to slap Junior. Junior, wide-eyed, keeps dodging out of the way, which angers Clay even more. Finally, he pushes Carole out of the way and tries to corner Junior. Carole picks up the sweeping section of the vacuum and whacks Clay with it on the back of the legs. He goes down to the floor. Junior, still stunned, stands looking at him_)

CAROLE (_to Junior_): I want you to go outside and look after your sister.

JUNIOR (_stunned_): Where is she?

CAROLE: Just go!

(_Still spooked, Junior quickly exits_)

CLAY (_subdued_): I'm sorry.

CAROLE: You're stinkin' drunk.

CLAY: I know it.

CAROLE: Clay McCormick, you ever hit that boy again, I will leave you so flat and take the whole family with me.

CLAY: That's just what I'd want you to do.

(_The anger goes out of her. She feels for her husband and decides to tell him a secret_)

CAROLE: Clay . . . sweetheart . . . listen to me. There's somethin' you should know. Clay, Junior cannot be Billy Nero's son because Billy Nero never did anything that would give me a son. He was always impotent.

CLAY: What are you talkin' about?

CAROLE: I said . . .

CLAY: I heard what you said. How can that be true? Billy Nero was a man. You're makin' that up.

CAROLE: I'm not.

CLAY: Why didn't you ever tell me this before?

CAROLE: I didn't think you had a right to know before. Not so long as Billy was alive.

CLAY: He's been dead for eight years.

CAROLE: Well . . . you've never hit our son before. *Our* son, Clay. Not Billy's.

CLAY: I can't hardly believe it.

CAROLE: It's true. I swear I would have told you sooner if I'd only known how deeply you really felt about it. You've been carryin' on so long, I thought it was mostly a stupid joke, like the way I used to feel about Mama talkin' about how cold it is. (*This reminds her of the conversation she and Mother once had about her "graveyard" line and makes her take stock of herself*) I suppose I should have paid more attention. (*She gives him a chaste kiss*) You can stop worryin'. Stay put. Rest. I'm goin' to see if I can go find the kids. (*She exits out front door*)

CLAY: I can't hardly believe it. (*A decision*) I *can't* believe it.

MOTHER: I can't, either. Not Billy. I think it's just he wanted it so bad that he didn't want it. I think he drank too much on purpose. I think he didn't bother to try. (*The lights fade to a spot on Mother's face*) God. It's so cold. My fingers are freezing. I'm so stiff. (*Beat*) I miss him. You can laugh, but I loved him. He wrote me a poem. It was our little secret. I wasn't supposed to tell. "Cottonwood snowflakes somersault in summer air." He didn't finish it for Carole. He finished it for me. (*Lights up, like a switch is flipped, on stage left area. There is an open casket there. Clay, Carole, and Junior stand looking down into it*) I did so depend on him. I did. He kept me warm. Just bein' with him kept me warm. Now I'm cold. My hands are so cold. What was it I used to say? "I think the graveyard won't be any colder than I am right now?" (*Over by the casket, Carole mouths the line at the same time as Mother speaks it, then starts to choke up. The lights click off on the casket area*) I would check to see if I'm holdin' a glass full of ice but I can't seem to move. Isn't that funny? I can't seem to move atall. I was so much older, like his mother, almost could have been his mother. He wasn't supposed to go away before me. And here I thought . . . I was so sure, so sure we had ourselves a little date. Someplace. Someplace I thought was cold, but it isn't cold. It's warm 'cause Billy's there. It's warm 'cause Billy's there. It's warm 'cause Billy's there.

(*Slow fade of spot on Mother's face.*)

Scene Four—Eight Years Later

Prelude: *In stage right spot. The same small bar table with chair that Billy Nero always used. Lots of empty glasses on the table. Clay is sitting there, so drunk he can't keep his head up. He sleeps. Junior enters and stands before him. He doesn't touch his father, but Clay senses him, anyway. Clay rouses, looks up blearily at his son.*

Crossfade to the main set where Carole is sitting on the couch with a damp cloth on her forehead. In Mother's chair is Mary McCormick, the now 16-year-old daughter of Carole and Clay. Mary is played by the same person who played Mother. Mary is reading a book intently. She turns a page crisply.

CAROLE: Not so loud.

MARY: Sorry.

CAROLE: Do you have to sit in that same chair all day long? (*Beat*) You'd think you'd be a little more sociable than to always have your nose stuck away in some book.

MARY: Sorry.

CAROLE: I'm the only one who has ever accepted reality around here. Everything from your grandmother's delusions to your father's worries to you stuck all day in a book. Not that the reality has been any great shakes for the last dozen years or so. I'm about at the end of my rope. If your father so much as sniffs of alcohol this time, I swear to God, I'm gonna . . .

MARY: I don't want to hear it.

CAROLE: What?

MARY: I don't want to hear it. Do you mind? I am reading this book.

CAROLE: You're always readin' some goddamn book.

MARY: Well, maybe that's because I prefer it to your past.

(*Junior enters through front door, towing along a drunken Clay*)

JUNIOR: Here he is.

CAROLE (*removes wet cloth from forehead*): No dinner with you, I see.

JUNIOR: Dinner?

CAROLE: He was supposed to get take-out for dinner.

CLAY (*subdued*): I stopped in first for one little drink.

CAROLE: You left here four hours ago.

CLAY: You know how it is. You tilt a glass of Scotch to your lips, there's a whole world inside of it. A choppy sea of amber backed with a heavy-bottom shotglass horizon. You can drift in that small sea forever, feeling every bob and swirl of current. There's no goddamn concept of time.

JUNIOR: Well, now that I've brought him, I'm going to be getting myself back home.

CLAY: Why's that? Can't stand to be with your old man, is that it?

JUNIOR: No, I . . .

CLAY: Do your mother's dirty work? Come runnin' when she calls? But the minute the old man's home, you'd rather sit in the dark in that shitty little studio apartment you got than stay here and have a visit with me.

JUNIOR: If you would be here, instead of the bar, whenever I come here to visit, maybe I'd bother to . . . oh, hell, what's the use?

CLAY: What? Can't finish a sentence now? Just like your daddy, huh? Couldn't finish his poetry, couldn't finish his life, couldn't finish jack shit!

JUNIOR: What the hell is *this* now?

CAROLE: Stop. Both of you. Just stop. Clay dear, don't go yet. Visit a while. Visit with your father.

JUNIOR: Ma, he doesn't even want me around.

CAROLE: Then visit with your sister and me. We want you around, don't we, Mary?

MARY (*nose in book*): Uh-huh.

JUNIOR (*gives in, sits*): I don't have anything to say.

CAROLE: Tell your father about work.

CLAY: Work? You call that work? Writing for the town newspaper? That's not work.

JUNIOR: It keeps me going.

CLAY: Hell. That joint account is what keeps *you* goin'.

JUNIOR: I never touch it. Not for myself.

CLAY (*introverted*): You never wanted to sell vacuum cleaners like your old man.

JUNIOR: I didn't think you wanted me to. It's not like it's a family business.

CAROLE: Besides, they fired you five years ago for lack of sales. What kind of life is *that* to wish on somebody else?

CLAY: It was a pretty good life. Better than writing poems and bein' a goddamn drunk. (*Beat*) I don't know what it was that finally happened to me. I just couldn't concentrate. I don't know what it was. Had too much on my mind, I guess. Plus, what the hell can you do when you sell a machine that works good for life? There aren't many people that'll buy more than one off you. It's not like *every* customer's gonna buy seven or eight. (*A moment as this reminds him of Billy, then he rouses himself*) Carole, why don't you pull out the old hand-held, industrial-strength air-filtration system so Clay here can see it? Did you ever take a real good look at the space-age machine your old man was selling, son? I mean, did you ever *really* stop and take a look at it? (*Beat. Carole hasn't moved*) Carole?

CAROLE: I can't.

CLAY: Shore you can.

CAROLE: We don't have it any more.

CLAY: Why not?

CAROLE: Because it broke, that's why not. It was never much good to begin with. The time it worked the best was when I used it to take a swing at you.

CLAY: It's supposed to have a lifetime guarantee.

CAROLE: Well, I can guarantee you, it reached the end of its lifetime.

CLAY (*devastated*): When did this happen?

CAROLE: Long time ago. I told you about it.

CLAY: I don't remember it.

CAROLE: Most likely you were drunk. Pouring the joint account down your throat. That *is* where that money's goin', isn't it? All those withdrawals I always see. I mean, Junior here says he never touches it, so it must be you. Beats me how you manage to get your hands on it. *Your* name's not on the account.

CLAY: I got the exact same name as my son.

CAROLE: So what? That doesn't mean you can go in without him and . . . (*Gets it. To Junior*) oh, honey. You haven't.

JUNIOR (*shrugs*): *I'm* not going to be using it.

CAROLE: But you know he's only goin' to use it to buy booze.

CLAY: It's all it was used for when Billy had it.

CAROLE: You hear that, Mary? You hear what your brother is doin' with his money?

MARY (*reading*): Uh-huh.

JUNIOR: Well, why not? It's not really *my* money.

CAROLE: Of course it is.

JUNIOR: Well, I never earned it. It belonged to Billy Nero. What's he doing giving it to me for, anyway? I barely knew him. Why should he care about me?

MARY (*still reading*): God, Clay, don't be so dense.

JUNIOR (*defensive*): What?

MARY (*puts book down*): It's only the only thing Mom and Dad have talked about for, like, the last hundred years. Billy Nero this, Billy Nero that. You'd think he was alive and in charge of our lives instead of being dead just forever. Don't tell me you don't know about this. I'm so sick to death of it, it's so old, I'm like, don't even talk to me any more. I don't even want to hear it.

(*She picks up her book and reads*)

JUNIOR: It's not like I don't know about it. It's more like I never really listened to it. I don't understand it. (*To Clay*) I feel like, because of this Billy Nero guy, you've just tried to swallow me up. Anything I say or feel that's at all different from anything you say or feel, you just try to swallow me up.

CLAY: I know it. You're right. Billy warned me not to put horns on you. Now it's too late. (*Beat*) And the air filtrator is gone to boot. I can't believe, after all these years, that the old air filtrator is gone.

JUNIOR: Does that matter to you? The way you always talked, I thought you hated those damn vacuum cleaners.

CLAY: *You're* the one that always hated them. You couldn't even bring yourself to touch them.

JUNIOR: I hated them because *you* did, dad. All I could see is how unhappy they made you. Why would I want to touch that?

CLAY: I wish that *that* was true.

JUNIOR: It *is* true.

CLAY: If I ever thought for a minute it had anything to do with feelings for me. . . I always thought . . . (*He stops*)

JUNIOR: What?

MARY (*reading*): Billy Nero.

JUNIOR: I barely knew who Billy Nero was. You're the one I was always thinking about, Dad.

CLAY: You mean it?

JUNIOR: Of course I mean it.

(*Suddenly, spontaneously, Clay grabs his son in a big hug. Junior hugs back. Mary looks up from her book, then goes back to reading. The two men separate*)

CLAY: I'm so sorry, Clay.

JUNIOR: For what?

CLAY: For everything. For the way I've always treated you. For takin' the joint account money when it's meant for you.

JUNIOR: I want you to have it.

CLAY: I'm drinkin' it all up, is all I'm doin'.

JUNIOR: I know, dad. I wish you wouldn't, but you can do with it what you want.

CLAY: Takin' charity. Always said I would never take charity.

JUNIOR: Don't think of it as charity. It's not charity. It's more like . . . (*Beat. He thinks*) a kindness to the giver who doesn't have anyone else to give it to.

(*This is the same thing that Billy Nero said to Carole and Clay recognizes it. It is like a slap in the face. All of the kindness he has felt for Junior disappears. If he was starting to feel that Junior really is his son, he now strongly feels that Junior is Billy Nero's son*)

CLAY: What?

JUNIOR: I said . . .

CLAY: I heard what you said. You can just keep all your dirty money, you little bastard.

CAROLE: Clay!

JUNIOR: What is this, now?

CLAY: As if you don't know!

CAROLE: He got that expression from me. He doesn't know it came from Billy.

CLAY: Of course. Of course. What the hell is next, Junior? Gonna look through the telescope? Did you get *that* from your mama, too? (*He holds his hands up in the telescope gesture that Billy does*) Gonna ask me what it's like to step out in front of a car? You little shit!

(*Clay takes a wild swing at Junior. Junior grabs him. They struggle together, almost in mockery of the previous hug*)

CAROLE: Clay McCormick, you stop!

JUNIOR: Don't make me hurt you, dad.

CLAY: Is that some sort of threat, Nero?

(*They grapple, but in spite of Clay's ferocity, Junior is younger, stronger, and sober. He tosses Clay down to the ground. Clay does not bother to get up. As soon as Clay hits the ground, Mary puts down her book and watches, in anguish. She continues to watch until her moment at the end of the play. The book is never picked up again*)

JUNIOR: That's it! That is it! You've been knocking me around since I was a kid. You want to know what kind of daddy you've been? What I remember? That's it! Slappin' me around! Knockin' me around! I have tried. God knows I have tried, but I am finished with it. You want to drink yourself to death? You can drink yourself to death! You can have the whole goddamn savings account to do it with, but don't you ever ask me for anything else ever again! (*He heads for the door*)

CAROLE: Clay, honey. Wait.

JUNIOR: What!?

CAROLE: I'm goin' with you.

JUNIOR: Ma . . . you don't have to.

CAROLE: I mean, I'm *leavin'* with you. This was the end for me, too. With your father. If I can stay with you in your apartment until I find a place of my own.

JUNIOR (*breathing heavy, looks back and forth at his parents*): Okay. All right. Sure. Come on, then.

CAROLE: Just give me a minute.

JUNIOR: I'll be in the car. (*He exits*)

CLAY: The minute I married you, I knew one day it would come to this. I knew it and I've been afraid of it.

CAROLE (*gentle*): It's your own fault.

CLAY: Everything I ever did, I did for you. I loved you so much. I had this voice in my head. It whispered, "Carole, Carole, Carole." Endlessly, "Carole, Carole, Carole." It was all for you. Even getting you to forget Billy Nero. He would have been so bad for you. That was all for you.

CAROLE: I know it. I know Billy was bad for me with his drinkin' and selfishness and no job and everything. That's a big reason why I didn't marry him. But you know what? I ended up married to him, anyway. And I can't stand it any more, Clay. I have just got to go.

CLAY: What about the kids?

CAROLE: What *about* them, you big idiot? They're *yours*!

CLAY: I don't believe you.

CAROLE: I know you don't. Here's something else you never believed, either. I loved you very much, Clay. You were clumsy and shy and you were like one forlorn half-burned match compared to Billy Nero's bonfire but I got around to seein' there was more warmth in your flame than Billy's would ever have. That was before you tried to make the flame bigger and put it out, instead. That was before you stopped believin' everything I told you, all in the name of bein' so much in love with me. Believe it or not, I loved you more than I ever loved Billy Nero. But I don't love you any more. Not even a little bit. (*From offstage, the sound of a car horn honking*) That's your son callin'. Mary, will you please stop by Junior's place later and bring me some of my clothes and things?

MARY (*wide-eyed*): Uh-huh.

CAROLE: I'm going to go right now.

(*She exits. A slight pause as Clay soaks this all in*)

CLAY: Oh, God. She's gone. She's gone and I believe her. Wouldn't you know it? I actually finally believe her. All this time, I thought that voice in my head said, "Carole, Carole, Carole" when all along it always whispered, "me, me, me." Twenty-five years, I thought I knew her, but I was too busy with myself to really see into her heart. I could never see into her heart.

(*Still sitting on the floor, Clay suddenly breaks down and cries. Mary, shocked and frightened by all this, jumps up and goes over to him. She puts her arms around him, comforting him*)

MARY: Don't cry, Daddy. Don't worry. Everything's okay. Really, it is. The past is dead. It's all over. We can forget it, you and me. From now on, everything is totally new. Everything is . . . (*she gets distracted, looks over at the dirty spot on the rug, finishes her sentence in a distracted fashion*) totally . . . new.

(*Hardly realizing what she is doing, Mary goes over to the dirty spot and rubs at it with her shoe. She rubs and rubs. Slow fade to black.*)

ML   10/02